DEALING WITH DRUG MISUSE
Crisis Intervention in the City

Anne Jamieson,
Alan Glanz,
Susanne MacGregor

Tavistock Publications
London and New York

For
Erik Jamieson
Rita and Bill Glanz
and
Brian Baird

First published in 1984 by
Tavistock Publications
11 New Fetter Lane, London EC4P 4EE

Published in the USA by
Tavistock
in association with Methuen, Inc.
733 Third Avenue, New York, NY 10017

Printed in Great Britain by Richard Clay,
The Chaucer Press, Bungay, Suffolk.
Typeset by Keyset Composition, Colchester, Essex, England.

British Library Cataloguing in Publication Data

Jamieson, Anne
   Dealing with drug misuse.
   1. City Roads—History
   I. Title   II. Glanz, Alan   II. MacGregor, Susanne
   362.2'938   HV5840.G7

   ISBN 0-422-78450-8
   ISBN 0-422-79300-0 Pbk

Library of Congress Cataloging in Publication Data

Jamieson, Anne.
   Dealing with drug misuse.
   Bibliography: p.
   Includes indexes.
   1. City Roads (Crisis Interventional) Ltd.—History.
2. Drug abuse—Treatment—England—London—Case studies.
I. Glanz, Alan.   II. MacGregor, Susanne.   III. Title.
HV5840.G72L64   1984   362.2'938   84-8870

   ISBN 0-422-78450-8
   ISBN 0-422-79300-0 (pbk.)

Contents

Abbreviations used in the text   vi
Acknowledgements   vii

Introduction   ix

PART ONE Planning the Service
 1 Defining the Problem   3
 2 The Making of City Roads   24

PART TWO The Service in Practice
 3 The Use of City Roads   47
 4 Difficult Clients   68
 5 Multi-disciplinary Team Work:
   A Professional Approach?   96
 6 Social Work at City Roads   113
 7 Links with the Environment   134
 8 An Assessment of City Roads   153

PART THREE Barriers to Policy Implementation
 9 Managing an Innovation   175
10 Social Responses to the Drugs Problem   192

Appendix A Performance Indicators in the NHS   202
Appendix B Common Drugs of Use and Abuse   204
References   210
Name Index   217
Subject Index   219

Abbreviations used in the text

A and E dept.	Accident and Emergency Department
ACMD	Advisory Council on the Misuse of Drugs
AHA	Area Health Authority
CDP	Community Drug Project
CQSW	Certificate of Qualification in Social Work
CURB	Campaign on the Use and Restriction of Barbiturates
DDU	Drug Dependency Unit
DTC	Drug Treatment Centre } also known as clinics
DHSS	Department of Health and Social Security
GLC	Greater London Council
GPs	General Practitioners
ISDD	Institute for the Study of Drug Dependence
LBA	London Boroughs Association
MRC	Medical Research Council
NHS	National Health Service
RHA	Regional Health Authority
RMN	Registered Mental Nurse
RMO	Regional Medical Officer
SCODA	Standing Conference on Drug Abuse
SRN	State Registered Nurse
UCH	University College Hospital

Acknowledgements

We should not have been able to carry out the research on which this book is based without the fullest co-operation of all at City Roads. We were offered a unique opportunity to observe what actually happened inside an agency, and being in at the start could observe in detail the development of policy and practice there. We are greatly indebted to the Management Committee, staff, and clients at City Roads for their collaboration in this research. We enjoyed much help and encouragement from everyone and names are too numerous to mention. We should, however, thank especially Annas Dixon, John Hedge, Dennis Muirhead, Derek Harper, Paul Hitchens, Giumpi Alhadeff, and Brian Langley. We are also grateful for permission to reprint pages 22–6 from City Roads's Drug Resource Pack. The Department of Health and Social Security provided generous support for the research and we are very grateful to them for this. Representatives of SCODA were most helpful in providing background information. We should mention in particular Bob Searchfield and David Turner, the latter of whom also offered useful comments on sections of the manuscript. The research was carried out while we were all members of the Department of Politics and Sociology at Birkbeck College, University of London. During this time we were very fortunate to have Pat Culshaw working with us as part-time secretary. Her contribution to the team effort was considerable. Apart from her administrative and secretarial skills, which are of the highest order, she played a full part in data preparation and analysis. Her comments on the research work and on the manuscripts were always pertinent and helpful. Later, Anne Jamieson became Associate Fellow at the King's Fund College and she is grateful to her colleagues there for encouragement, especially to June Huntington for useful comments on sections of the manuscript. The library and information service at ISDD offers an invaluable resource for research in this area and we have benefited from this. We should thank in particular Mike Ashton for his helpful comments on certain chapters.

Martin Mitcheson also read some sections and provided knowledgeable criticism. We should also mention the co-operation we enjoyed from other agencies working in the field, hospitals, street agencies, and rehabilitation projects in particular. All in all, we have been most fortunate in the generous support and encouragement of many individuals and agencies. To all we are duly grateful. We should add, however, that the manuscript in its final form is entirely our own responsibility. The judgements we make and the conclusions we reach are our own, as are any faults or errors.

January 1984

Introduction

This book is concerned with the activities of City Roads, a crisis intervention service for problem drug-takers in London. Discussions about that service began in the early seventies in response to the problems experienced by street agencies and Accident and Emergency departments in Central London which were having to deal with chaotic and sometimes disruptive people. City Roads eventually opened in 1978 and has since then established itself as a highly regarded service. This book is mainly about what happened between 1978 and 1981, the years when it was an experimental project. Since then some changes have been introduced at City Roads and the style of drug misuse most common on the streets has shifted from one dominated by the problems caused by barbiturate misuse to one where the misuse of opiates and opioids is more prominent. However, the main issues dealt with here remain central to the debate on policy and practice in the field of problem drug-taking. How best to provide services for the 'unstable', the 'chaotic', the most difficult among drug misusers, those who are very likely to be homeless, unemployed, and almost destitute, living on the streets, and out of touch with their families? Why is it that trying to improve the provision of services, both in quantity and range, seems to be such an uphill task? What is the role of the voluntary sector and what part should it play in relation to the statutory sector? And what is the role of social work in the treatment and care of problem drug-takers?

The experience of City Roads is directly relevant to these key issues, which are not, of course, confined to the field of drugs policy but can be found in other policy areas concerned with 'unpopular causes' and 'difficult clients'. Drug misuse is a subject from which many people steer away, perhaps because they see it either as a minority problem of no concern to them or as something rather distasteful with its connotations of illegality, inadequacy, and squalor. We argue that, on the contrary, the issues concerning the treatment, care, and control of 'problem drug takers' and the prevention of drug misuse are part and parcel of wider debates about social policy, medical practice, and social work. General explanations of deviance and social problems, and social responses to these, and issues surrounding the provision of services, may be illuminated, we hope, through the discussion that follows. By focusing on our case study of City Roads, we can see in some detail the way in which policies and practice develop over time and the contribution of research to this process.

Increasing drug misuse

The social problem of escalating drug misuse cannot easily be ignored. In 1983, Customs and Excise officers seized a record amount of heroin in Britain, 201 kilos with an estimated street value of £25 million. Mr Cutting, Chief Customs Investigation Officer, has referred to the 'bush-fire' escalation of heroin addiction in Britain. The bulk of the drug comes from Pakistan, and Britain is now a target for international drug smugglers. Some indication of the extent of the international trade was given after the cracking of what was claimed to be the largest world organization of illegal arms traffic in November 1982. The Italian State Prosecutor showed that this ring exported huge quantities of arms, including helicopters and armoured cars, to Middle East countries in exchange for narcotics, mainly heroin.

With street prices of heroin at about £80 for a gramme of increasingly high quality and purity, users find little problem in obtaining supplies. The Home Office index of addiction, which notoriously underestimates the size of the problem, has seen an annual 20 per cent growth in recent years. At the same time, the clinics, the main hospital-based service dealing with drug misusers, have seen their waiting lists grow longer and GPs have steadily increased as a source of new notifications of addicts to the Home Office, from 15 per cent in 1970 to 53 per cent in 1981. (New notifications from the treatment centres (clinics) fell as a proportion of all new notifications from 45 per cent to 33 per cent while even more impressively, those from prison medical officers fell from 40 per cent to a mere 14 per cent between 1970 and 1981 (Advisory Council on the Misuse of Drugs 1982: 120 Table 4).)

Yet in spite of the growing size of the drugs problem, the

political will to respond effectively is lacking. We are seeing 'a tragedy born of inaction' as a leader in *The Guardian* put it (Thursday, January 5 1984: 10). Few politicians are prepared to think seriously about drugs policy. It is rarely debated in the House of Commons. Meanwhile,

> 'normally quite moderate sources from the Home Office, the street agencies, the medical profession, the police and rehabilitation houses are all of one accord. Unless there is a major change in policy and resources, Britain is going to have a really serious problem by the middle of the 1980s.' (Clark 1981: 11)

It is remarkable that only a few years ago in 1978, the authorities felt able to claim with some satisfaction 'in comparison with several other countries facing similar problems, the United Kingdom appears at present to have a relatively stable situation as far as narcotic drug dependence is concerned' (COI 1978: 1). More recently, however, a provisional estimate by researchers at the North East London Drugs Indicators Project (NELDIP), extrapolating from a study of problematic drug use in two inner London boroughs, produced a total of between 10,000 and 15,000 people in London alone, using opiates on a heavy and regular basis during 1980 and a similar number in the rest of the country. The authors suggested that as many again may have problems arising from their use of non-opiate drugs (ISDD 1982). At the beginning of 1984, even the Home Office's conservative estimates suggested 50,000 people in the UK addicted to drugs; a more likely figure might be 100,000. In addition, the casual use of drugs by young people now far outstrips the scale of the so-called 'drugs problem' of the late sixties.

There is little doubt then that illicit opiate use has increased substantially since the late seventies and the greatest increase has been in the use of illicitly imported heroin. In addition, thefts from pharmacies, warehouses, and doctors' surgeries, and deception of doctors form a significant source of illicit psychotropic drugs, an especially important one at present being Diconal (the prescribing of which has recently been restricted by the Home Secretary). The major 'problem' drugs are opiates and barbiturates. (Misuse of barbiturates overshadowed that of opiates throughout the seventies but the balance has now changed. However, the two drugs and others will often be used by the same person depending on availability.) The basic issue of 'problem drug taking' is one about which British society is soon going to have to take some hard decisions.

The City Roads Project

Let us begin, however, by saying something about City Roads itself since much of what we are discussing refers to that innovation. City Roads (Crisis Intervention) Ltd is a short-stay residential unit staffed mainly by nurses and social workers. It is a registered charity and a company limited by guarantee. Its services are designed to meet the immediate needs of young, multiple drug misusers in the London area, especially those who have a 'chaotic' life style, that is who lack stable employment, accommodation, and personal relationships.

The House is situated in an inner London borough and can take 15 residents. After the first six months, it was accepted that 12 should be the maximum number accommodated at any one time. In the three years we studied the unit, there were employed, besides the Director and Deputy Director, an administrator, secretary, part-time cleaner, cook, part-time Medical Officer, part-time consultant psychiatrist, and 16 team workers. It opened its doors to residents on 8 May 1978 and from then until 8 May 1981, its status was that of an experimental project funded jointly by the DHSS and LBA, and over those three years it dealt with 660 separate admissions.

Research was an integral part of this experiment from the beginning. The main aim of the research was to consider the appropriateness and effectiveness of the model of service provision on which the City Roads experiment was based. Throughout the three-year experimental period, the project operated without major problems, continued to attract clients and established itself as a recognized service, acceptable to both clients and other agencies.

City Roads was set up with three main aims:

1. To provide for the immediate needs of young multiple drug misusers who frequently overdose and who may be admitted to hospital Accident and Emergency departments.
2. To operate at a crisis intervention level providing a warm, sheltered environment where nursing, medical, social, and psychiatric support is readily available.
3. Not to attempt to offer a complete treatment and rehabili-

tation programme under one roof but to see its function as making contact with multiple drug misusers and attempting to encourage them to accept longer-term help from existing treatment and rehabilitation services. As a community-based service to establish and maintain close working relationships with all relevant statutory and voluntary agencies and community groups (Operational Document 1978).

It was expected that City Roads would function as part of a wider network of services. It would be a short-stay unit only, accommodating residents for up to three weeks, after which they might move on to other services. It would be a link between different kinds of services, such as street agencies, hospitals, drug treatment centres, the probation service, social service departments, hostels, and long-term rehabilitation projects. It would provide a link between specialist and non-specialist, residential and non-residential, statutory, and voluntary agencies.

Summary of research method

Because City Roads was seen as a system operating in an environment (Homans 1961; Etzioni 1970), the research had three main areas of interest: the characteristics of the users of the service; the internal operation of the system; and the links between the system and its environment. A fourth area of interest followed from these, which was to consider the way all three conceptually distinct areas acted together in reality, through a consideration of the careers of the users as they moved into and out from the system; the circumstances surrounding their admission to the project; what was done to them and their experience of treatment; the circumstances surrounding leaving the project; and what happened afterwards.

A wide range of conventional social research methods was used: participant observation; quantitative analysis of records; computer processing of some data; qualitative textual analysis of records; questionnaire surveys; and interviews. These accumulated to produce 660 admission sheets, 660 discharge sheets, 220 readmission sheets, thousands of telephone message slips, 71 interviews with staff, 57 interviews with residents, 11 in-depth case studies, 80 case histories, follow up of 150 residents, analysis of 20 case files, postal questionnaires to 50 agencies, and an analysis of a card index on 580 people referred but not admitted. Further qualitative data were particularly valuable, derived from participant observation over a three-year period. Time was spent in the house with the residents and staff, talking to them and generally joining in their activities. (A full account of the research methods can be found in Jamieson, Glanz, and MacGregor 1981.)

In writing about this material here, we have chosen to concentrate on the process of policy implementation, looking at City Roads 'in the round' and its impact on clients and other agencies. We focus especially on the problems and choices that might be encountered in other attempts at innovation, especially where providing services for unpopular or disadvantaged groups. In order to comment more fully on these questions of policy implementation, we have continued to observe in some detail, since 1981 when the research exercise had formally come to an end, the process of negotiation and decision-making surrounding the future funding of City Roads.

Outline of the book

This book is devoted to an account of what happened in the process of putting the design for a service into practice. Chapter 1 sets out the position in which the City Roads experiment was to intervene, the paradigms within which explanations of drug taking were set which influenced the development of public policy in Britain. We show how pressure was brought to bear on central government to support an experimental innovation in this field. Once the policy change had been agreed, the process of implementation began, and Chapter 2 gives an account of the obstacles that had to be overcome, and how this process affected the shape of the service which was eventually made available in 1978. Chapter 3 gives an outline of how that service functioned over the three years on which we focus (1978–81), using firstly the basic monitoring data and then attempting to bring these statistics to life by presenting some brief case studies of how typical clients made use of the service. The next set of chapters moves from these accounts to begin to present an explanation and assessment of how and why the service operated in the way it did. This is organized around the 'banner goals' of the new service. Chapter 4 considers the first objective: to provide for the immediate needs of young multiple drug misusers who frequently overdose and who may be admitted to hospital

Accident and Emergency departments, looking especially at the question of the needs of the client group and proposing that their way of life is better understood not as 'chaotic' or 'disorganized' but as orientated around a set of perspectives about the world and a set of strategies for accommodating to the problems and difficulties presented to them in their daily lives. These clients are not 'blank sheets' upon which practitioners can write. They come into the situation created at City Roads with a set of expectations and desires: they approach the service from a set position. The issue for the practitioners is how to negotiate a deal with these clients, to come to an agreement about future lines of action. Establishing a negotiating position and reaching an agreement require accommodation on both sides but the outcome has much to do with the balance of power between the sides, as well as with the extent to which their interests and desires can be matched up. Chapter 5 moves on to look at the second objective: to operate at a crisis intervention level providing a warm, sheltered environment where nursing, medical, social, and psychiatric support is readily available, that is, at what is offered or laid on the table by the workers at City Roads. This chapter also looks at how the service operated, especially at how far and how it acted as a multidisciplinary agency. Chapter 6 considers the first part of the third objective: not to attempt to offer a complete treatment and rehabilitation programme under one roof but to see its function as making contact with multiple drug misusers and attempting to encourage them to accept longer-term help from existing treatment and rehabilitation services, and presents a detailed analysis of the treatment practices adopted, considering especially how far they were responsive and sensitive to the perspectives and strategies assumed by the clients. The second aspect of the third objective – as a community service to establish and maintain close working relationships with all relevant statutory and voluntary agencies and community groups – is taken up in Chapter 7, which looks at the connections between City Roads and other services and summarizes the assessment of City Roads made by other agencies. Chapter 8 discusses the key issue of assessment of new policies and their implementation, and Chapter 9 focuses on the problem of managing an innovation, especially of negotiating the stage between being a new experiment and becoming an established service. Chapter 10 concludes by setting out the issues in the debate about action to tackle the current problem.

PART ONE
Planning the Service

PART ONE

1 Defining the Problem

Theories and treatment of drug dependence

To understand how far City Roads represented an innovation and why there should have been pressure to set up such a service, we need to know something about the background of policies and ideas about drug dependence in the UK, especially since the late sixties. Earlier periods have been well documented and analysed, especially by Berridge and Edwards (1981) and Stimson and Oppenheimer (1982), so we do not propose to cover this ground again. However, during the seventies, following the setting up of the clinics, discussion about drug misuse and appropriate ways of dealing with it has shifted somewhat and we need to understand in what ways this has occurred and why.

There are two main statutes regulating the availability of drugs in the UK: the Medicines Act 1968 which governs the manufacture and supply of medicinal products; and the Misuse of Drugs Act 1971, the aim of which is to prevent the non-medical use of certain drugs. This Act controls not only medicinal drugs but also drugs with no current medicinal use. Drugs subject to this Act are known as *controlled drugs*.

The form of the controls we have on drugs today dates largely from the Dangerous Drugs Act of 1920. This was introduced mainly in response to pressure from the international movement for drugs control, especially from America. Policy and practice since have followed the lines established in this legislation, namely that the availability of opiates should be confined to medical prescription; that there should be regulations controlling the import, manufacture, and supply of drugs; and that there should be heavy penalties for infringement of these controls (Edwards and Busch 1981). The Rolleston Committee, set up to deal specifically with the question of what constituted legitimate prescribing, proposed in its Report of 1926 an interpretation of the law which served quite adequately for the next forty years. Their key recommendations on prescribing for addicts were that there are two groups of people suffering from addiction to whom administration of morphine or heroin could be regarded as a legitimate medical response. These were: those undergoing treatment for cure of their addiction by the gradual withdrawal method; and those for whom after every effort had been made for the cure of the addiction, the drug could not be completely withdrawn without serious adverse effect on their well-being. It was this latter dispensation which came to be seen as a distinctively British way of dealing with addiction. From then until the sixties, as Griffith Edwards notes drily, 'Britain's drug problem was of interest exactly and only because of its trivial size' (Edwards and Busch 1981: 9). Whether or not this was the result of the availability of opiates on prescription is, however, a matter for debate.

In the sixties, a dramatic change occurred in the character of the drug scene in Britain. Drug taking began to be perceived as a social problem, prompting calls for a new response from government. The numbers known to be using drugs increased, young people especially were taking a variety of drugs, particularly injected heroin, and an active black market appeared, the result largely of an overspill from lax medical prescribing.

The Brain Committee, an interdepartmental committee of experts which had published an earlier report in 1961, was reconvened and produced its second report, *Drug Addiction*, in 1965 (Interdepartmental Committee on Drug Addiction 1965). Significantly, this committee chose to interpret its terms of reference in a narrow and limited way. They assumed that they were 'not being invited to survey the subject of drug addiction as a whole but rather to pay particular attention to the part played by medical practitioners in the supply of these drugs' (p.5). In retrospect, it may seem that an opportunity for a wide-ranging enquiry was missed. Following the lines of the Rolleston Committee, the Brain Committee regarded addiction as 'an expression of mental disorder rather than a form of criminal behaviour' (p.4). The orthodox line was thus maintained, promoting a medical definition of the addict and the offer of treatment rather than a moralistic one leading to punishment. It was assumed that these were the only alternatives. Suggestions that drug taking might be seen as having social causes calling for a more wide-ranging response or that people other than doctors might take the main responsibility for dealing with drug users were never seriously entertained.

The key concern of the Report was that the medical profession should put its own house in order and that greater control should be exercised over those doctors whose prescribing of opiates was, to say the least, injudicious. The major issue was, as the Report recognized, one of effecting a balance between controlling the illicit market and inadvertently encouraging addiction. This continues to be the central dilemma in debates on drugs policy and practice today.

'If there is insufficient control [over doctors' prescribing] it may lead to the spread of addiction, as is happening at present. If on the other hand, the restrictions are so severe as to prevent or seriously discourage the addict from obtaining any supplies from legitimate sources, it may lead to the development of an organised illicit traffic.' (Interdepartmental Committee on Drug Addiction 1965: 7)

They recommended a system of notification of diagnosed addicts to the central authorities (emphasizing their preference for the term 'notification' rather than 'registration', since the latter term might be seen to indicate more acceptance of the provision of drugs for drug addiction on the part of the medical profession and the authorities than was the case). Notification of addiction was no more an infringement of liberty than was notification of cases of smallpox and TB and of similar relevance: 'addiction is after all a socially infectious condition . . . the addict is a sick person . . . addiction is a disease which (if allowed to spread unchecked) will become a menace to the community' (p.8).

The development of policy and practice towards drug misuse in Britain in this century can be characterized as one of bureaucratic policy making (Berridge and Edwards 1981). What stands out clearly from the twenties to the present is the importance of the alliance between the medical profession and the state in proposing and implementing solutions to the 'drug problem' as they perceived it. The medical analogy dominates. The social system is seen as rather like the human body: protest is a 'social disorder'; unacceptable behaviour like drug misuse is a 'symptom' amenable to treatment and care. Drug addicts are the pimples on the face of society. The relatively greater concern of the medical profession with this particular social problem, as compared for example to the very similar one of alcohol misuse, results from the importance of drugs as one of the doctor's tools of trade. A major aspect of a doctor's everyday practice is the prescribing of drugs, and drug controls in general have served to create the doctor's privileged position as the monopolistic source of drugs and have been desired by the medical profession for this reason. Restrictions on their right to prescribe whatever they think appropriate in the treatment of their patient's condition threaten their highly valued prerogatives and thus the social position of the profession as a whole. A further factor historically accounting for the interest of the medical profession in addiction is that so many of the mid-twentieth-century addicts were medical or para-medical personnel or their families, for whom they felt a special responsibility. Moreover, until the early sixties the majority of known addicts had become addicted in the course of medical treatment, reinforcing the doctor's responsibility for dealing with this side effect of earlier treatment.

From the sixties onwards, as drug misusers became less respectable characters, more often members of the underclass and petty criminal underworld, obtaining their drugs from other addicts, the grip of the medical profession over their care began to loosen.

The changes in policy and practice introduced in the late sixties were then a direct response to 'the apparent inability of some doctors to deal responsibly and adequately with the changing nature of addiction in the 1960s' (ISDD 1980: 1). It was presumed that the problem could be dealt with by and through the medical profession. The solution was to limit prescribing of heroin and cocaine to doctors holding a special licence to do so from the Home Office. In 1968, over 500 hospital-based doctors were granted these, most of them working within the discipline of psychiatry. Most important was the establishment of hospital-based drug dependency treatment centres (the clinics), each headed by a consultant psychiatrist specializing in drug dependence, with a team of supporting staff from the disciplines of medicine, nursing, social work, and psychology. These were to signify an energetic response to that outbreak of addiction which the *British Medical Journal* had called 'a grave symptom of social disorder' (11 February 1967). The treatment centres were expected to have the proper facilities for 'energetic therapy and rehabilitation' of the addict.

The hope was that the clinics would contain the spread of addiction: that they would attempt the treatment and rehabilitation of addicts, detoxification, the medical care of complications, offer emotional and practical support and health education. The Advisory Committee on Drug Dependence in 1968 had stressed the need for flexibility and experimentation and concentration on the social aspects of rehabilitation. Addicts should be persuaded to accept in-patient detoxification and long-term rehabilitation with social and psychological support. The clinics were then presented with quite a tall order, especially since most were under-financed and in many health authorities, especially outside London, there was a reluctance to establish specialized treatment centres.

Since 1968, the clinics have been seen as the main elements in the response to the problem of drug misuse in Britain. In considering their role, the main issues are: how far have they in practice attempted to pursue the objectives set out originally? How effective have they been? What actually happens in the clinics? And especially, what policy should they adopt to the prescribing of controlled drugs, injectables like heroin in particular?

Almost from the start, the clinics began to try to shed their image as 'prescribing units'. Between 1971 and 1978, the amount of heroin prescribed fell by 40 per cent. Prescriptions for injectable methadone increased by 20 per cent. But most dramatically, prescriptions for oral methadone increased by five times (470 per cent) (ISDD 1980: 6). Doctors and clinic staff became suspicious of the intentions of patients they saw as 'manipulative' and felt a conflict between their professional commitment to the promotion of good health and continuous prescribing of dangerous drugs. But the dilemma remained; how to preserve a proper balance between the 'social control' role of containing the problem and the doctors' desire to focus on the health of their individual patients. As early as 1972, the *Lancet* commented that the restrictions on prescribing introduced by the reforms of the late sixties were losing for the British system its monopoly of supplying drugs to addicts. The increasing use of imported heroin and of substitutes like the barbiturates constituted a threat to society (ISDD 1980: 3).

As time went on, the experience of practitioners at the clinics, and the findings of surveys conducted on patients attending there, began to build up a more sophisticated picture of the addict and the effectiveness of treatment. But the picture was a partial one because it was seen through the lens of practice at the clinics with a lack of information on what was going on elsewhere. Wiepert and his colleagues reported on 575 British opiate addicts entering treatment between 1968 and 1975 at two clinics in London (Wiepert, Bewley, and d'Orban 1978). They confirmed the view that there had been a gradual change in treatment practice since 1968. The aim was to reduce gradually the quantities of a drug prescribed. The patients would be expected to attend the clinic each week but would collect their daily prescription from a specified pharmacy. Routine urine testing would be conducted to monitor the patient's drug taking. It was found that 40 per cent of patients used other drugs as well as those prescribed. The change from heroin to methadone was very clear. In 1968, all opiate prescriptions were for heroin. In 1969, injectable methadone (physeptone) replaced heroin and in 1975 in the two clinics studied, only five of the 258 patients being treated there in that year were being prescribed heroin. Of the 575 people (455 men and 120 women) who had been treated at those clinics in the eight years studied, slightly over half were still in treatment (52 per cent). Eleven per cent had died, 6 per cent were in custody, and 3 per cent had left the country. Twenty-eight per cent were not in treatment at that time. The assumption was that those no longer in treatment were no longer using opiates. 'The consensus is that there are not a significantly large number of opiate addicts outside the clinics and that the numbers have increased slowly since 1968.' The view at the time then was that 'there is some evidence that the system has been of value and that it has helped to contain the problem'. The picture looked fairly hopeful:

> 'relatively fewer people may have been developing dependence . . . and that the London drug dependence clinics are for the most part still treating an accumulation of chronic patients whose first contact with opiates occurred during a period when illicit opiates were more easily obtained' (Wiepert, Bewley and d'Orban 1978: 31)

Opiate dependence was, then, seen mainly as a chronic condition which resulted from an earlier acute epidemic from which some had died and others recovered but a large number would remain in treatment as chronic invalids.

This perception of the problem was supported by the results of a seven-year follow-up of heroin addicts (Stimson, Oppenheimer, and Thorley 1978). This reported on 128 patients, a one-third representative sample of patients at 13 of the 15 clinics in London. These patients were being prescribed heroin on a daily basis in 1969. (In this sense they are a relatively unusual group among problem drug-takers since the practice of prescribing heroin was later rejected in favour of methadone. The sample consisted then of people who in these early years were offered heroin rather than methadone. At that time, 45 per cent of patients at London clinics were being prescribed heroin: the present figure is about 5 per cent.) Seven years later, 41 per cent had stopped attending the clinics, 43 per cent were still attending, a fairly similar figure to that of Wiepert, Bewley, and d'Orban in the study reported above. (Twelve per cent had died, again a similar proportion to that reported by Wiepert, Bewley, and d'Orban.) Forty-eight per cent were still using opiates, only 5 per cent of whom were not obtaining a legal prescription. Experts felt able to conclude therefore that

> 'these data show that few people . . . continued to use opiates without attending clinics . . . [and that] continued opiate use is rare among patients who stop attending clinics and live in the community. [In addition] opiate dependence does not seem to have been replaced by dependence on other drugs.' (Wiepert, Bewley, and d'Orban 1978: 6)

These findings therefore produced a relatively hopeful picture of the drug scene in Britain. However, they contrast with other findings, such as those of Mitcheson and Hartnoll (Hartnoll *et al.* 1980). This was a particularly influential study, a survey conducted between 1972 and 1976. Although the date of publication is relatively late, the original intention for the study and general beliefs about its findings, which circulated earlier than publication, supported the growing view in favour of prescribing oral methadone as the drug of preference at clinics. This study used a strict random allocation method to divide patients into two groups. One group was offered injectable heroin and the other oral methadone. After twelve months, three quarters of those given heroin were still in treatment, compared to less than one third of those offered oral methadone. Most of the latter group left before three months had elapsed. However, those offered injectable heroin (and thus more likely to remain in treatment) showed little change in their behaviour and were just as likely to be adopting a 'junkie' way of life as at the start of treatment. Those offered oral methadone (and thus more likely to drop out of treatment) had, however, polarized into two groups: some had given up drug misuse altogether and 23 per cent were spending no time at all with other drug users, compared to only 2 per cent of the 'heroin' group, a successful outcome therefore; but others continued in the world of illicit drugs, spending time with other users and being criminally active. These findings are of great significance for the debate about the role of the clinics and the extent to which they should or could act to 'contain' the growing drug problem. The confrontational response resulted in a higher abstinence rate but also a greater drop-out from regular treatment. Which should be the preferred goal: relative 'success' with less than one half or keeping in touch with the majority but making less impact on their behaviour?

These various research findings began to influence ideas about appropriate treatment practices. One view was that if you left people long enough they would eventually grow out of (mature out of) drug taking, the implication being that a policy of support and encouragement for a patient over time, which might involve prescribing but always with the aim of reducing, could succeed. Another view encouraged a more active role for the clinics where patients would be confronted, pulled up more sharply about the effects of their behaviour, which was not condoned by staff, and prescribing would be of oral methadone only. Here success would appear earlier with those who were likely to give up, while the remainder would be left to bear the responsibility for their choice to continue drug taking by chancing their luck with the criminal underworld and the police and prisons.

The two views differ essentially in the degree to which they see the addict as able to exercise control over his or her actions. The Brain Report gave this definition of the addict:

'a person who, as the result of repeated administration has become dependent upon a drug controlled under the Dangerous Drugs Act and has an overpowering desire for its continuance but who does not require it for the relief of organic disease.' (Interdepartmental Committee on Drug Addiction 1965: 7)

The key term here is 'overpowering desire' which derives from the WHO Report of 1964 (WHO 1964: 13). This definition accords also with the lay view of addiction wherein the addict is enslaved or 'hooked' by repeated use.

Acceptance of the involuntariness (the craving) argument is found in both popular and expert circles. The accuracy of this portrait of addiction has been questioned however. Finigarette and Hasse, for example, argue that focusing on four aspects of drug use belies this myth. They refer to

'1. the existence of a population of drug users who do not become addicts; 2. the successful elimination of addictive patterns among formerly addicted groups; 3. the relative rarity of a heavy physiological addiction in narcotic addicts in this country [USA]; and 4. the correspondingly wide-spread influence of social and psychological inducements to addictive behaviour.' (Finigarette and Hasse 1978: 156)

The perception of addiction as compulsive, they argue, gives rise to an 'all or nothing' approach to cure and the concentration on relapse as a single instance. A preferable approach, they argue, which is one that we shall see later to have been on the whole held by the workers at City Roads, begins by noting the general finding in contemporary Western societies that new addicts are

'young, psychologically immature, occupationally unskilled, socially uprooted, poor and disadvantaged. . . . Young people who are disadvantaged and alienated may find the foundation of a socially authenticated identity in addiction. For such persons, drug use provides at last a "constructive" focal activity in life, generating its own occupational respon-sibilities, opportunities for success and achievement, social status and ideological, philosophical or religious meaning.' (Finigarette and Hasse 1978: 168)

They note also that 'a person who has developed roots in conventional society and skills for leading a productive life is substantially less likely to find a meaningful social identity in the drug culture and such a person can more readily abandon addiction as it develops' (1978: 168).

The implications of this alternative view of drug addiction are to concentrate on offering an alternative social identity and points of reference and directing attention to the roots of alienation and disadvantage rather than focusing attention solely on the substance used, heroin, barbiturates, alcohol or whatever, and the individual's so-called compulsion or over-powering motivation to rely upon it.

An example of this kind of approach is found in the work of the Lifeline Project, a voluntary agency that runs the only remaining day centre in Britain dealing specifically with drug takers. A similar approach is adopted by many of the concept houses that predominate in the rehabilitation field. The workers adopt a 'no drugs confrontational' approach. 'Negative street talk' is discouraged and they insist on abstinence as the only positive way forward. They refuse to place the clients or residents in a 'victim' role, preferring to negotiate contracts that set realistic, mutually agreed goals and expectations or to insist on adherence to a rigid programme of staged improvement as at

Phoenix House. The philosophy is one of self-help and acceptance of one's own responsibility for crises and in some cases
submission to the norms of the resident group.

It is possible to see then the emergence of a distinctive
response to addiction within the voluntary sector, which
parallels the 'confrontational' approach increasingly adopted at
some of the clinics. The aim is to encourage greater self-control
and personal integration among clients. They generally take a
firm stand against drug misuse. However, they emphasize the
general problems of the clients not just their drug use. They also
criticize the fragmented and compartmentalized nature of the
services and prefer multi-faceted projects where a variety of
services are available to the client in one place. (This, they feel,
tends to shift power to the client and increases the range of
options open to them.) On the grounds of cost, they are willing
to consider the use of non-residential services but argue for a
switch of resources from the clinics to the community services.
They would also like to see a new funding structure to aid the
establishment of a range of community-based services and the
recognition of drug misuse as a national problem and thus a
central government funding responsibility.

It is interesting to note the shared view of some psychiatrists
and some social workers that drug misuse reflects 'problems in
living'. (Within this, opinions differ between those who see the
addict's problems as in some sense an individual inadequacy,
and who therefore set out to make radical changes in their
personality, and those who prefer to stress the social causes of
addiction, that in a drug-taking society there are cultural
pressures encouraging drug taking and vested interests, commercial, professional, and criminal, exacerbate these.) The
perspective wherein the patient's lack of social skills and
problems in interpersonal relationships are seen as the key
features tends to predominate among practitioners.

> 'There remains a strong clinical impression that hospitalised
> drug takers are particularly handicapped in the social skills
> necessary to initiate and maintain close and meaningful
> interpersonal relations and that the self gratification from
> drugs becomes a surrogate relationship in its own right.'
> (Thorley 1979: 283)

Their 'pre-existing neurotic illnesses' are influenced to a large
extent by their experience of 'homes where there has been
parental disturbance and family disruption'. Long-term treatment of drug dependence involves the need to work with

personal and social problems, encouragement of personal responsibility, and the use of out-patient facilities and communally based counselling and skilled social work. In the short term, the key focus is on the patient's fear of withdrawal which needs careful management. Barbiturate withdrawal especially requires in-patient care and close supervision.

Many of these principles were fundamental to the City Roads approach. Partly this reflects the development of a new approach to dealing with drug misuse which both workers in the clinics and in the voluntary projects shared, building it up over time, and being influenced by American experience. But there was also a direct input into City Roads from the social workers appointed as the original Director and Deputy Director and from the consultant psychiatrist. This set of principles on which City Roads was able to build was well established before City Roads opened and can be called a 'new orthodoxy'.

The special problem of the 'chaotic' drug misuser

The debate about social provision in general in the seventies began to focus on 'those in special need'. Health and social services adopted more a crisis management approach, offering services on selectivist criteria to special categories of 'casualties', those with more severe conditions, those in greatest need. This partly reflected the rising rate of social expenditure and the desire to cut costs, while protecting the most vulnerable, and partly a change in attitudes, where emphasis on self-help and individual rather than collective responsibility for welfare became dominant, and communal services for all gave way to special services for problem cases.

In the field of drug misuse, some attention focused on the special problem of the chaotic or problem drug taker. It was in this context that the need for a crisis intervention service came to be voiced and pressure built up which culminated in the opening of City Roads for a three-year experimental period.

When the idea of City Roads began to take shape there were two main types of service for drug misusers, the statutory and the voluntary. The statutory services offered specialist help for drug dependants and were controlled by the medical profession. They were all connected with hospitals, the main service being the out-patient clinics (DTCs). There were also a few in-patient detoxification units and some provision for longer-term rehabilitation. These were set up from the late sixties to deal mainly with the problems of opiate dependence. Although some clinics were social-work oriented and most included social workers on their staff, the voluntary sector differed from the statutory in being predominantly *controlled* by social workers. It contained the non-residential street agencies, offering advice and counselling and the residential rehabilitation projects, which provided long-term accommodation together with various kinds and degrees of support and therapy.

The idea of a crisis unit arose when the view began to grow that the problem of drug misuse was changing. It was thought that a new style of drug use had appeared on the scene, new both in medical terms and in terms of the social problems presented. From a medical point of view, these people were seen as multiple drug misusers, in the sense that they used a variety of drugs more or less indiscriminately depending on what happened to be available on the market. Barbiturates in particular were widely available and taken in large quantities by young, homeless people who frequently overdosed and were brought into Accident and Emergency departments where they were found difficult to manage and sometimes violent. They seemed to have a particular set of needs for which none of the existing services could provide adequately. There was here an implicit criticism of the way the clinics were operating, that the clinics adopted too much a purely 'medical' (partial) and substance-based approach, that they were not effective in treating the 'unstable' patients, and that in being predominantly out-patient based, they could not respond quickly enough when help was asked for nor provide detoxification.

The main problem was the inability of any non-residential service to cope with the barbiturate-intoxicated client. The street agencies first voiced the demand for a crisis intervention service. This network of voluntary projects, working in Central London, came face to face with the daily problems of drug takers especially those in the West End and around the Piccadilly area. In the early seventies, all the non-residential services were working as day centres – New Horizon, CDP, Hungerford, and Blenheim. With the exception of Blenheim, they had 'fixing rooms' where notified addicts could inject their prescribed drugs in hygienic conditions. The services offered were a variety of activities including art and crafts, (usually) cheap food, advice and counselling and, most clearly, a safe setting for drug users during the day.

Concern about barbiturate misuse arose initially because it

presented a serious management problem. Addicts used the fixing room to inject barbiturates, over-dosed, had to be taken to hospital and discharged themselves in time to return to the day centre intoxicated but not comatose. The day centre staff were then faced with individuals whom they could neither return to hospital nor discharge to the streets. It was from this base that discussion began which involved the idea of a crisis unit, control of barbiturates, and restrictions on the supply of drugs to temporary patients. (These latter were taken up with some effect through the CURB campaign whereby doctors voluntarily agreed to restrict their prescribing of barbiturates. It had some effect on general levels of dependence on barbiturates among more stable patients but supplies still continued to reach the streets.)

Criticism of the existing services was heard among workers in the street agencies. Clients of the day centres used heroin, amphetamines, and barbiturates obtained from both licit and illicit sources. This criticism was not specifically related to barbiturates but the misuse of barbiturates did focus attention on the gap in services. Whilst there was anger and frustration because services were not available or inappropriate to the needs of the barbiturate user, the main call was for *more* services. The shortage of services has indeed been a common and continuing theme, especially the unwillingness of authorities to accept a responsibility for the provision of services for drug misusers and the constant wrangling as to whether they are a central or local responsibility.

State departments from the late sixties onwards tried to monitor the changing drugs scene through the activities at various times of the Advisory Committee on Drug Dependence, the Prisons Board, Home Office Drugs Branch, and ACMD. One of the first working groups appointed by the ACMD was on barbiturates and this was a key element in collecting information and, possibly, important in encouraging the funding of relevant research, especially that by Ghodse which will be discussed below.

The argument for a short-stay residential project in London, open 24 hours a day with a capacity for up to 15 residents, was first put forward by a Steering Committee set up by SCODA in 1973 to evaluate the extent of multiple drug abuse in Britain. SCODA is a voluntary organization funded by the DHSS which acts as a co-ordinating body for voluntary services dealing with drug misusers. In pressing for this kind of service, the Steering Committee emphasized that the clinics were largely unsuccessful with the more chaotic type of drug misuser. There was a need for a service which would not only fill the gap in the existing services but would also ensure that the existing services would be used more fully and in the appropriate way. The group of drug misusers who were most in need of this service were generally homeless, sleeping rough, and spending occasional nights in hostels. They regularly overdosed and attended A and E departments for resuscitation and to be treated for abscesses, septicaemia, hepatitis, and other conditions. A range of drugs other than opiates, including barbiturates, were being used intravenously, often in extremely unhygienic circumstances. These young people presented special difficulties to the helping agencies, since they were often intoxicated and appeared poorly motivated to accept any treatment. They were said to dislike the structure and rules of clinical and institutional settings, failed to keep appointments, and their often aggressive behaviour created severe problems in the hostels which accommodated them. The street agencies attempted to offer a counselling service but because the clients were often intoxicated, found it difficult to advise them. They also encountered difficulties in referring them to accommodation since many hostels were reluctant to accept people who were disruptive elements. They emphasized the need for an immediately accessible residential service which would specialize in dealing with such young people, with their medical and their social problems, offer short-term shelter, assessment of needs and onward referral to appropriate services.

SCODA, having put forward its initial proposal for a short-stay unit, undertook a survey in 1973 among the central London street agencies, which showed that half the number of people, about 200, seen by these agencies were using barbiturates regularly. About half those who visited these agencies did not have contact with specialist medical agencies such as the clinics. They concluded that there was a large group of people whom these existing medical services did not reach.

At the same time, medical practitioners working in the drugs field began to build up a picture of the sort of person who was most 'at risk' and most difficult for doctors and staff to deal with. These 'very unstable' patients, sometimes described as 'chaotic', were most likely to show a particular set of characteristics. They were more likely to be treated in hospital as an in-patient on numerous occasions: 'hospitalisations for treatment of drug abuse are a sign of instability' concluded Wiepert,

Bewley and d'Orban (1978: 30). Whereas 71 per cent of the patients they surveyed over eight years at the two clinics had never been hospitalized for abuse, 'those treated as in-patients in hospital two or more times for drug abuse had an average of 9 hospitalisations'. These people were also at greater risk of dying – 'those who had died had been more inconsistent in attendance, had abused drugs more and had a lower rate of employment'. Other features of instability were lack of accommodation and lack of significant personal relationships. Overall then, the most unstable or 'chaotic' were deviant in terms of the central social values of home, work, and family.

Attention in the seventies began to focus on two issues. First the perception of drug misuse as one of 'multiple drug misuse', and the associated view that opiate use was less prominent within this than barbiturate misuse. It is interesting to note that as early as 1969 Mitcheson had found that the use of barbiturates and methaqualone was widespread among heroin addicts attending the clinics (Mitcheson *et al*. 1970). By 1979, Teggin and Bewley were reporting that

'the number of patients referred to Tooting Bec Hospital with physical dependence on barbiturates has increased each year. Some have been opiate addicts and others polydrug abusers who were not using opiate type drugs habitually but who required hospital admission for withdrawal treatment' (Teggin and Bewley 1979: 106).)

Second, attention concentrated on the specific problem of the 'chaotic' or 'difficult' client with whom the clinics were having little success, who either did not present at the clinic for treatment or who did not continue long in treatment after one or two appointments.

Nurses too showed concern and protested at the conditions in A and E departments. The nurses at the Middlesex Hospital, the A and E department closest to the Soho area and in the front line at the time, were particularly influential in raising the level of concern. They wrote that 'casualty departments in London and other cities were inundated by young addicts, registered or otherwise, who had lost their source or could not pay for their drugs' (Mitchell and Rose 1975: 1488). At the Middlesex Hospital A and E Department, Beryl Rose kept a register of all drug users seen there which indicated 'the swing towards barbiturates, especially Tuinal, although addiction now is commonly a multi-drug problem' (Mitchell and Rose 1975:

1489). The crisis in casualty departments was dramatically emphasized:

> 'many unconscious addicts are brought in to the department by ambulance two or three times in 24 hours. Immediately they have recovered sufficiently to walk out of the department, they obtain more drugs from the black market, collapse and become unconscious and are brought in again. Multidrug abusers are often violent, anti-social young people. Many are undernourished and have infected wounds. They seldom wash and many of them have body lice. The age group is usually 18 to 25 but 14 year olds have been known' (Mitchell and Rose 1975: 1489–90).

Such graphic and emotive descriptions were perhaps necessary to bring the issue to the attention of those concerned with the provision of services. (The authors also significantly noted the continuing existence of a market of young people dependent on drugs, awaiting exploitation by traders in narcotics, just what was in fact to occur in the later years of that decade.)

Of most significance in influencing government to pay some attention to the issue was the research carried out by A. Hamid Ghodse at London casualty departments. This work, conducted through the Addiction Research Unit at the Institute of Psychiatry and financed by grants from the DHSS and MRC, was a most thorough and meticulous survey, definition of the problem and proposals for action. Ghodse surveyed all drug-related attendances at 62 casualty departments in Greater London in August 1975. Amongst these, he isolated 395 drug-dependent individuals, the majority of whom were seen following an overdose. Barbiturates were the drug used most frequently and there was a high incidence of multi-drug use. Drugs were obtained illicitly in most cases. Patients had commonly a history of repeated overdosing and one-fifth behaved aggressively in the casualty department. He stressed the importance of this category of people, separated from the clinic population of addicts, in helping to provide a fuller picture of drug dependency, though he recognized that even so the two did not constitute the whole story. These 'drug dependent patients may reach the casualty departments before they come to the notice of the drug clinics or after they have disappeared from those clinics. Indeed, some casualty attenders may represent a sub group of the addict population who never become "registered" ' (Ghodse 1977a). Awareness of the characteristics of this group could help to throw light on service needs and the operation of the system of health care.

Although barbiturates figured prominently in these cases (half used them) opiates were used by more than one quarter. 'About half . . . who took an overdose of methadone and/or barbiturates had overdosed repeatedly.' Almost a quarter of those taking an overdose of barbiturates administered the drug by injection although the preparation was in fact meant to be taken by mouth. Impaired levels of consciousness were found in 80 per cent of cases, almost always the case if the patient had used a combination of barbiturates and methadone. Ghodse concluded 'the drug dependent population of London casualty departments although undoubtedly containing some "registered" narcotic addicts, also probably includes some subjects, as yet unknown to any authority who in years to come may approach the clinics' (Ghodse 1977b: 279).

It is interesting here to note the comment of one of the street agencies at the same time that 'the majority of people we contact at Piccadilly are not receiving treatment from a clinic . . . this is largely because they do not have a heroin or methadone addiction' (Helping Hand 1978: 4).

Ghodse continued, 'this study suggests that there must be serious doubt as to the aptness of the present system for the needs of this group of patients. It is an accident of health care evolution, rather than any intentional policy, that has handed to casualty departments the front line responsibility for dealing with this extraordinarily complex medico-social problem . . . the repetitive ways in which drug-dependent individuals take overdoses and present to hospital is an indication that the treatment they are at present receiving is not an appropriate response' (Ghodse 1977b: 279).

He proposed the following solution: 'After the physical complications of drug dependence have been dealt with medically, there ought to be available some immediate form of appropriate social intervention.' He recognized that there were no easy solutions in this area but suggested that immediate action at the moment of crisis might find the patient more receptive to help than at other times.

Ghodse's research also showed that the problem, although not exclusive to the city centre, was concentrated in central London. Five hospitals dealt with 42 per cent of all incidents of drug overdose involving drug-dependent individuals. Four of them, within one and a quarter miles of Piccadilly Circus, dealt with more than a third of the incidents. Two dealt with 20 per cent and he suggested that 'one or both of these hospitals would be the obvious place for the trial of new methods of case contacting, motivation and treating people with these problems'.

Doctors and nurses questioned by Ghodse generally agreed that such patients should receive full psychiatric evaluation and that a psychiatrist should always be on duty and available to advise them. Two-thirds thought there should be a full-time security officer available at A and E departments to deal with aggressive patients and four-fifths that drug-dependent patients should be taken to special emergency centres rather than to A and E departments. Only 40 per cent of these patients who had overdosed and were seen in the London casualty survey were in fact admitted to hospital. 'Reluctance to admit them may have been due to doubts about the value of the in-patient assessment and treatment but could also have been because drug dependent individuals are thought to be "difficult" patients who may disrupt a ward' (Ghodse 1979: 173). (Of these drug-dependent patients only 34 per cent were known to the Home Office; of those who used narcotics still only 53 per cent were noted there (Ghodse 1977b).)

The weight of all this evidence led the authorities to accept that multiple drug abuse was a major problem. Indeed as early as 1974 in answer to an annual UN questionnaire on drug abuse in the UK, the government had stated that 'the pattern tends to be of multiple drug use' and by 1975 were clear that 'the problem in the UK is mainly one of multiple drug abuse'. By 1975, 'polydrug' had become a separate item on the list of DHSS statistics of drug dependence. While useful in describing what had always been the reality more precisely and emphasizing the contribution of barbiturates, the term tends however to play down the role of opiates, which continued to play a significant part as Ghodse's findings indicated. (It should be noted that barbiturates are not controlled under the Misuse of Drugs legislation although they may only be dispensed by an authorized pharmacist on a prescription given by a medical practitioner. In 1980, ACMD recommended that barbiturates be controlled under the *Misuse of Drugs Act* and this may be implemented in 1984 (cf. ISDD *Druglink* 18 1983: 17).)

The interim report of a working group of the Advisory Council on the Misuse of Drugs set up 'to undertake a comprehensive review of the treatment and rehabilitation services for the misusers of drugs and to make recommendations for dealing with both the immediate problem and the longer-term situation' concluded that the problem in the seventies had changed rather than diminished. Multiple drug misuse was the main problem facing the services and the committee noted that the London clinics were then more heavily loaded than ever before and that some young people had difficulty in finding appropriate treatment rapidly. A and E departments dealing with overdose patients and services providing detoxification were frequently overburdened and inadequate and there was a lack of choice in rehabilitation services (Advisory Council on the Misuse of Drugs 1977). (This interim report specifically supported the establishment of a crisis unit and the Advisory Council maintained pressure for and interest in this development.)

The official response then to the continued pressure from the voluntary projects, the views of experts, and in particular the evidence of Ghodse's survey (which they had commissioned) was to fund, on an experimental basis, a short-stay crisis intervention service, City Roads, which would deal with the problems of the drug misuser who is prone to take overdoses: 'these often disturbed and self-destructive people, many of whom are young' (Advisory Council on the Misuse of Drugs 1977: 26).

Shortly before City Roads opened in May 1978, a Man Alive programme (*The Fix*, Nick Ross, April 4, 1978) reported that there were 400 overdoses per week in London of which 100 were of drug-dependent people. This was a sevenfold increase in ten years. The Middlesex Hospital A and E Department was reported to be seeing three people per night suffering from barbiturate overdose, mainly of Tuinal, selling then at three to four per £1. This department had, in fact, set up a special observation room for such patients, designed originally, interestingly enough, as a decontamination room for victims of nuclear accidents involving radiation. There the patients could sleep it off safely, lying on mattresses on the floor. Dangerous items were taken from them and they were observed by remote-control television. They were thus kept separate from other patients, with their own lavatory, and the whole area could be easily hosed down afterwards. The patients were characterized in the programme as aggressive and difficult. Attention focused on the regulars and the frustration of staff at their thankless task.

It seemed then that the need for City Roads was well documented and that when it opened in May 1978 both street agencies and A and E departments would feel a great sense of relief in having a special service to which to send their 'problem cases' and their 'difficult patients'.

Conclusion

We have seen how, through the seventies, attention among specialists increasingly focused on the unstable drug misuser, the more chaotic, more difficult client, very different in terms of commitment to drug taking and the world of drug misuse than the recreational drug user with firmer roots in the main stream of conventional society. A consensus grew up that the clinics were not having much success with these particularly unstable patients and that there were problems in trying to fit them into the conventional health and social services. Apart from some comments about the aloofness of the medical profession, there was a view that the clinics, as well as being underfunded, had not been sufficiently flexible or experimental in developing alternative ways of dealing with these patients. A key issue then is where among the 'caring professions' should the main responsibility for dealing with drug misuse lie – with medicine or social work? Within either profession is it desirable to confine this concern to a specialized group?

In these discussions, the setting too is seen as particularly significant. City Roads, by being a specialist agency, but set up at community level, outside the conventional structures of the NHS and outside the conventional rules and regulations of the medical and nursing professions and local authority social service departments, can be seen to have been a deliberate compromise between these different sets of views. It was run mainly by social workers but a psychiatrist was there to keep an eye on things. It was a voluntary project but it was not allowed total freedom in the way it would operate, being supervised in its early days by the DHSS and continually by a management committee increasingly dominated by the representatives of the statutory sector. City Roads might then be seen as a hybrid, an experiment in cross-fertilization. The question was, could this 'artificial plant' survive and grow roots in the community? A number of issues were on trial. Could social workers handle these difficult cases? Could such a service, particularly one dealing with casualties, both medical and social, be run effectively in a community setting? Could a treatment approach be developed which would be flexible, accommodating to the needs of drug misusers as a whole, not narrowly substance-based? Could that approach come closer to the client, involve a partnership between the professional and the client in an informal setting without things getting out of hand and the balance of power tipping too much towards the client, leading to disruption of the kind that had been observed in some of the original day centres and hostels where 'fixing' on the premises was tolerated?

The time was ripe for the City Roads experiment. Pressure was building up from experts and from the media and especially from the agencies represented through SCODA. Pessimism and despondency had set in in the clinics and a new initiative was unlikely to come from there (see Stimson and Oppenheimer 1982). And, as it turned out, City Roads opened just as the emerging crisis of increasing opiate addiction began to surface, building on the multiple drug misuse of the seventies. Even so, the obstacles that had to be overcome in the setting up of City Roads were considerable and even now its future is far from secure. In the next chapter we give an account of the difficulties faced by the project and how it managed to overcome them and eventually open in May 1978.

2 The Making of City Roads

It took six years to set up City Roads, that is six years from 1972, when the idea of setting up such a unit was first expressed, to 1978 when funding had been raised, premises found, and aims specified.

This chapter will explore what happened during these six years. Why did it take such a long time? What problems were entailed in establishing a new service? We shall show that the process was not simply one of rational and careful planning. A great deal depended on the initiative of particular individuals, different interests were involved, and many issues relating to the operation of the unit were still unresolved when it opened in 1978.

As we have seen, changes in the perception of the drug problem and of the needs of drug misusers took place during the seventies, the very period during which proposals for City Roads were being discussed. In other words, City Roads was not the result of people sitting round a table with a pile of research papers on the basis of which a decision was made. Rather, these findings were coming out and the debate was going on at the same time as talks about City Roads. When, for example, the Advisory Council on the Misuse of Drugs published their Interim Report in 1977, recommending among other things that a short-stay unit be set up, negotiations about City Roads had already begun. There was widespread agreement among all that some kind of short-stay unit was probably needed. But exactly what it should be doing, who it should be for, and who should fund it were not at all clear. The answers to these questions emerged gradually between 1973 and 1978.

The history of City Roads

In 1973, SCODA produced its first proposal for a short-stay unit. This was a year of informally sounding out the amount of goodwill in various quarters. SCODA approached the DHSS and the London Boroughs Association (LBA). Both expressed their willingness to support in part the operating costs. The position of the DHSS was that, since the project could be seen as an experimental, innovatory project, they would be able to fund it on this basis for a fixed period of time, and with an independent research team evaluating the service. They emphasized that they saw the project as a London-based service and that therefore the responsibility for it was ultimately a local one. Furthermore, this local responsibility was not seen purely as a concern for the health service, but also for the Social Services, since the project aimed to offer combined social and health care. The DHSS would fund it as a 'pump-priming' exercise, to get it off the ground, but with the aim that local health and social services would take over the funding responsibility after three years. It was clear, therefore, that for the DHSS to fund the project at all, the LBA would have to make a contribution from the start to show a commitment in principle. What was *not* clear, however, was which local health authorities would be expected to take up the bill after the three years. The Camden and Islington Area Health Authority became involved from the start by administering the nursing budget and taking responsibility for the professional nursing standards at City Roads. But the money came from the DHSS and the link was purely administrative. The reason it was this particular health authority was simply that City Roads was situated within its boundaries. Clients were not expected to come solely from this area, and it was assumed that other health authorities would have to become involved financially after the three years. But nobody else was drawn into the negotiations by 1978. This was partly to do with the fact that at this stage it was not known where the clients would actually come from, but principally it was because everybody was keen simply to get City Roads opened. The problem of what would happen after the first three years was put to one side, even by the DHSS, who were satisfied to have at least secured the support of the LBA.

At the beginning of 1974 a Steering Committee was formed to work out detailed proposals and to undertake the negotiations necessary for the proposal to become reality. There were several obstacles on the way, which will be discussed through a summary of the main events between 1974 and 1978.

The first obstacle was to find some premises. The funding authorities did not wish to negotiate details until suitable premises had been secured. This took eighteen months. Then, in

September 1975, a funding application was sent to the DHSS and the LBA. By the end of 1976, the DHSS had agreed in principle to support the project as a three-year experimental service, on condition that the LBA contribute as well. The DHSS seemed confident of the viability of the proposal, for at this time they granted money for the research. Birkbeck College was approached and in December 1976, the Research Officer was appointed, funded by the Small Grants Committee of the DHSS. In March 1977, the LBA agreed to support the project financially, and a full-time Administrator was appointed from 1 April. However, before the final go-ahead could be given and the rest of the staff appointed, a further major obstacle had to be overcome: the specification and agreement between the parties involved, Steering Committee, the DHSS, and LBA, about the operational policies of the unit. Negotiations about this Operational Document went on until March 1978, when it was finally approved. In the meantime, preparations were made for building work to be done on the premises, and in January 1978, a Director and Deputy Director were appointed. They were involved in the final and crucial stages of the writing of the Operational Document. They also got permission to advertise for further staff in order to avoid any delays, and as soon as the final go ahead was given, the fifteen team workers were appointed to start their training programme in the middle of April.

We shall now consider in more detail some of the main problems encountered during the making of City Roads. To a large extent the opening of City Roads represented only a temporary solution to these problems. Throughout, and indeed after the three-year experimental period, issues relating to the continued survival of the project were to dominate in one form or another.

PREMISES

The task of finding a house proved to be very difficult indeed. Local authorities and residents' associations were approached without results. The problem was twofold: first, no one was attracted by the prospect of housing drug misusers, and second, the project did not at the time have any guaranteed financial support. A house in North London was eventually found, more by chance than through any deliberate attempt to place the project in this area. The place, which consisted of two interconnected terraced houses on three floors, seemed suitable for several reasons. It was the right size to house fifteen residents, which was the maximum number intended at the time, and it provided good opportunities for offering a non-institutional, informal setting. There were not many residential houses in its immediate vicinity, so the risk of possible complaints from neighbours seemed minimal. The house, which was owned by the SOS Society, was rented for three years from September 1975. Since the project was only in its initial planning stage at this time, the house was sublet to Centrepoint, a housing organization, until April 1977. At this time the Administrator was appointed, and building work started. Certain alterations and repairs had to be made, and central heating and a fire detection system installed. The DHSS/ LBA undertook the payment of rent and granted some capital for the building work.

However, the lease obtained in 1975 represented only a temporary solution to the housing problem. It was due for renewal in September 1978, by which time the owners (the SOS Society) were indicating that they planned to sell the premises. During the next two years, the management was frantically busy trying to raise capital to buy the building. It was very near to being a Catch 22 situation. In order to obtain funding beyond the three-year experimental period, City Roads had to have safe premises. But many of the trusts they approached for capital were reluctant to grant money to a project whose future was was uncertain. The SOS Society was extremely sympathetic and understanding, extending the lease several times to give City Roads a chance to find the capital money. A special sub-committee of the Management Committee was engaged solely in raising this money and eventually, after much activity, they managed to raise enough (£77,000) to buy the house in 1981.

THE FUNDING OF CITY ROADS

Funding was a key issue throughout the history of City Roads, both before and after it became established. The nature of the problems, however, changed somewhat once the three-year experimental period was due to expire.

When the process of setting up City Roads began, two prospective funding bodies were identified – the DHSS and the LBA. The Steering Committee counted on getting the main bulk of its revenue from them. Although they made contact with the Home Office and had a person from the Drugs Inspectorate as observer on the Steering Committee, an application for funds to the Home Office was not considered seriously. A number of charities were approached for capital contributions, but no other statutory bodies were considered. Although the DHSS was expected to meet all the running costs, provided the LBA made some contribution, no actual sum was mentioned at the beginning. The Steering Committee was asked to put in an application including an estimated budget. Negotiations over this budget turned out to be lengthy and very frustrating for the Steering Committee. Basically, the problems stemmed from the status of the project, combining *voluntary* and *statutory* elements. It was in principle a voluntary project, but with financial and some administrative input from the statutory side. In the statutory sector there are rules and regulations regarding pay, conditions of work, professional standards, and accountability. Voluntary services, on the other hand, are usually thought to be less bureaucratic and rule-bound, more flexible, cheaper (though not necessarily more cost-effective).

When the Steering Committee drafted its first budget, it did so on the basis that the unit had to provide a multidisciplinary service and employ a number of professional staff. Yet the voluntary nature of the project was manifest in its expected reliance on unqualified workers and volunteers, and in that any statutory requirements regarding staff working conditions were not really anticipated. They soon had to revise their first budget, when the Camden and Islington Area Health Authority, through whom the nursing staff were to be appointed, made it clear that the budget had not taken into account the stipulated nursing salaries and hours of work. This revised budget was discussed with DHSS administrators and finance staff at a meeting in May 1977. The Steering Committee was asking for £57,000 from the DHSS, having been promised £12,000 from the LBA. They were told categorically by the DHSS administrators that £43,000 was the absolute maximum the Department could offer. The Steering Committee went back to the drawing-board, thinking about how to make savings. However, before another budget was drafted, discussions about the operational policies of the unit were initiated with the professional advisers from the DHSS: medical, nursing, and social work. Their concern was with professional standards and conditions of work, and they insisted that an adequate level of professional staffing was the main consideration in determining the necessary funding. Needless to say, the Steering Committee was in total agreement with this, but also the administrators/finance section of the Department seemed to accept tacitly the views of the professional advisers, and the sum finally granted for the first year of the operation of City Roads was thus determined through discussions about operational policies alone.

AGREEING THE OPERATIONAL DOCUMENT

Until March 1977, when the funding authorities agreed to support the project, negotiations had taken place on the basis of a written proposal dating back to 1975. This proposal outlined aims and methods, admission criteria, referral sources, research and evaluation, staffing and job descriptions, education and in-service training, premises, and administration/organization. In March 1977, the DHSS asked the Steering Committee to provide an operational policy document. Until such a document had been approved, no money could be granted. This message was telephoned to the then full-time administrator for the project. Although he was uncertain of what the DHSS wanted, he started to write some sections describing in more detail some of the points mentioned in the proposal. This was done with the support of some working groups of the Steering Committee. At a meeting in May 1977 with the DHSS officials, the staffing section, which had been completed by then, was handed over. At a meeting in August 1977 with the DHSS, the LBA, and the AHA, the Steering Committee was again asked to produce an Operational Document. The representatives of the Steering Committee present at this meeting said that they found it very difficult to map out in detail the operation of the unit and that they would like to maintain a certain amount of flexibility. However, the message they received was that they had to produce a document outlining 'the purpose of the unit, the function of the unit and how it is going to work'. No mention was made of the sections already handed in to the Department. The Operational Document of the Leeds Alcohol Detoxification unit was mentioned as an example of the kind of document required.

The next meeting with the DHSS took place in January 1978, by which time an Operational Document had been produced. The DHSS officials had a range of objections to the document, some concerned with minor technical details, some with more fundamental policy questions. Without going into details, the main issues were first, admission policy: the DHSS insisted that the unit should only take clients referred by certain A and E departments for the first three months, and that after that, any

changes should be negotiated with the DHSS; second, job
descriptions: the DHSS thought that the responsibilities of the
individual staff members were not clearly defined, especially
the division between professional and co-ordinative responsibilities; third, technical details: a number of sections were
shown to be either irrelevant or badly phrased, and the
Steering Committee was asked to stress concepts like 'multi-
disciplinary' and 'experimental' more than had already been
done. In short, a number of changes had to be made, and this
was done by the three senior staff, who had by then been
appointed. They succeeded in producing a satisfactory document, so that in March 1978, precisely a year after the document
had first been requested, the final approval was given.

The question that many would raise is whether it had to take
such a long time to obtain the final approval. There are a
number of factors involved in explaining the length of the
process: first, the decision-making process is inevitably rather
slow, given the number and kind of organizations involved.
For example, it does take time merely to arrange a meeting
between all the parties involved. Also, given the bureaucratic
nature of the statutory organizations, many different groups
and individuals are involved in the decision-making process.
Likewise, the decision-making process of the Steering Committee was inevitably a lengthy one, since the members were all
committed full-time elsewhere. However, there were other
reasons for the delay, which could to some extent have been
avoided. The DHSS could have specified more clearly and at an
earlier stage exactly what was required in the Operational
Document. They might have done this in the form of some
more concrete comments on the proposal they had already
received, so that the discussion which took place at the January
meeting, and which clarified what sort of document was
wanted, could have taken place much earlier. Another factor
that contributed to the delay was the Steering Committee's
reluctance to specify operational policies in detail before any
staff had been appointed. Their attitude, that the staff themselves should decide on details of policies, was incompatible
with the expectations of the DHSS. As it happened, the delay
meant that the Senior Staff were appointed before the Operational Document was finalized, which allowed them to be very
much involved in working out the document which was
finally approved.

The demand for a satisfactory Operational Document was a
source of great frustration for the Steering Committee. They

found it a real burden, a time-consuming exercise, and only seemed to do it because the DHSS wanted it. It was a document 'for the DHSS'. However, in retrospect it was a useful exercise, because the process clarified a number of issues and the Document actually became extremely helpful for the staff. It was not, as it turned out, to be regarded as 'just a piece of paper' written to satisfy the funding authorities. It became the 'constitution' of City Roads, and throughout the three years it was constantly referred to in discussions about policies and procedures and in introducing new staff to the unit.

Before turning to the content of this document and issues relating to the specification of aims and methods, we should consider the composition and role of the Steering Committee.

THE STEERING COMMITTEE

The composition of the Steering Committee changed consider-ably after it was first formed in 1974. As we have seen, the initiative to set up the project came from SCODA, and the initial negotiations with the funding authorities, the search for premises, and so forth were done by the then co-ordinator of SCODA. Different people had been involved at different times, and only a very small core of the group continued to be involved: a social worker from a Drug Dependency Unit, a nurse from an A and E department, a social worker from a voluntary agency, an observer from the DHSS, and the SCODA co-ordinator. By March 1977, when it seemed certain that the project was going to be realized, more people had become involved. The Committee was then composed of two members whose background was in the statutory services, and six who represented the voluntary field. In addition, the solicitor to the project was represented, and there was one observer from the DHSS and one from the Home Office. Basically, the members were selected by the SCODA co-ordinator either for their personal qualities or because they represented a particular kind of service, or had useful connections with individuals and organizations, especially within the statutory field, whose co-operation was needed. At the beginning of 1977, then, the majority of the Steering Committee consisted of people with a background in voluntary organizations. This changed during 1977. First, the SCODA co-ordinator withdrew from the spot-light and the DDU social worker was elected chairperson. A number of new people were recruited. One was the honorary treasurer, but the remaining five new members were from

statutory organizations, representing clinics, A and E departments, the area health authority, local social services, and
the probation service. At the same time, one of the representatives from the voluntary field withdrew his membership. The
stress had shifted towards a greater involvement by the
statutory services.

The shift was deliberate. The idea was to put City Roads on
the map right from the start. Strategic considerations weighed
more heavily than operational concerns. After all, the unit had
to think of its continued survival, exactly the aspect that was to
keep the Management Committee, as it was called after 1978,
busy during the next three years.

Just as survival was the dominant theme in the work of the
Management Committee, the pre-1978 preoccupation was with
the process of the birth rather than with determining what sort
of baby was to be born. True, the Operational Document had to
be written, but as much as possible was left to the staff
appointed, and the parts drafted by the Committee were
mainly the work of one person. At no point was the document
debated by the full Steering Committee, with the exception of
admission policies. Meetings mainly had the function of
informing members of the progress of negotiations with the
DHSS and of giving general support to the small core of
members who were actively involved in the negotiations. It is,
of course, inevitable that the degree of involvement of people
who are there purely on a voluntary basis will vary. Some had
more time than others, some were more interested or may have
seen City Roads as more relevant to their own careers. From the
point of view of getting established and fighting for future
survival, City Roads was lucky to have a very active and
competent Steering/Management Committee compared with
many other voluntary organizations, where the staff are often
left to fight their own battles. When it came to operational
policy matters, however, the members were, as a whole, much
less clear about what they expected. This became evident at an
early stage, when members were interviewed about their views
of the aims and methods of the unit they were involved in
setting up. It is to these aims that we shall now turn.

The aims of City Roads

1. City Roads is an experimental project aimed at the
   immediate needs of young multiple drug misusers who

frequently overdose and may be admitted to hospital Accident and Emergency departments.

2. City Roads will operate at a crisis intervention level providing a warm, sheltered environment where nursing, medical, social, and psychiatric support is readily available.

3. City Roads will not attempt to offer a complete treatment and rehabilitation programme under one roof, but will see its function as making contact with multiple drug misusers and attempting to encourage them to accept longer-term help from existing treatment and rehabilitation services. As a community-based service the unit will need to establish and to maintain close working relationships with all relevant statutory and voluntary agencies and community groups.

These are the aims as they were stated in the Operational Document agreed before City Roads opened. These aims were specified further in the document, but, although it offered guidelines in a number of respects, there was still a great deal of uncertainty about what would actually happen once the unit opened its doors to the clients. A number of potential contradictions were apparent, both from reading the document and from listening to the interviews, discussions, and negotiations that took place over the preceding years.

We shall now consider more closely the aims of City Roads and attempt to point to the key issues over which there was disagreement or which harboured contradictions or dilemmas, the solutions to which were to present the staff with quite a challenge.

City Roads had a number of aims, falling into three broad categories: those relating to the *clients*, those relating to the *internal operation* of the unit, and those concerning relations between City Roads and its *environment*.

THE CLIENTS

1. What sort of people were to be helped?
2. Where should they come from, and how should they come to the unit?
3. What condition should they be in on admission?
4. What sort of help should be offered?
5. How long should they stay at the unit?
6. What condition should they be in when they left?
7. Where should they go when they left?

1. The written aims state that City Roads would be for young multiple drug misusers aged between 16 and 30, who frequently overdosed, and who would often, but not necessarily, be homeless. This is quite a clear definition of the client group. The kind of drugs used was left open with the exception that the unit would not undertake opiate detoxification, which meant that people with an excessive amount of opiates in their bodies would not be accepted. It was assumed that there were adequate services already for 'these people'. We say 'these people', because there was an implicit assumption that somehow people could be categorized depending on the kind of drug(s) they were using, that the population of opiate users was different from the population of 'chaotic, multiple drug misusers'. Barbiturates were believed to be the principal type of drug used by the potential City Roads clients, hence the provision of barbiturate detoxification. However, the assumption that the population could be neatly divided in this way was to be seriously challenged during the first three years of the operation of City Roads.

The age range (16–30) was quite specific. There had been some discussion about whether to put the upper limit at 35, but that was decided against. The range 16–30 is quite wide and could cover very different types of people. The issue was whether the unit aimed to intervene at an early stage in people's drugs career, while they were still experimenting and perhaps on the fringes of the drug subculture, or whether the more chronic, long-term users would be more inclined to use and benefit from City Roads. Although members of the Steering Committee did not agree among themselves about this, most of them did not have any strong views one way or the other. As a whole they were unsure, and the 16–30 range left things open for the staff as well as for the clients.

2. The question of where the clients should come from was a contentious issue during the final stage of negotiations. The Operational Document states that 'While the House will be providing a service for the whole of the Greater London area, in practice we anticipate that the majority of referrals will come from Central London and in particular from the five London hospitals' Accident and Emergency Departments, identified by Dr Ghodse'. These five A and E departments were: St Charles, St Thomas, Middlesex, University College Hospital, and Westminster. In addition, the two hospitals nearest City Roads were included in the list, i.e. the Whittington and St

Bartholomew's. After this the Document lists other possible referral sources, such as other A and E departments, police, social services, DDUs, walk-in medical centres, relevant street agencies, day centres and rehabilitation centres, the probation service, GPs, and self-referrals. The Appendix states that during the first three months of operation priority would be given to the A and E departments listed.

What is interesting is the low priority that appears to have been given to the voluntary sector, not to mention self-referrals, which came last on the list. This Document did not reflect the views of SCODA and the voluntary agencies, who did not expect A and E departments to be necessarily the primary source of referral to City Roads. However, the DHSS insisted during the negotiations that the A and E departments, and in particular the seven specified, be given priority. It seemed that for them to fund City Roads, they had to show that they were responding to the problems of the NHS as they had been exposed by Ghodse. The problem of service misuse was as important to them as the problem of drug misuse. Some representatives from the voluntary sector were angry with this decision, but found that they had to accept it if City Roads was to get off the ground. Their hope was that in the long run the Operational Document would not prevent City Roads accepting referrals from a wide range of sources. In fact, their anger and despair over this issue turned out to have been quite unnecessary. Over the three years, City Roads did indeed take an increasing number of referrals from the voluntary sector as well as self-referrals.

3. The question of what condition the clients should be in on admission concerns first, their physical state and consequent need for treatment; and second, their psychological state and social condition at the time of referral. The Operational Document is quite clear that the unit could not accept people whose mental or physical condition required medical treatment beyond the level of domiciliary nursing offered at the House. The level of intoxication acceptable was, however, to some extent left open, although it was made clear that people who were believed likely to go into an unconscious state could not be accepted. Also, all the parties involved in setting up the unit were adamant that admission should be voluntary. This principle, clearly stated in the Operational Document, had two consequences. First, it meant that the unit would not accept conditions of residence in any supervision or probation order.

Second, in order to be sure that clients did want to be admitted, one would not expect them to be in such a state of intoxication that they were unable to make a rational decision to come to City Roads. We shall consider later to what extent this principle of voluntarism could in practice be carried out. After all, how much of a 'choice' is it for someone who is cold and hungry to go to City Roads, if the only alternative is to sleep rough or perhaps to be picked up by the police? Another important issue relating to the clients' condition on admission as well as to the treatment offered, is the meaning of *crisis*. Both the name of the unit and the Operational Document imply that people admitted will be in crisis. When asked, however, members of the Steering Committee were by no means clear about the meaning of this term. Some suggested things like overdosing, being short of drugs, or having nowhere to sleep, but others were reluctant to offer a definition and would, in fact, have preferred to avoid using the term crisis too much, as it might put off the clients. The ambivalence about the term was reflected in the way City Roads was referred to during the years of negotiation before it had a name. Thus, when the idea of City Roads first arose, it was referred to as a 'crisis centre'. Later documents avoided the term crisis and referred to the project as the 'short stay unit'. It was not until shortly before the project was about to open and the name City Roads was decided upon that the term 'crisis intervention' crept back in again. We say 'crept in' because there really was no debate about this, and the rationale for it was not made explicit. The question was open, therefore, whether and how the City Roads staff would use the term crisis when deciding whether or not to admit people.

4. Similarly, turning to the question of what sort of help should be offered, the term 'crisis intervention' was at best only specified in an indirect manner. 'The House', says the Operational Document, 'will provide a crisis intervention and assessment service.' The aim of City Roads was somehow to meet people's immediate needs and, in addition to this, assess their more long-term needs. The most important aspect of the City Roads service was the holistic approach to the clients, in the sense that medical, nursing, and social problems would be treated under one roof in an integrated manner. The concept of a multi-disciplinary approach was central: medical, nursing, psychiatric, and social work skills were all to be available. From the residents' point of view, they were to be offered general primary care which would help them recover from the effects of

drug use and general self-neglect. This included a warm house and regular meals, barbiturate detoxification, medical examination and general nursing attention to problems like, for example, abscesses. On the social work side, residents were expected to go through a number of phases: a settling-in stage, during which they would receive reassurance and familiarize themselves with the House procedures; an assessment stage, during which their needs and level of motivation would be assessed, and during which a great deal of one-to-one counselling would be expected; and finally, a planning and onward referral stage during which plans would be discussed and applications made for residents to be referred on to other services if needed.

5. The City Roads treatment – primary care, assessment, planning, and onward referral – would take three weeks. This was to be the maximum length of stay on any one occasion, although it was anticipated that some residents might leave after a few days, and subsequently seek readmission. Three weeks was decided upon mainly because the Director and Deputy Director felt that this was an appropriate length of time if the residents were not to settle down too well and change it into a long-stay unit. The various members of the Steering Committee had not been at all clear about what constituted a short stay. Their suggestions ranged from ten days to three months and some thought the period should be flexible, depending on the individual needs of residents. However, everybody seemed quite satisfied with the idea of a three-week stay, but the fear was, of course, whether in practice this would hold. On the one hand, they might be faced with a problem of actually retaining people for that length of time; on the other hand, it could be difficult to discharge residents after three weeks if they had not managed to find them somewhere suitable to refer them on to within this period. Much would depend not only on the attitude and behaviour of the clients, but also on the response and availability of the services to which residents might be referred.

6. Clients leaving City Roads were not expected to have seen the last of the social/medical welfare services. They were not expected to be 'cured' in the sense of having 'kicked the habit' and found stable accommodation, and employment. Rather, the hope was that for some, City Roads would mark the beginning of an attempt to abandon their lifestyle and stop misusing drugs. Again, no one was certain about the extent to

which even this would happen. Many were expected to leave
City Roads within a few days, but the hope was that they would
come back, once they had made contact with the House. The
expectation was that residents would leave City Roads in a
better physical condition, that they would at least have started
to think about a change, and that in most cases they would have
been referred on to services appropriate to their needs and level
of motivation.

7. What were the services to which the residents were expected
to be referred? The Operational Document lists the following:
hospitals; rehabilitation hostels; general hostels; emergency
accommodation; family/friends; day centres; street agencies;
social services; probation services; community services; and
GPs. A range of possible outlets was anticipated, but what was
far from clear was what the residents might be wanting, and to
what extent these services would be willing and/or able to take
the City Roads residents, especially at relatively short notice.
One of the hopes from the very start was that the intervention of
City Roads might result in better use of existing facilities, partly
through City Roads making referrals in the light of a thorough
assessment of what people needed, and partly through offering
some kind of background support for agencies, like for example
general hostels, which might otherwise be reluctant to accept
drug misusers. Exactly how successful City Roads was to be in
this respect remained to be seen.

THE INTERNAL OPERATION OF THE UNIT

The most important aspects of the City Roads service were that
it would be *multi-disciplinary*, and that it would be provided on
a 24-hour basis. The staffing agreed at the time City Roads
opened was as follows: Director; Deputy Director; 15 team
workers, i.e. five nurses, five social workers, and five care
assistants; a part-time medical officer; a part-time consultant
psychiatrist; an administrator; a secretary; a cook; and a
cleaner.

This staffing level had been agreed after some negotiation
with the DHSS, during which as we have seen there had been
some conflict of interest between the finance staff, who were
concerned with cash limits, and the professional advisers, who
were concerned with professional standards. The latter group
succeeded in convincing the finance people that the five care
assistants were necessary. Thus the dispute was about the
number of team workers needed. There was never any discus-

sion or doubt that the unit needed nurses as well as social workers. Nor was there ever any doubt that the medical input was to be on a part-time basis, and that a social worker would be in charge of the place. Everybody agreed that it was to be predominantly a social-work-type agency, although psychiatry, general medicine, and nursing were important and necessary as well. There was some concern, therefore, on the part of the Steering Committee over the procedure for appointing the nurses. At one stage it was suggested that the area health authority should do this, but a compromise was reached whereby the AHA would be formally appointing the nurses, but City Roads would select them. This was a very important principle for the Steering Committee to get established, because they wanted to be sure that the nurses appointed would be committed to working in a multi-disciplinary setting, and even do social work themselves.

In order to understand what might be meant by this multi-disciplinary approach, it is useful to look at the staffing structure shown in Figure 1. The most significant aspect of this structure is the organization of the workers in *teams*. Each team would have a social worker, a nurse, and a care assistant. Either the social worker or the nurse would be the team leader. There would be no separate night staff; the five teams would work shifts, so that at any one time there would be at least one team on duty. The multi-disciplinary aspect of the team work was supposed to be practised in two ways: they were expected to share their knowledge and experience and learn from each other; and they were expected to co-operate and co-ordinate their work. Indeed, if the concept of team work and its built-in hierarchical structure were to make sense, the professional barriers would have to be minimal. Otherwise it would be difficult to resolve the apparent contradiction between the professional-horizontal division, and the hierarchical-vertical division. The team leader on duty was supposed to have overall responsibility for making sure that House policies were followed, irrespective of whether s/he was a nurse or a social worker. It remained to be seen to what extent nursing could be done and/or decided upon by social workers, and to what extent nurses would be able to do social work. Much would depend on which aspects of the care would be emphasized, something that depended not only on staff attitudes, but also on the residents' wishes and needs. It would also depend on what type of social work would be practised. Another open question was the role of the care assistants, who were supposed

Figure 1   Staffing structure

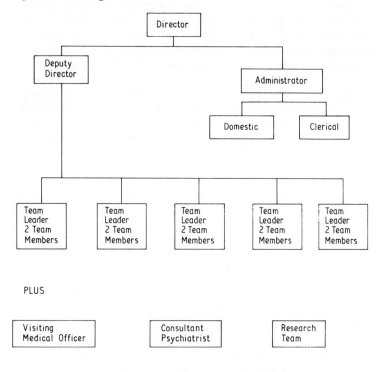

In the Director's absence the Administrator will report to the Deputy Director

to be unqualified. Would they be able to get on with the professionals and learn from them? Or would they be barred from
doing certain things? The whole question of what actually
constituted professional care was something which could really
only be determined by looking at how actual practices developed.

When considering the internal operation of the unit, it is
important to note the general atmosphere it was supposed to
offer. It was to offer a contrast to existing statutory institutions,
a homely, informal setting, thought to be more attractive to the
client group in question. To this end, it was important that the
staff presented themselves in an informal, relaxed manner, and
to encourage this, the hierarchical structure was to be counter-
balanced by democratic mechanisms so that all the staff felt
they were treated equally and had a say in policy matters. Thus

for the staff there were to be regular review meetings involving the whole team in discussion about the residents, and there were to be full staff meetings to consider general policy questions. In relation to the residents, there were to be daily meetings between them and the staff, and generally it was hoped that the barrier between the residents and the staff would be minimal. Yet there were clearly to be House rules, the most important one being that residents could not bring in their own drugs. In order to enforce that, another rule had to operate – no one was to leave the House without being escorted by a member of staff. If a resident broke these rules, s/he would automatically be discharged.

This was as much as had been decided when City Roads opened. The staff were faced with quite a challenge, trying to balance their wish for informality with the need for some order, which was necessary if the house was to function reasonably well as a breathing space from street life. Exactly how this balance would work out was left open, the details to be sorted out on a trial-and-error basis. For example, no one liked to say whether clients should be searched for drugs when they were admitted. Nor had they decided whether and when someone who was discharged for breaking a House rule could be readmitted. It was difficult to decide on matters of this kind before it was known what the residents would actually be like, and what their behaviour would be like at City Roads.

LINKS WITH THE ENVIRONMENT

The need for City Roads was articulated not by the drug users themselves, but by the services dealing with them. The work to establish the unit was done by the people working with these clients and by the DHSS. True, it was all being done in the belief that this was what the drug users needed, but it was certainly also very much what the services, voluntary and statutory, felt that *they* needed. The voluntary agencies felt overwhelmed and unable to cope with the 'chaotic' drug users, and, as already shown, the DHSS was concerned with what they saw as inappropriate use of the A and E departments. In other words, the expectations attached to the setting up of City Roads did not only concern the effects on the clients, but also the effects on other services. Thus one of the aims of City Roads was to relieve the burden on other agencies, in particular the A and E departments ('to help the helpers'). Second, it was widely believed that the existing services could be better used, if only they were better co-ordinated and there was sufficient knowledge about what the clients needed and what services were actually available. Thus, for example, services like hostels, probation officers, and GPs, while not designed specifically to deal with drug misusers, might be able to offer some help. City Roads was expected to be a 'centre of wisdom' as regards these services, and also a link between them, since much of the problem was thought to be that workers in different agencies did not communicate as well as they could. In particular, relations between the Drug Treatment Centres and the voluntary agencies were rather delicate, and hopefully City Roads, having close links with both sectors from the start, would help relations in this respect. Third, City Roads was expected to perform an advisory and educational function in relation to workers who were uncertain about how to deal with this client group.

Conclusion

By the time City Roads was ready to open its doors to the clients, a model had emerged, indicating the kind of client group it was expected to cater for, the kind of services they would be offered, and the methods by which these services were to be delivered. Fairly detailed policies had been agreed upon in some respects; yet the success of the enterprise depended as much on the clients and on other agencies. Was this really what the drug misusers needed? Would they want to use City Roads at all? Would they use the place too much and change it into a long-stay unit? Would there be suitable places to refer people on to? Would other workers start using City Roads for referrals and advice, or would the information about its existence get lost? Would it be possible to recruit a suitable, stable staff group, and would they be able to work together despite their different professional backgrounds? These were just some of the questions that had to be answered in order to judge whether the experiment could be said to be a success. Indeed, when it came to specifying possible criteria of success, all the parties involved were most reluctant to do so and when they did, they had different sets of priorities in mind. Some would say, for example, that if the clients were attracted to City Roads, this would be a sign of success, irrespective of the outcome of their contact. Others would say that if City Roads managed to survive as an organization when faced with the pressures from clients and other services, this would be a sign of success. However, maintaining stability in the organization could be in conflict with the aim to deal with as many clients as possible. Also, the quantity of clients seen might affect the quality of the outcome; for example would a situation in which ten clients stayed at City Roads for three weeks and then went back to the street be a more successful outcome than three people staying at City Roads and then going to a rehabilitation project? In addition to this, of course, there was the whole question of the expected effect on the environment (on other services and agencies). Apart from the difficulty of measuring this, how much was it to count compared with the effects on the clients? All in all, therefore, the research team, who had been asked to *evaluate* the project, were faced with many problems in measuring and assessing the achievements of City Roads. In the chapters that follow, we consider these issues in more detail, looking at City Roads' performance in the four main areas referred to in the broad aims of the Operational Document. Before we do this, we shall try to give an overall view of what happened at City Roads in a typical day and over the three-year experimental period, illustrating this with some case studies of how different residents made use of the service.

PART TWO
The Service in Practice

3 The Use of City Roads

Inside City Roads

Before we go on to consider how City Roads was used and how
it worked, let us try to paint a picture of the unit as it looked on
opening in May 1978. We will describe what happened during
a day at City Roads, not at this stage passing any judgement on
whether things could have been done better or differently. We
shall then set out some of the findings on patterns of use of the
service.

The house turned out to serve its purpose very well indeed.
There had been some fear that supervision would be difficult,
given that there were four floors, including the basement.
However, as the maximum number of residents was established as twelve and with the relatively high level of staffing
and the strictly controlled use of drugs, the problem of supervision was insignificant. A four-bedded reception area was
directly opposite the office on the ground floor and therefore
easy to keep an eye on. The basement area, with the kitchen/
dining room and record player, was the most frequently used by
the residents during the day. On the first floor were the medical
room, the staff lounge, and the residents' lounge/TV room,
where most of them tended to spend the evenings. On the floor
above were the bedrooms and two side-rooms for counselling
sessions.

The position of the house was, on balance, very convenient.
It was not immediately close to any of the main referring
agencies and the area where most of the clients would tend to
spend their time (Piccadilly/Soho area). But it was only 10–15
minutes' drive from this area, and since City Roads did not
encourage people to drop in, but collected prospective
residents in their yellow taxi, the distance was quite an
advantage. The area had reasonable shops where residents
could buy cheap clothes; and it had a cinema, with which City
Roads made a special arrangement for free tickets for certain
performances. Apart from trips to the shops or the cinema, the

involvement in the community was minimal. On the other hand, City Roads did not receive any complaints about the behaviour of the residents. In fact, it was ironically the City Roads residents who complained about their noisy neighbours. They were next door to a private club, where the level of intoxication seemed considerably higher than that at City Roads!

The day started at 8 a.m., when the day shift came on. Four of the five teams were working shifts, and the fifth team was on relief duty in case someone was ill or on leave. If no one was off sick, the members of the relief team would work an eight-hour day from nine to five. The Director, Deputy Director, administrator and secretary would also work nine to five. So the House could be quite full of staff between these hours. At 8 a.m. the night team would hand over to the day team. This could take anything between ten minutes and one hour, depending on whether the day team had been on duty the previous day, and depending on what had happened in the House during the night. New residents might have been admitted during the night, but most residents were admitted during the day. After the handover session a team member would check that the residents had got out of bed. They were not allowed to stay in bed after eight except on Sundays, because it was thought important that they learn to live a structured life. After getting up, the residents would make breakfast, and a staff member would join them. After breakfast they would all have a morning meeting, deciding upon tasks to be done, e.g. washing up, cleaning, and shopping. After this, everybody would meet again to decide on activities for the rest of the day. These meetings were mainly for practical matters and not meant as group counselling. If the atmosphere had been bad for some reason, this would be discussed, but if problems concerned a particular individual, the staff preferred to deal with this in a one-to-one session. The activities for the day were not terribly exciting for the residents. Priority was given to the one-to-one sessions, and this tied up the staff a great deal. They might have time to take a group of people out shopping or for a walk, especially if there were volunteers around. Otherwise the residents would have to keep themselves occupied in the House. There were various games like monopoly, chess, or table tennis and there was a record player and a TV. Most of the day the residents would sit downstairs smoking cigarettes and listening to pop music, and in the evenings they would go upstairs to the lounge to watch TV. Generally they gave the appearance of being tired and uninterested in anything and quite happy to do nothing. They did complain at times that they were bored, and they could not think of ways themselves of passing the time constructively. The staff were reluctant to organize too many activities for them, because it was part of the treatment philosophy that people should concentrate on themselves and their own individual problems and not be distracted by other activities too much. Also, they did not want the residents to settle in too well, given that it was a short-stay unit.

If the residents were passive and bored, the staff certainly were not. After the morning meeting with the residents, they would meet with the Deputy Director to discuss each resident and what should be done. They would decide who would do sessions with which residents. Although there was some attempt to ensure continuity in the counselling sessions, residents were not allocated to one particular worker through-out their stay. First, this was impossible because of the shift system, and second, there was a conscious policy of preventing bonds developing too closely between a particular worker and a resident. All three team members would do their sessions during the day, but they all had other things to do, which might mean that they had to leave the House. All newly admitted residents had to go to the local social security office to get their supplementary benefit. This would often tie up a staff member for one or two hours. Then, of course, referrals had to be dealt with as they came. When a client was referred over the telephone, details were noted and the team would discuss whether s/he was appropriate. This might involve some more telephoning to obtain additional information. Then the team leader would decide which staff member to send out to 'assess' the client. The staff member would leave in the taxi to go to talk to the client. This could take hours; in most cases the client would be considered suitable and brought back. The admission process would then tie up this staff member further, because an admission sheet had to be filled in and the person needed a general introduction to the House, and reassurance. Apart from work done directly with the residents, a lot of time was spent on the telephone. People would ring up for advice, ex-residents would ring up for a chat, and a lot of work had to be done finding places to refer people to and liaising with solicitors and probation officers. Many residents had court cases coming up whilst at City Roads, and apart from the paper and telephone work it involved, it also meant that a staff member had to escort them when they went to court. The fact that the residents had to be escorted wherever they went—to the DHSS, the courts, hospital appointments, etc.—meant that those left in the House would often be extremely busy. The team leader would normally stay in the House and tended to do more 'office work'; s/he was supposed to co-ordinate the work, allocate tasks, and offer advice to the rest of the team. Often the Director and Deputy Director would be involved in discussions, since they were usually around in the office.

After 5 p.m. things began to become less hectic. When the team workers had finished their sessions they would retreat into the office to write up case notes and generally unwind. During the period immediately preceding the 8 p.m. handover, the office would often be very quiet, with workers writing frantically. If a referral was made at this time, clients were most often asked to ring back after the handover session. Throughout this period the residents might be left to themselves, although in principle a worker was supposed to be with them. The evening handover session would often be longer than the morning one, because so much more happened during the day. Sometimes the day team would not leave City Roads until 9 p.m., although they were supposed to go off duty at 8 p.m.

Night duty was less busy. There might be an admission during the evening, and there would often be a few one-to-one sessions with residents who had not been seen during the day. After midnight, however, residents would normally be asleep, and there were very few referrals. Some teams would spend this time cooking themselves a meal, after which they might take it in turns to sleep. Occasionally a resident would be unable to sleep, and a worker would talk to him or her. They did not use night sedation but there were always staff around to talk to people if they could not sleep. Early in the morning the workers would write up the case notes, after which they would wake up the residents before the 8 a.m. handover session.

What we have done so far is to describe an ordinary, average kind of day at City Roads. Of course, there were quiet days and hectic days; there were times when the House was full and times when there were very few residents (the average rate of occupancy was about nine residents); there were times when the atmosphere was tense and residents difficult; and there were times when rules were broken and residents had to be discharged. However, these were all exceptions, and most of the time things were under control, and although there was a lot of anxiety, there was little drama.

Patterns of use: a statistical profile

REFERRALS

Just over a third (34 per cent) of all referrals to City Roads resulted in admission (within the month in which the referral was made). City Roads did not operate a system of waiting lists: it was ostensibly a crisis intervention unit. In addition, it was thought that the client's situation and motivation would fluctuate to such an extent that it would be impossible and meaningless to operate any kind of reservation system. So, people were admitted on a first come, first served basis. Since the house situation could change very quickly, persistence on the part of either the client or the referring agency was important in gaining admission. The occupancy rate or shortage of staff might prevent City Roads taking admissions during the day, for example, but by the evening the situation might have changed and the first one to 'phone in the evening might well be lucky enough to be admitted.

ADMISSIONS

The majority (75 per cent) of admissions occurred between 8 a.m. and 8 p.m. Only half (52 per cent), however, took place during normal office hours (9–5) and 17 per cent occurred at night (between 11 p.m. and 6 a.m.).

Over the three years studied, 308 people became residents of City Roads, making up altogether 660 admissions. It had been expected that residents would be admitted to City Roads more than once, since it was realized that the building up of trust and motivation would take time. Over the years, then, as the group of ex-residents grew in number the proportion of readmissions also increased. *Table 1* (p. 52) shows that the proportion of residents who were new to the service in each year fell over time.

'Project activity' as such measured by 'throughput' increased each year from 190 admissions in the first year to 252 in the third. This was not, however, the result of increased recruitment of new clients but of more extensive use of the service by a similar number of individuals (cf. *Table 2*).

One half (155) of all City Roads residents were *not* readmitted at all in the three years studied. (This proportion holds when an extended readmission period is allowed for. In the first two years, 215 individuals were admitted of which 101 (47 per cent) did not return at any time during the three-year period.) There

Table 1   *Proportion of all admissions that were new admissions in each year*

year	number of new admissions (1)	number of all admissions (2)	(1) as % of (2)
1	117	190	62%
2	98	218	45%
3	93	252	37%
3 years	308	660	47%

Table 2   *Residents' use of the service in each year*

year	number of residents	number of admissions	admissions per resident	bed nights per resident
1	117	190	1.6	21.9
2	131	218	1.7	23.2
3	131	252	1.9	24.8

Table 3   *Length of stay and outcome for first admissions and readmissions*

	mean length of stay (days)	percentage referred to rehabilitation
first admissions (N = 308)	10.7	19.2
second admissions (N = 153)	14.6	23.5
third admissions (N = 87)	15.7	26.4
fourth admissions (N = 47)	16.8	34.0
fifth admissions (N = 26)	17.8	30.8

was thus a wide variation in patterns of use: of the 308 residents, in addition to the 155 who came once, and did not return, 66 people were readmitted on only one occasion, while 87 (28 per cent) returned more than once. A substantial number became regulars, 47 (15 per cent) totting up four or more admissions and the top 10 per cent of users (32 people) between them producing 147 admissions (22 per cent of all admissions). The highest number of admissions by any one person was 13 in the three years studied.

LENGTH OF STAY

City Roads offered clients a three-week stay, although in many cases residents left before that. While only just under a third (31 per cent) of all admissions lasted three weeks, just under half (49 per cent) of all residents completed a three-week stay on at least one admission. The mean length of stay for all admissions was just under two weeks (13.4 days). There was considerable variation among residents in the way they used the service when all admissions were taken into account. Twenty per cent (61 residents) spent no more than one week in total at City Roads, while 23 per cent (70 residents) totalled up more than six weeks in the project, and one woman spent a total of around five months there between 1978 and 1981.

As *Table 3* (p. 52) indicates, the pattern was for *readmissions* to be of increasing duration. This reflects the process whereby clients initially approached City Roads warily and tested out the experience of being a resident. Some found that the service did not suit them, others made further and increasingly extensive use of it.

The use made of City Roads on the whole was, however, quite definitely *short stay* use, even by readmissions. The service was in general operating as a short-stay unit dealing with immediate problems. Although about one-fifth of the residents were 'regular' users, even the extremely regular users stayed on average for only about one month out of twelve in any one year. The vast majority used the place only once or twice and stayed for relatively short periods of time.

Different patterns of use could be distinguished. The main types were:

1. Those admitted once only, that is they came once but never came back (155 people). Of these, 52 stayed less than one week whereas 103 stayed for longer than one week.

2. Those who were readmitted on at least one subsequent
   occasion (153 people). These divided as shown in *Table 3*
   into various groups with more or less frequent use of the
   service.

Four types of user of the service were defined: low use;
medium use; high use; and very high use, and these were
compared on a number of factors. One factor which clearly
affected the use made of City Roads was that of 'previous
accommodation'. Those who were homeless on first admission
were more likely to make higher use of City Roads; those with
alternative accommodation were likely to make less use of City
Roads. Those who made less use of the service were also more
likely to be in touch with their parents. The indications were
that those with more support in the community would make
less use of City Roads whereas the more 'chaotic', those living
on the streets and in touch with the street agencies, and those
who had criminal records and were on probation, were making
more use of City Roads (Jamieson, Glanz, and MacGregor 1981:
118–27).

Men and women differed in the extent of their use of the
service. Women were more likely either to use it very little or
very much (being found in the low-use and very high-use
categories more often than the men). The more 'stable' stayed
for shorter periods of time at City Roads, where 'stability' was
defined as having had some employment in the previous year.
(Thirty-eight per cent of the 'stable' group stayed for over 30
days in total, whereas 62 per cent of the 'unstable' group stayed
for that length of time.) The very high users with four or more
admissions to their credit were less stable in this sense than the
rest.

A higher proportion of younger people were readmitted.
This was influenced by sex differences in that the women were
younger than the men (on the whole 2–3 years younger).

MODE OF DEPARTURE

The most common mode of departure from City Roads was
self-discharge, whereby a resident would leave either without
warning or notifying staff or, more commonly, after discussing
the decision with staff. A detailed examination of 100 con-
secutive departures revealed that 44 were self-discharges,
with such grounds for this action recorded by staff as 'unable
to cope with remaining in the House, becoming increasingly
tense and frustrated'; 'unable to handle tensions, increasingly

wound up'; 'said no point in staying as she wasn't getting anywhere'; 'saw no point in staying as she felt she wasn't ready to go on to anything'; 'said he couldn't stand being shut in any longer'; 'said he couldn't handle confrontation with the staff'; 'unable to cope without drugs'.

Of the 100 departures examined, 10 were House discharges, involving breaking the rule of no drugs or alcohol in the House (8 cases) or unacceptable behaviour in the House ('was asked to leave after constantly not getting up, winding up other residents, etc.'; 'unable to cope with his bizarre/aggressive behaviour').

The other forms of departure found in the sample of one hundred involved onward referral arrangements (30 cases), completion of the three-week residential period (15 cases), and one person who received a prison sentence following a court appearance.

OUTCOME

As will be discussed in more detail in Chapter 6, City Roads' approach to crisis intervention went beyond immediate response and reassurance. A more intensive form of work with residents was undertaken which involved exploration of the roots of the clients' 'maladaptive' behaviour, and assessment of options for further rehabilitation.

A key objective of the work with residents thus became onward referral to an agency offering longer-term rehabilitation. Just under a quarter (22 per cent) of all admissions resulted in a rehabilitation referral to therapeutic communities (some of which are known as concept houses, such as Phoenix House), Christian communities (such as Life for the World), and group-supportive projects (such as Elizabeth House). In other cases (31 per cent of all admissions), where such a referral was not acceptable nor feasible, other arrangements were made, involving short-term accommodation and/or supportive contact with appropriate agencies. However, the most common outcome of residence was a return, with no onward referral, to previous or unknown living arrangements (47 per cent of admissions).

The outcomes for *individuals* who stayed at City Roads should also be considered. While 148 admissions resulted in a rehabilitation referral, this involved 111 individuals (36 per cent). Thus 25 per cent of rehabilitation referrals were *re*-referrals. Analysis of case histories reveals that 42 per cent of residents had already had some experience of rehabilitation agencies prior to admission to City Roads. City Roads, in fact, created an *initial* rehabilitation opportunity for only 17 per cent of all residents.

The proportion of admissions resulting in a rehabilitation referral fell somewhat over the three-year period: 27 per cent in Year 1; 24 per cent in Year 2; 18 per cent in Year 3. The proportion terminating with no arrangements remained relatively stable at about one half; 48 per cent in Year 1; 43 per cent in Year 2; and 48 per cent in Year 3.

Table 4   *Pattern of onward referral of all admissions*

	N	%
referral to residential project for rehabilitation	127	19
referral to psychiatric hospital unit for rehabilitation	14	2
in-patient opiate detoxification arranged (prior to rehabilitation)	7	1
supportive contact arranged with short-term accommodation	79	12
supportive contact with return to previous/unknown accommodation	83	13
short-term accommodation arranged	28	4
admitted for hospital treatment	10	1
taken to police custody	5	1
no accommodation arrangements made	307	47
total admissions	660	100

Some individuals were, however, admitted several times *before* a rehabilitation placement was finally arranged; others were readmitted several times *after* a rehabilitation referral had been made on a previous stay at City Roads, and others were referred on *more than one* occasion to a rehabilitative setting. It is interesting to note therefore the proportion of individuals who were *ever* referred for rehabilitation (*Table 5*).

Those who were referred to rehabilitation from City Roads differed from the residents overall in being more likely to be the least 'stable' (more chaotic), as indicated by their being more likely to have injected drugs, used drugs for longer, had some experience of institutions as a child, been in prison, and be homeless on admission. Those who started using drugs before the age of 15 were more likely to be referred on to rehabilitation (Jamieson, Glanz, and MacGregor 1981: 118–27).

A very clear difference appeared between men and women regarding referral to rehabilitation (men being more likely to be referred to rehabilitation) which was not explained by their extent of use of City Roads. (The difference between the men and the women held in each category of type of user.) Similarly, women were less likely to have some arrangements made for

Table 5 *Onward referral for individuals over all admissions*

	N	%
referred for rehabilitation at least once	111	36
only other arrangements ever made	102	33
no arrangements ever made	95	31
total number of individuals	308	100

them on leaving City Roads than were the men: even in the high-use category there were still 15 per cent of women who left without any arrangements ever being made for them whereas all the men in this category had some arrangements made for them.

We shall now present a number of typical case studies to illustrate these rather dense statistical data. These studies indicate the complexity of patterns of use and the way in which the attitudes, intentions, and circumstances in which residents and staff found themselves, interacted to produce a rich mix of outcomes.

Case studies

CHRIS

Chris was 30 years old at the time of his admission to City Roads, and he is one of the 'old timers' on the drugs scene. He was born and brought up in London. His father left his mother at the time she was pregnant with Chris, and Chris's childhood was an unstable alternation between children's homes and a parental home dominated by a step-father whom he disliked intensely. He was involved in delinquent episodes at an early age, and spent periods in approved school and borstal. Chris was one of the 'first wave' of hospital DTC patients in 1968. His drug use was more or less continuous from early adolescence, punctuated by several prison sentences and short periods of self-achieved abstinence. He had had no experience of any form of rehabilitation agency before admission to City Roads.

First admission (16 days)

Chris was referred to City Roads by the hospital DTC, at which he had been (but was no longer) a patient. He was described as a 'stereotype junkie'. At the time of his admission he was in very poor physical condition, with an abscess in the groin, several cuts and bruises, and a generally emaciated appearance. The nurse on duty at City Roads said at the time of his admission 'I'm not at all sure that he is well enough to be here'. He was using barbiturates heavily and was homeless, staying recently at Dean Street Reception Centre and Salvation Army hostels.

He was immediately started on the phenobarbitone reduction regime and received other nursing attention.

At an early stage in his stay, Chris expressed his desire to change his way of life. He said that he had children from a marriage that had ended in separation several years ago and he wanted to take a part in their upbringing. He also felt that he could no longer keep up the lifestyle he had been living and could now envisage only further deterioration or death. Another element of his motivation was his expectation that sooner or later he would receive a long prison sentence. For the first time, he said, he was taking the idea of rehabilitation seriously.

After ten days of residence a plan emerged for Chris to apply to a rehabilitation community close to London. By this time, his physical condition had vastly improved. However, within a few days of writing a letter of application to the rehabilitation agency, he was discharged from City Roads because (together with a woman resident) he was found to have smuggled alcohol into the unit.

Second admission (24 days)

Chris contacted City Roads on several occasions after his departure. He had been barred for three weeks and when this time had elapsed he was readmitted. He had been using barbiturates and had again physically deteriorated.

During this second stay, the plans for Chris's referral to the rehabilitation agency he had selected were continued. He attended the agency for an interview, but was subsequently informed that he was not acceptable to them, his record of violent behaviour being the main cause of concern. Chris was initially very angry about this rejection and talked about 'forgetting the whole idea' of rehabilitation. However, several staff members worked intensely with him and towards the end of this period of residence, he agreed to plans for referral to Phoenix House.

The plans could not be implemented before the completion of the three-week period (extended over an 'extra' weekend) and interim accommodation was arranged for him at a 'holding house' with which City Roads had a special arrangement.

Third admission (8 days)

Chris was admitted to City Roads for a third time following referral by a voluntary street-level agency (Hungerford). City Roads had been aware that Chris had continued heavy drug use while staying at the hostel and that he had eventually been evicted with the aid of the police. However, during this period Chris had managed, with the help of the street agency, to obtain an interview for admission to Phoenix House. He was not immediately accepted as there was concern about his medical history and condition.

When Chris was admitted to City Roads for the third time, he was bitter and depressed about this second rejection. There were several intense and tearful sessions with staff members. He took his own discharge when he met a woman friend while on an outing with a City Roads staff member.

Fourth admission (10 days)

Before his fourth admission to City Roads, Chris had been admitted to hospital following a serious overdose of barbiturates. He also, by this time, had a court case pending. During this fourth admission there were several episodes of disruptive behaviour by Chris, and a number of staff members expressed the view that he was now unsuitable to be a resident at City Roads. However, Chris was expressing a commitment to seeking admission to Phoenix House and an interview was arrranged. Chris apparently could not go through with the plans and discharged himself from City Roads the day before the interview was to take place.

Fifth admission (1 day)

Chris's fifth admission to City Roads occurred seven months after the fourth. In this intervening period, he had actually been accepted and spent nearly five months as a resident at Phoenix House. He contacted City Roads within a few days of discharging himself from Phoenix House. He had immediately resumed heavy drug use and had been admitted to hospital casualty departments following overdoses on several occasions.

On admission Chris appeared to be extremely depressed, though he expressed to staff his intention of returning to Phoenix House. However, it was decided by the staff later on his first day in residence that Chris was becoming increasingly intoxicated and, although he denied having taken any drugs at City Roads, he was asked to leave. Ten days after this discharge from City Roads, the street agency with which Chris had been in contact informed City Roads that Chris had returned to Phoenix House.

Five years after first being admitted to City Roads, at the time of writing, Chris is now abstinent and is a community worker in South London.

PENNY

Penny was 23 years old when admitted to City Roads. She was born and brought up in London. From an early age Penny had presented disturbed behaviour patterns and from the age of 11 she was placed in a residential school for maladjusted children. Her home background was one where violence was a common experience: her father was violent towards Penny's mother, and her mother was violent towards Penny. Her drug use began while at the school and continued consistently from that time. Penny had served a short prison sentence and had spent a short time in a residential rehabilitation agency outside London. She was very well known at certain hospital casualty departments through her repeated drug overdoses.

First admission (18 days)

Over a five-month period before her first admission, there were eight contacts with City Roads by, or about, Penny. On certain of these occasions City Roads was unable to spare a staff member to conduct an assessment: on other occasions, it was felt that Penny was expressing inadequate motivation or was too intoxicated to be admitted.

When Penny was admitted, following referral by the Middlesex Hospital, she was in very poor physical condition. She had been using barbiturates very heavily and was homeless. (She had no contact at all with her family.) As well as the phenobarbitone withdrawal regime, Penny was placed on a course of vitamins.

City Roads' approach to Penny was initially a very tentative one, and Penny herself was very reticent in sessions with staff members. There was little expectation that Penny would stay long at the unit and a definite view on the part of staff that she was not 'ready' for any form of rehabilitation. It was more than a week after her admission that Penny expressed any view of her own needs and this amounted to a desire for a 'decent place to live' where she could 'learn about motivation'. The staff at this time were expressing their own frustration at Penny's 'negative' response to their own approaches.

After about two weeks a policy emerged that staff should not consider rehabilitation as an option for Penny 'this time around', but should focus on encouraging her to make contact with a voluntary street-level agency for daytime support, and anticipate further admissions to City Roads. Penny herself had selected a residential agency in London which accepted drug misusers although not geared to any rigorous form of rehabilitation. A number of staff members expressed misgivings about the appropriateness of making such a referral. However, a few days later it turned out that this agency had no vacancies for several weeks in the future. Although Penny wanted to persist in applying to this agency, it was made clear to her that City Roads would not support such an application on grounds of unsuitability and because it had 'not been thought through'.

Over the next couple of days no specific plan for Penny was developed. The general view of her at this time was that it was remarkable that she had stayed so long at City Roads, and this effort on her part was an adequate first step in the right direction.

After 18 days, Penny left with no arrangements having been made about accommodation, but with an agreement that she should contact a street agency for support and counselling.

Second admission (21 days)

Penny was readmitted to City Roads two and a half weeks after her first departure. There had been an almost continuous series of telephone contacts concerning Penny from street-level agencies, hospital casualty departments, and Penny herself. Although it was clear to City Roads that Penny was still in a state of 'crisis' – homeless, overdosing regularly, and seeking readmission – there was hesitation about readmitting her because she was usually intoxicated at the time of contact and there was doubt concerning the nature of her 'motivation'. In fact, Penny was 'assessed' on one occasion but was not accepted for readmission because the staff member concerned felt that she would 'misuse' City Roads and was not really interested in 'doing anything about herself'. Other staff members, however, felt that Penny should be given a second chance and she was readmitted following several telephone calls from nurses at the Middlesex Hospital and from Penny herself.

At readmission, Penny was again in very poor physical shape. The medical officer noted that she weighed just 6 st 11 lb fully clothed. As before, Penny was somewhat reticent in sessions with staff, and although she agreed that she was in need of rehabilitation, she was reluctant to commit herself to a specific plan. However, after about ten days, Penny agreed to an arrangement for an informal visit to a residential rehabilitation agency in London. A week later, Penny went for a second, more formal visit to the rehabilitation agency. Both staff and Penny herself were pleased that she had gone this far towards seeking rehabilitation. However, it would be necessary for Penny to attend for a third visit before she could be accepted as a resident by this agency. By this time her three-week period was completed and interim accommodation in a 'holding house' outside London was arranged. Although Penny was taken to the railway station, the agency concerned later telephoned City Roads to say that she had not arrived.

Subsequent contact

A few months after this second departure from City Roads, Penny resumed contact and there was again a series of telephone calls from Penny, from hospital casualty departments, and from other agencies. City Roads was uncertain as to whether Penny should be readmitted since she was repeating the pattern of her previous behaviour. Penny was told on several occasions that she would have to be 'straight' before she could be 'assessed'.

Four days after her last telephone contact with City Roads, Penny died from barbiturate poisoning.

JOHN

John was 17 and had been in London for only six months when he was referred to City Roads. He had been brought up in Manchester, partly by foster parents and partly in children's homes. He had a history of criminal convictions dating from when he was 13. He had started sniffing glue at 13; at 15 he was taking cannabis and valium; at 17 he was using barbiturates.

At the time of his first admission to City Roads he had been squatting in London for six months, adopting the dress and manners of a punk. He was on bail and his court case for criminal damage was due the following month. When giving him bail the court had told him 'to do something about himself'. He was referred by a probation officer and when assessed said that he had come to City Roads because of his court case, but that he was not particularly interested in coming off drugs.

First admission

On his first admission John stayed for only two days, after which he left because he was 'bored'.

Second admission

His second admission lasted for the full three weeks: one week after leaving City Roads, John asked to be readmitted. He was not coping and said that this time *he* wanted to do something about himself. He stayed at City Roads for three weeks, and during this time his appearance, attitude, and behaviour changed considerably. At the beginning he was clearly an exceedingly angry young man, bitter, aggressive, and distrustful. He tended to isolate himself and was reluctant to speak to anyone except one other resident, a girl, who was also into punk. However, the staff persisted in taking an interest in him and he was characterized as an 'intelligent guy who never had any strong relationships' and who, therefore, did not trust anybody. He was informed of the existence of rehabilitation projects, which he had never heard of. Slowly he started to take an interest in this. Gradually he began to co-operate and open up to the staff and eventually he decided that he was interested in Phoenix House. Towards the end of his stay he was interviewed and accepted by Phoenix House, but at the last minute he decided that he was not ready for this and he was quite happy to carry on as he had been doing. On the last day he left without saying goodbye to anyone.

Third admission (13 days)

Two weeks later John was back at City Roads. He had been 'assessed' in prison where he was remanded for theft. This time, he said, he really wanted to go to rehabilitation. He was let off by the court on condition that he stayed somewhere which satisfied the probation officer and he was taken straight to City Roads from the court. He was clearly relieved to get out of prison. At the end of this stay at City Roads, John went on to Phoenix House.

One year later, when the follow-up study was done, John was still at Phoenix House and was said to be doing well.

JOE

Joe, aged 20, had lived in London for most of his life. He left his parents' council flat when he was 17. He left school at 16 without any qualifications and had been employed in casual jobs since then. He was frequently dismissed from jobs because of his drug use. From the age of 16 he used cannabis and speed occasionally at parties, but soon started to go to Piccadilly Circus regularly and had started to use drugs daily. During the twelve months before his first admission to City Roads he had been using barbiturates, speed, and methadone. He had a criminal record, his first conviction had been when he was 17. He was first referred to City Roads by a psychiatrist he had seen at University College Hospital.

Within two years Joe was admitted to City Roads five times (he spent 13 weeks there altogether). During this time he experienced seven different rehabilitative settings, including two psychiatric hospitals. In addition to this he was admitted to five different hospitals following overdoses. He had also spent five months in prison.

First admission (21 days)

After this admission Joe was referred on to the Henderson Psychiatric Hospital where he stayed for one month. He spent the following month at Link, a rehabilitation project, from which he was discharged for drinking. Shortly after this he spent a month in a psychiatric hospital. Eventually he was referred to City Roads by a street agency, six months after his first admission.

Second admission (21 days)

City Roads characterized Joe as someone who tended to rush into things without much thought, and who needed to slow down and realize that he was not ready for rehabilitation. He was eventually referred on to Bed and Breakfast. He immediately overdosed and was admitted to hospital. After this he spent a month with his sister and took up a job, but he began to use large quantities of drugs again, lost his job and was thrown out of his sister's home. He spent the next month on the street, regularly telephoning City Roads. City Roads did not respond to his requests until after one month, when he was finally readmitted having said that 'he wanted rehabilitation'.

Third admission (7 days)

At the time of admission Joe had already decided that he wanted to go to Phoenix House. City Roads saw it as their task to test his motivation and make him reflect on his decision. During his stay Joe's behaviour was characterized as 'attention-seeking, aggressive, and winding other residents up'. He was clearly irritated with City Roads for doubting his suitability for Phoenix House. After one week he left, saying that he would go elsewhere to talk about Phoenix House. He soon overdosed and tried to get back into City Roads. He was told to contact Phoenix House directly – which he did with the result that they admitted him. He stayed there for only one week and spent the following five months using drugs, overdosing, and being admitted to various hospitals. During this time he was regularly in contact with the Hungerford. He also referred himself to City Roads several times, but was turned down. Eventually he was readmitted to City Roads.

Fourth admission (21 days)

Joe was readmitted on condition that he would be willing to think hard about his problems and what to do about them. He was referred to Suffolk House which was considered suitable because it was small and therefore able to give him more attention and to accept his 'more neurotic side'. He left Suffolk House after one week, got into legal trouble, and was sent to prison where he spent the next five months.

Fifth admission (21 days)

Soon after he was released from prison Joe was readmitted to City Roads. He said he had learned a lot from his prison experience and was now really serious about 'doing something about himself'. This time he was referred to Life for the World. He spent less than one month at this rehabilitation project after which he left to go back to the street and using drugs.

Conclusion

These are just four cases selected from the 308 people who became residents of City Roads between 1978 and 1981. Some could be counted as successes (Chris and John); some as failures (Penny and Joe). What stands out, however, is the complexity of the processes at work. The people seen came into City Roads with a baggage of experiences, dating generally from childhood, which affected their attitudes and expectations of City Roads and of life in general. City Roads could, if it handled things well, help to encourage a person along the way to a change in life, usually through rehabilitation. Chris gradually came round to building a new life for himself. It is impossible to weigh up how much City Roads itself contributed to this. When Chris first went to City Roads he had no experience of rehabilitation. City Roads suggested this to him but the Hungerford also propelled him down that path and he was strongly influenced by the feeling that his body was packing up and prison and death faced him as the likely alternatives. With Penny, however, City Roads made mistakes for which they grieved. Again she was a very 'difficult' case. Other agencies dealing with her were very worried and concerned but did not know what to do. City Roads turned her down when she asked for help, but one can understand how they came to do so. She seemed to be 'manipulative' – the word used so often by psychiatrists and social workers to describe people they cannot help, who seem bent on living a 'destructive' life, dragging everyone they meet (professionals and friends) down with them.

These cases illustrate the changeable and impulsive behaviour of the clients and the difficulty and frustration experienced by the staff as they tried to persuade them to change the course of their lives. They also show how City Roads had a unique opportunity to 'work on' the clients day in and day out while they stayed there, whereas other agencies, A and

E departments, street agencies, and probation officers, saw them only for one or two hours at most. But City Roads was still acting together with these other agencies and had to try to co-ordinate what it did with these other workers. Together they might succeed or they might fail. But in the end, the outcome would depend as much on the clients themselves – on their view of things, their needs, and their wishes.

4 Difficult Clients

The chapters that follow (Chapters 4–7), focus on the main goals of City Roads, as stated in the Operational Document. Each of these four chapters takes one objective in turn and discusses what happened at City Roads in the light of it, considering how far the project was able to achieve this end and what factors were at work, influencing and constraining its activities and results. This chapter then is prefaced by the first stated objective:

> 'to provide for the immediate needs of young multiple drug misusers who frequently overdose and who may be admitted to hospital A and E departments.'

In assessing City Roads in these terms, we shall first present a profile of the people who became residents there, principally to find out were they young multiple drug misusers, did they frequently overdose and use A and E departments? If we recall that in setting up City Roads, the intention was to provide a service for people who were thought to be out of contact with existing treatment agencies and, perhaps, to be in some ways different from the patients seen at the clinics, we shall note that there was some uncertainty about what the residents would be like. The group as a whole was characterized as 'chaotic' and 'unstable', 'socially disorganized', but precise details about this client group were not known. A carefully described ethnography of these 'problem drug takers' would then be a useful product of the City Roads project, a valuable contribution in itself.

Having drawn a profile of the client group, we shall then move on to fill in some of the details, concentrating especially on the question of their immediate needs. We shall describe their condition on presenting themselves at City Roads and give an account of how they themselves saw their immediate needs and what they hoped to get out of being there. From this we shall go on to consider what other needs might lie beneath their immediately visible, surface needs, as these were revealed in the case histories. It will be seen that these are much more complex but seem commonly to revolve around problems of deprivation and failures of emotional attachment. The justification for probing more deeply is the assumption that surface needs and deeper needs are closely connected. To define and to understand the immediate needs of the clients at City Roads it is necessary to be able to link them to underlying, perhaps deliberately hidden, deeper needs. Similarly, the assumption is that careful and sensitive treatment of a client at City Roads in the short term should be linked to longer-term plans if it is to be beneficial and not run the risk of being counter-productive.

Profile of the clients

There were twice as many men as women among the 308 people seen at City Roads between 1978 and 1981 (68 per cent were men (N = 209)), 32 per cent were women (N = 99)). This is a similar sex ratio to that found in the official statistics on addiction. (At the end of 1979, males constituted 71 per cent and females 29 per cent of addicts known to the Home Office (Home Office 1980).) However, relatively more women seem to attend at A and E departments than at City Roads (47 per cent of attendances in Ghodse's study were by women (Ghodse 1977a)).

Just over half of all residents were under 25 years of age: slightly less than half were over 25, so they were not predominantly very young people, as may perhaps have been expected. (The mean age was 24 years.) While there were as many very young women as men (of those under 21 years of age, 38 were women and 37 were men) among those over 21, the number of women fell steadily with an increase in age.

Since they were not so young on the whole, it is perhaps not so surprising to find that three out of ten had been married at some time (29 per cent) but only 4 per cent were still married. Twenty-six per cent had children, although only five people still had their child living with them. Fifty-two per cent had been brought up in either London (39 per cent) or the South East (13 per cent). Twelve per cent came from Scotland. The rest came fairly evenly from other regions of the British Isles and 5 per cent were from overseas. It is important to note that the clients seen at City Roads were not typical of the young homeless population in London, more of whom are recent migrants to the big city. For example, only 7 per cent of the City Roads residents had been in London for less than one month and 62 per cent had lived in London for more than five years. This is markedly different from the situation found at a walk-in medical centre in Soho for young homeless people, where 44 per cent of patients had been in London less than one month and only 30 per cent had been in London for over six months (Kitchener, MacGregor, and Croft-White 1980).

Drug takers are not a homogeneous population. Gerry Stimson illustrated this well when he identified four sub-groups within a representative sample of addicts receiving heroin prescriptions in 1969 from hospital Drug Treatment Centres (clinics) (Stimson 1973). City Roads residents, interestingly a group at that time selected as *not* primarily opiate users, conformed very closely to one of Stimson's

Table 6   *Sex and age of all residents*

| | Percentage in each age group | | | | |
	16–19 (n = 60)	20–24 (n = 98)	25–29 (n = 99)	30+ (n = 51)	Total (N = 308)
male (n = 209)	12%	32%	37%	19%	100%
female (n = 99)	35%	31%	22%	12%	100%
total (N = 308)	19%	32%	32%	17%	100%

categories of heroin addicts, the *junkies*. (The junkies were rated lowest among these sub-groups on a scale representing degree of organization of social behaviour.)

Multiple drug use, as *Table 7* indicates, was indeed the pattern found among residents. Only 17 per cent reported current use of just one type of drug and just over 40 per cent reported current use of three different types. *Table 8* (p. 72) indicates the range of drugs currently used and, here, expectations about the predominance of barbiturate misuse were confirmed, with 78 per cent including barbiturates in their pattern of drug misuse.

However, the predominance of barbiturate misuse should not prevent one from noting that over half of these clients reported current use of at least one sort of opioid drug (see *Table 8*). While opiates were not the drugs principally misused by this group at that time, it is clear that a significant number of people were obtaining methadone, heroin, and Diconal and were then on the margins of opiate addiction and were not being seen at the clinics.

The drug-taking careers of City Roads' clients were certainly more extensive than many had anticipated. The average length of time using drugs was almost ten years (9.8 years) and for the most part this had been continuous use. Over three quarters of the group had injected drugs and over 60 per cent were regular injectors. They began taking drugs generally when very young, the youngest age being when 12 years old, the oldest at 23 years. The average age at which drug taking began was 15 years.

Table 7   *Extent of multiple drug misuse among individuals seen at City Roads*

	% of all individuals
one type (n = 51) (barbiturates n = 38)	17
two types (n = 129) (barbiturates + opiates n = 48)	42
three types (n = 87) (barbiturates + opiates + stimulants n = 29)	28
four types (n = 37) (barbiturates + opiates + stimulants + hypnotics/ sedatives n = 17)	12
five types (n = 4)	1
total individuals (N = 308)	100

When asked about their pattern of multiple drug misuse, some said they deliberately took a variety of drugs. They enjoyed varying the effects of 'uppers' and 'downers' or would take one drug to modify a mood produced by another, for example, relieving the depressant effects of barbiturates or opiates with Ritalin. Certain drugs might be taken as substitutes for preferred drugs when resources or availability were low or where there was a need to stave off withdrawal effects (Valium was commonly used in this way).

So, although not *very* young, the clients at City Roads were predominantly multiple drug misusers. Did they frequently overdose and use A and E departments? Forty-three per cent had attended an A and E department within the previous three months, 18 per cent on more than one occasion, following an overdose. This happened largely as a result of taking barbiturates: 'It's really nice on barbs but I lose control really fast. If I've

Table 8   *Pattern of current drug use among individuals seen at City Roads*

type of drug		n of users	% of individuals (N = 308)
barbiturates		240	78
mainly: Tuinal	173		
Nembutal	43		
not named	54		
opiates/analgesics		163	53
mainly: methadone	86		
heroin	78		
Diconal	43		
not named	2		
stimulants		152	49
mainly: amphetamine group	98		
Ritalin	34		
not named	16		
hypnotics/sedatives		130	42
mainly: Valium	83		
Mogadon	23		
Mandrax	18		
Doriden	13		
others		65	21
mainly: cannabis	24		
LSD	16		
cough mixtures	12		

Note: Individuals may appear in more than one category.

got a dozen barbs, I can't help taking everything I've got. After a few you don't care anyway.' Occasionally, excess amounts were deliberately taken in public places so that a hospital bed might be secured as somewhere to crash for the night. On the other hand, one man stated that he used barbiturates so that he could get to sleep in uncomfortable public places but sometimes found himself being whisked off to hospital just as he thought he was nodding off peacefully!

The more damaging and lethal effects of drug abuse tend to arise through intravenous injection, particularly when the preparations are not intended for injection. The practice of injecting crushed pills or the contents of capsules (such as Tuinal and Nembutal, the most frequently taken barbiturates), usually under non-sterile conditions, can cause abscesses, gangrene, and septicaemia (blood poisoning). Fifty-four per cent of these residents were found to have been injecting daily, 15 per cent were injecting occasionally, and only 31 per cent were not injecting (case history survey: this excludes eight cases where information was not recorded).

A distinctive feature of the junkie group, as described by Stimson, is the fact that 'the use of drugs appears to be more of a social activity than for other groups . . . (Junkies) seem to be more involved with the use of drugs' (Stimson 1973: 138–39). This is indicated by their high degree of contact with other addicts and visits to Piccadilly. The City Roads group tended to follow this pattern: the social interactions associated with drug taking were as important as the sheer consumption of the drugs and they had a high level of presence on the drugs scene. (The drugs scene may be regarded as a set of institutions and practices surrounding the behaviour of drug taking.)

Drug takers also need a source for their drugs. For most of those interviewed, sources were mixed. Doctors were frequently mentioned as a source of drugs. Doctors were approached in a variety of ways depending on what 'type' they were seen to be. The *bent* doctors were said to write out the desired prescription 'if I slip him a couple of quid', 'put a bottle of Scotch on the table' or 'let him give me a once-over examination'. Others were seen as *stupid* doctors, who appeared to be gullible: 'if you concoct a story about being temporarily in London or something'. Others were seen as *do-gooders* who 'really think they are helping you'. Or they may be 'too pushed for time to ask any questions and just want you out of the surgery as quick as possible'. One man stated that sometimes he got his prescription by threatening the doctor that he 'would wreck the surgery' if he didn't comply with the request for drugs.

The most usual source of drugs, however, was a known dealer. A few individuals reported that they would buy drugs from someone they had not met before, if for example offered something in a pub. Some said they had forged prescriptions, or in one case had burgled chemists' shops, to obtain drugs at some time in the previous four weeks.

These clients, being highly visible on the drugs scene, frequently had contact with the police. A majority reported at least one contact with the police over the past four weeks. This had usually involved a 'stop and search' episode. Several thought they were well known to the police and were hassled in a routine way. 'They arrest me for being drunk and disorderly when I'm barbed up or for loitering or obstruction. They lock me up for a few hours and then kick me out. Sometimes I've had a £10 fine or a day inside and I've usually already done the day.' 'They know me at the Dilly. They search me but if they find anything they just give me my stuff back.' Few, however, expressed strong antipathy towards the police or complained about their methods (except one young woman who said she had once been 'battered' in a police cell).

Given all this, it is not surprising to find that a high proportion had had contact with the probation service. Thirty per cent of all those admitted to City Roads reported that they were in current contact with the probation service (not necessarily under a probation order and not necessarily actively). Views on the probation service were mixed. One person stated that her probation officer 'is always around if I need her', but several others were more negative and the general feeling was that they had very little time to devote to these clients; one said, 'she gives me money to get rid of me'.

Another feature of the drugs scene is the non-statutory helping agencies, or 'street' agencies, such as the Hungerford Drug Project, St Martin-in-the-Fields Social Service Unit, and the Piccadilly Advice Centre. Contact with these agencies was very common among these clients. Of all those admitted to City Roads, 53 per cent reported current contact with a street agency. It was clear from the interviews that those who did use the street agencies tended to visit more than one, and that there were functional distinctions among them. Hungerford Drug Project offered 'counselling', St Martin's 'a cup of tea and a chat'; different needs might be met at different times by the different street agencies.

Only 23 (7 per cent) of the 308 individuals admitted to City Roads were currently patients at a DTC (clinic). On the other hand, we have seen that 53 per cent reported current use of opiate drugs (most commonly methadone), though the degree of dependency is unknown. One quarter of these City Roads clients had however previously been treated for opiate dependency. Previous treatment for drug-related psychosis and for detoxification was also common. Thirty-four per cent had been in-patients in psychiatric hospitals and a small number had been admitted for rehabilitation in psychiatric hospital settings. Psychiatric treatment for non-drug-related problems was also found, 13 per cent as out-patients and 6 per cent as in-patients.

The views expressed about the clinics were generally negative. One man who was currently a patient stated that his 'treatment', apart from the methadone, consisted of an appointment every two months when he 'may or may not see the doctor'. Another, who had been a patient in the past, was very bitter: 'the clinics are killing off more people than they are curing, through people getting their scripts cut off. You don't get a decent script, anyway. There's bound to be people who take advantage, but it's a rigid policy of giving 40mg and no more. They don't discriminate between people's needs.' Another person stated that he would not 'get registered' because he didn't want to get 'hooked' on methadone which, according to him, 'is the hardest of all opiates to come off'. A more positive view was expressed by another person, however, who occasionally visited one clinic where he received no prescription, but thought the contact was beneficial.

Piccadilly Circus (the Dilly) is the market place of the drugs scene, the place where drug misusers are most likely to 'score' when they need supplies. But there is more to the Dilly scene than buying, selling, and taking drugs. It is a focal point for the exchange of information, expertise, ideological and social support. Participation in this is a source of social contact, time-structuring, and stimulation, and these functions have a significance equal to that of drug taking itself as the basis for attachment to this lifestyle.

Some people were around Piccadilly every day, and others said they visited the area more than once a week. Only a few stated they did not spend any time in the Piccadilly area. One young woman indicated an important function of involvement in the Piccadilly drugs scene thus: 'I'm there at least some part of every day. I know people at the Dilly, they all sort of relate. I feel comfortable there. It's a meeting-place. You have a sense of belonging.'

Participating in the West End drugs scene is a means of feeling something in common with other people, of sharing an identity and, as one young woman put it, 'it's easy to meet people if you're like them'. Yet, at the same time, there was an awareness of the superficiality of these relationships, a feeling that 'you don't make real friends', just 'acquaintances and contacts'. Despite the social contact, for one man who spent most of his time around Piccadilly, 'the Dilly is the loneliest place in the world'.

Attachment to the drugs scene went beyond drugs themselves. Several talked of drug taking as 'a way of life'. Habituation was not simply to drugs: 'out there, it's what I know, a habit, a routine, like brushing your teeth. When I wasn't using drugs I stayed in bed. There was nothing to do. Life's boring without drugs'; 'you're too busy to think. The whole day is taken up with drugs, sorting things out. It's routine, habitual. I carry on because it's familiar'; 'I enjoy the drugs scene – there's the excitement of scoring as much as fixing'; 'you have experiences every day, things are always happening'.

The City Roads clients, then, clearly resemble the *junkies* in Stimson's sample of heroin addicts. These accounts of involvement in the drugs scene seem also to fit in with certain American findings. In the view of Isidor Chein:

> 'the major factor in chronic urban opiate users is that taking it provides social benefits that are an answer to emptiness. There are three interrelated benefits the addict acquires from his involvement with narcotics: he gains an identity, one posing little to live up to. He gains a place in a subsociety where he is unequivocally accepted as a peer, a not-too-demanding place among his fellow men. He acquires a career, at which he is reasonably competent, devoted to maintaining his supply, avoiding the police, and the rituals of taking the drug.' (Chein 1966: 65)

To look at, City Roads residents were down and out. They seemed to have few possessions and often just owned the clothes they were wearing. They would certainly be defined as poor by any conventional standards. They were rarely employed. Only 10 per cent had been in some form of employment up to the time of admission to City Roads and 42 per cent had not had any kind of employment for at least one year. (This is a high level of disorganization even among drug misusers. A survey of opiate users approaching DTCs (clinics) found that 39 per cent were in full-time employment at the time (Blumberg 1974).) The most common form of income is social security, yet only half had claimed benefit within the month prior to admission. Clearly, many were relying on other sources of support.

In interviews, a range of alternative means of support were described, which usually amounted to some form of hustling,

such as begging or borrowing money, selling drugs, or prostitution. Younger women mentioned begging as a source of
income. The practice, as they described it, was to approach
likely people in the street and ask for 10p or 20p on the basis of a
fabricated story calculated to win sympathy. One person
claimed to make about £10 a day and another stated that she
could easily survive on her beggings. Prostitution was mentioned as a source of income by both males and females.
Dealing in drugs was also mentioned as a source of income, less
often by women. These dealers indicated that their involvement was generally small scale. If begging, prostitution, and
dealing are regarded as forms of hustling, two-thirds of those
interviewed were depending wholly or in part on hustling for
their income.

Criminal behaviour was common among the City Roads
clients. A strikingly high proportion had been convicted of
some offence (84 per cent) and a large number had been
imprisoned for their offences (40 per cent). Drugs Act offences
and offences involving drugs (e.g. forgery of a prescription) can
be distinguished and convictions for these offences were
common (51 per cent and 31 per cent respectively (these are
overlapping categories)). Although it cannot be determined
with any certainty what part drug misuse played in other
offences, for example if committed under the influence of drugs
or to support their dependency, the extent of non-drug-related
offences was high, property offences having been committed
by 76 per cent, aggression offences by 24 per cent, and crimes of
violence by 38 per cent. These are similar findings to those of
Blumberg where 80 per cent of people approaching DTCs had at
least one conviction (Blumberg et al. 1974). Half of those interviewed at City Roads reported that they had engaged in theft or
robbery within the four weeks prior to admission. This
includes shoplifting, usually for food for themselves, occasionally for items to sell in order to buy drugs, and theft of
handbags. Among all City Roads residents, 36 per cent had a
court case hanging over them at the time of admission.

These people generally lived in an unsettled fashion. *Table 9*
shows their accommodation circumstances at admission. There
was considerable mobility between these different forms of
accommodation, particularly for those not in 'secure' accommodation. For example, one woman who stated that her main
form of accommodation over the past four weeks was her
parents' home, also said that she spent periods staying at
squats and with friends when she wasn't 'fit' to get home, or if

relationships were difficult at home. Even within the four-week period prior to admission to City Roads, a variety of accommodation would have been used. For example, some had been in emergency accommodation – reception centres, non-statutory hostels such as Centrepoint, and various public places (including Charing Cross embankment, underground garages, and all-night cinemas). Others had stayed at friends' houses, at squats, and bed and breakfast hotels. It is realistic to describe two-thirds of the clients as effectively homeless. This situation was not a temporary crisis. The case-history sample

Table 9   *Accommodation situation of individuals on admission to City Roads*

	n	%
'secure' accommodation (parents' home, own rented or owner-occupied)	86	28
'insecure' accommodation (squatting, staying at friends' home)	62	20
'homeless' (using emergency hostels or sleeping rough)	154	50
accommodation not recorded	6	2
total	308	100

revealed that 57 per cent had been living *mainly* in very insecure accommodation (squats, friends' flats, short- and longer-term hostels) *ever since first leaving home*. Homelessness for this group appears to be a chronic problem, as was the case with Stimson's junkie group of heroin addicts (Stimson 1973).

Seeking help

The help-seeking episode occurs in the process of managing the benefits and costs of a life of drug misuse. City Roads offered a 'crisis intervention' service. Crises for these clients tended to take the form of a more or less serious breakdown in their capacity to manage the costs of their lifestyle: that is, a failure of their usual coping strategies. One important feature of this relates to the activities of social control agencies. We have seen that over a third had a court case coming up at the time they were admitted to City Roads. There was often considerable encouragement from probation officers: 'my PO said go to City Roads and take three weeks to figure out what to do and make some decisions about the future'; 'the Probation Officer said, it's come to City Roads or stay in prison'. The view was expressed several times that gaining admission to City Roads was a way of showing 'willing' to the court, which would minimize the sentence. The prospect of prison was often a spur to action: 'I'm terrified of prison'; 'I don't want to be sent down'; 'I know I won't get put away this time, but if I don't do something now, I'll end up in prison sooner or later'. One person explicitly stated that he came to City Roads because he thought the social workers would help with his court case.

Other pressures arose from very poor health: the 'need for a barb detox', wanting a 'safe withdrawal', being 'scared of fits', and 'wanting to get barbs out of my system'. One young woman elaborated on this: 'I can get a detox here so that when I do go out, there's no pressure to score right away. I don't want to get too much of a habit, so I break things up by coming to City Roads'. Given the extent of homelessness, low incomes, lack of adequate clothing and diet, injection practices and injuries, it is not surprising to find that many residents expressed concern for their physical condition as an important reason for seeking admission. Health care was a very important objective for many of these clients: 'I was really wrecked, in a terrible state'; 'the nurse in the casualty told me my body couldn't take any more'; 'food and a bed aren't important to me, medical attention is'.

City Roads was also seen as a short-term solution to the problem of homelessness, as well as offering the prospect of longer-term accommodation through onward referral. Many reported that they had no accommodation of their own to return to on leaving City Roads. The sense of having nowhere to go was expressed several times: 'I just needed somewhere decent to stay'; 'I've got no real thoughts about the future – except I want somewhere to live'. Homelessness was an integral part of the process of deterioration that they were experiencing.

An overwhelming sense of hopelessness was a common result of these multiple problems. One third specifically mentioned their poor mental state as a factor in seeking admission to City Roads: 'I was feeling really depressed, almost suicidal'; 'I was very depressed, feeling I was just getting deeper and deeper into a mess'. There came a point when their way of life seemed unacceptable: 'I couldn't face hassling for money any more'; 'I came here because I was sick of dossing, sick of barbs, and sick of landing in hospital'.

Longer-term aims were rarely expressed as the motivation for admission. Only a few mentioned the goal of rehabilitation: 'I want rehabilitation and a normal life'; 'I want to stop using drugs and go into rehabilitation'. In a few cases, there was even open antagonism towards the idea of rehabilitation: 'I'm not going to spend a year in rehab'; 'I've got no intentions of going into rehab'. However, for some 'rehabilitation is always in the back of your mind'. It is in this sense that a number of those interviewed expressed uncertainty about their needs, and saw City Roads as a means of clarification: 'I want to learn about the options'; 'I'm not sure about wanting to come off drugs, but I want time to think about it'.

The most persistent theme emerging from the interviews is the role of the 'fatigue factor' as the motivation for seeking help. City Roads is resorted to as a sanctuary from the pressures of their life: 'My first aim was just to retreat, to get time out'; 'I came to get a breathing-space'; there was a need for 'a break', and for 'time and space'. One man said, with evident relief, that compared to the way he'd been living, staying at City Roads was like being 'on a desert island'.

Several pressures were often at work at the same time, as in this case: 'I'd left the rehab and couldn't go back. I'd been picked up by the police. I was on the streets, no money, nowhere to go. I wanted to get out of the circle of the streets, and I wanted somewhere to impress the court. I wanted some assistance on ideas. I wanted to take off the pressure of street life. I wanted City Roads to give me time and space.' In this sense, their situation seems to fit with the theory of 'crisis' developed principally by Caplan, in which the essential factor determining the occurrence of crisis is an imbalance between the perceived difficulty and significance of the threatening situation, and the resources available immediately for coping with it (Caplan 1964).

Yet the clients remain ambivalent. They tend to be concerned with managing what could be termed the 'occupational stress' of the career of drug misuse. An American study of 'Drug Abuse as a Career' makes the same point: 'Detox centres play an important role in helping users who have hit bottom. . . . It is an opportunity to rest, to eat regularly, to reduce the costs of one's habit, and then to return to the streets renewed' (Coombs 1981: 383). The crisis situation is also, as Caplan's theory suggests, a moment when an individual is more amenable to outside inter- vention than at times of stable functioning. The dilemma for the practitioners of crisis intervention lies in offering a restorative service that re-equips the drug misuser, and at the same time using the crisis situation as a lever to move the client out of a pattern of living that produces the crises.

The point we wish to make here is that seeking admission to City Roads is an act of asking for help and this arises from the circumstances and the social context in which people find themselves. Seeking help is essentially adaptive behaviour. It is an effort to control one's environment. Work in medical sociology on help seeking, illness behaviour, and the sick role is relevant here. David Mechanic, for example, 'views much of human activity, particularly the activity surrounding illness, within an adaptive framework; such behaviours are seen as aspects of and reactions to situations in which persons are actively struggling to control their environment and life situation' (Mechanic 1978: 1). The crisis in which City Roads is to intervene is from the point of view of the client a more or less serious breakdown in coping capacity. The need for City Roads as defined within the frame of reference of the drug misuser is the result of pressure. The main pressures they were aware of were: legal pressures, one third had legal matters pending and anxiety about prison was often mentioned; health pressure, one half of those interviewed mentioned deteriorated health as a matter of concern; psychological pressure, one third mentioned feelings of depression and despair; the general presence of a 'fatigue factor', the cumulative demands of street life, homelessness, lack of money, and the absence of alternative sources of social support came across as a frequently stated need for 'breathing-space', 'time out', and 'a break'.

The environment and way of life of the clients of City Roads are essentially those of the *junkie* even though the term is one not used by all the residents and deliberately avoided by staff at City Roads, who were wary of conferring 'status' on their clients in this way. Eight features of the junkie pattern as elaborated by Stimson are found in this population of City Roads clients: *catholic drug use* – residents could be understood as multidrug abusers or polydrug misusers, confirming David Williams' comment about similar drug-dependent patients seen at the Middlesex Hospital's A and E Department, 'their drug consumption is almost as varied as the range of cocktails at the Savoy' (Williams 1981); *they have the highest incidence of physical complications* – data from the survey of 80 case histories indicated a range of treatment needs, abscesses, injuries, recent overdoses, barbiturate dependency, and need for withdrawal; *nearly all unemployed and have been for the last three months; they support themselves almost completely by stealing . . . and by 'hustling'; they have a high rate of criminal activity; residentially unstable; eat poorly, sleep irregularly* and have *a poor appearance; high degree of contact with other addicts* and *drug use is a social activity.*

Problems revealed in the case histories

Admission to City Roads, while arising from the context and motives outlined above, is however rooted in a long-term pattern of deviant response. The City Roads resident not only presents a set of immediate needs but also brings a history. Their histories are striking both in the extensive involvement in a career of drug misuse and also in that a range of other 'problem behaviours' pre-date and co-exist with drug misuse.

To give a broader profile and to consider the question of aetiology, an account is presented here of the family background of City Road clients. At first glance, the material or cultural factor of social class of family appears not to be related to subsequent behaviour, since the class distribution based on father's occupation is very close to that of the general population. However, when other indicators are brought into account, given the high rate of absence of father and a certain inadequacy of these data, the picture appears somewhat different.

On the basis of data on father's occupation, City Roads' residents appear to conform to the national distribution of social class, with the proportion in non-manual and manual categories being 36 per cent and 64 per cent. (The 1971 Census found that the population of economically active and retired males was composed of 35 per cent non-manual and 65 per cent manual workers (Social Trends No. 6 1979).) This finding for City Roads clients is consistent with other findings on samples of drug misusers (Blumberg 1981; Plant 1981).

However, a different picture emerges when other indices of social background are considered. City Roads residents show a pattern different from the national distribution in respect of type of family home (52 per cent were brought up in council property: the national proportion in 1962 was 27 per cent), and family size (56 per cent were reared in families where the total number of children was four or more). The conventional indicator of social class – father's occupation – is an unreliable one in these cases, because of the high incidence of paternal absence. Real living standards are better judged by the other indicators mentioned, and on this basis there are signs of social disadvantage.

Table 10   *Indicators of early social background (Case history survey N = 80)*

	% of cases in which indicator occurred
absence of at least one parent for 2 years or more before age 16 years	54
serious parental discord without separation (to age 16)	26
parental characteristics:	
heavy drinking – mother/father	39
mental disturbance treated – mother/father	26
experience of institutional rearing (to age 16)	36
attendance at child guidance agency	19
conviction before drug use	29
family size – 4+ children	56
family housing – council*	52
father's occupation – manual*	64

*Note: information not recorded on 18 of these cases.

It is often found in research on drug misusers (and other 'deviant' groups) that their early family experience tends to be characterized by disruption and separation. This may of course be a finding specific to drug misusers found in institutions or undergoing treatment. It certainly appears to apply to City Roads residents.

One source of family disruption or poor-quality relationships is disordered parental behaviour. Alcoholism/heavy drinking (39 per cent) and mental disturbance (26 per cent) were frequently reported in the parents of these people.

The extent of separation experience found in these clients is striking. Less than half (46 per cent) reached the age of 16 years with both natural parents providing continuous care. For 50 per cent separation was final, through desertion (9 per cent), death (16 per cent), or parents' separation (25 per cent). City Roads residents were almost three times more likely to have lost one or both parents by the age of 16 than the national sample (54 per cent compared to 16 per cent) (Fogelman 1983). The National Child Development Study found that at age 16, 95 per cent of their national sample were living with their natural mother, and 87 per cent were with their natural father (Fogelman 1976). The corresponding figures for City Roads residents are 75 per cent and 54 per cent respectively. A further comparison with the National Child Development Study reveals that in the national sample, 4 per cent had been placed for some period in the care of the local authority or a voluntary society (Essen and Wedge 1982). Among City Roads residents, 22 per cent were placed for some period in children's homes because of inadequacy of available parental care and 36 per cent in total had some experience of being in an institution as a child. Furthermore, there is among these clients a commonly found indication that in families that remained intact, the quality of parental relationships was more or less seriously discordant (in about one half of intact families).

It is difficult to separate the drug-use connected elements from other elements in these histories of problem behaviour and societal response. In many cases, the problem behaviour began early: at least it seems that parents or schoolteachers had a problem in dealing with their behaviour, in that 19 per cent were referred to child guidance workers and 24 per cent were placed in schools for the maladjusted or approved schools. This is certainly beyond the normal distribution, for example, the National Child Development Study found that only 5 per cent of their children had been referred at some time to child guidance professionals (Fogelman 1976). Furthermore, 29 per cent of City Roads residents had been convicted of a criminal offence before the reported age of first use of drugs.

To indicate the complexity and severity of the problems which lay beneath the surface of the junkie image, we set out here four 'ideal typical' portraits constructed from the case histories of clients at City Roads. Four ideal types are presented: first, a typical junkie, who had been seen at the clinics and had been on the scene for a number of years; second a 'disturbed' young man whose problems appear to have been mainly to do with drugs but who had little previous contact with treatment or help; third, a case sadly typical of most of the women, who were generally more 'disturbed' than the men, often with histories of severe abuse and deprivation as a child; and finally, someone with a long 'deviant' career of crime and prison, which predated his drug use.

ROBERT

Robert was born and brought up in North London and had used drugs almost continuously for 15 years. He described his childhood as happy and reasonably stable. The family home was fairly comfortable – his father had a managerial position with a motor car company. Robert was never aware of any conflict between his parents. He felt much closer to his mother than to his father and he got on well with his two older sisters. It is one of Robert's regrets that he 'never got to know' his father, who died of cancer a few years ago.

School meant little in terms of education. He obtained no qualifications but he enjoyed belonging to a group of friends. When he left school he started an apprenticeship as an electrician, but his commitment was sporadic and although he attended over several years he did not complete the training.

Before he left school, Robert was already using drugs on a regular basis. This chiefly involved taking stimulants with his friends at weekends. He had already experimented with cannabis at 14 years of age, but he preferred 'dealing' to taking cannabis. Before he was 16 he had been introduced to heroin and for the next year he was receiving a prescription for heroin from a GP. He was then admitted to a local psychiatric hospital for withdrawal treatment, but within a few weeks had returned to his doctor and resumed daily injecting of heroin. Again, at the age of 17, he was admitted to a psychiatric hospital but, according to Robert, this was not a genuine interruption in his drug taking since he was still able to obtain drugs while he was in the hospital.

When Robert left hospital and continued as an addict, getting prescriptions and buying and selling on the streets, his parents felt that his behaviour was no longer acceptable at home and they asked him to leave. Almost immediately, Robert was arrested and convicted of illegal possession of heroin. He was sent to borstal for two years and then accepted back at home by his parents. This was followed by almost three years of abstinence and stable living. Robert married when he was 21 years old, moved into a council flat, and held a job for two years as an electrician in a factory. They had a child after one year of marriage.

After 18 months of marriage, Robert's wife left him. He had started to take heroin again. His wife would not accept this and issued an ultimatum about the choice Robert had to make. The result was her departure and a very intense involvement with drugs for Robert. In an effort to regain some stability he became a patient at an East London hospital Drug Treatment Centre. However, he continued to supplement his prescription with extra heroin and with other drugs. The first of numerous admissions to Tooting Bec hospital was arranged to allow Robert to stabilize on a low prescription, yet he was now at 23 years of age heavily immersed in multi-drug use, including heroin and other opiates, barbiturates, and Ritalin (a stimulant). His pattern of drug taking was punctuated over the next six years by a series of prison sentences all for drug-related offences – and periods in Tooting Bec and other hospitals where he was treated for overdoses, septicaemia, abscesses, and a gangrenous hand through careless injecting which left him with restricted movement of his fingers. He lost his prescription from one Drug Treatment Centre because of multi-drug use, and managed to be accepted by another in a different part of London. After a number of interruptions to his status as a patient, two years ago the DTC finally refused to accept him back as a patient after a prison sentence.

Robert's attempts at stabilization and drug-free living have always been short-lived. He consistently resumed drug taking after periods in hospital and in prison. Some degree of stability was attained during two periods as a resident at Roma, a project offering support to drug dependants with opiate prescriptions. But these stays of a few months each broke down because of barbiturate abuse. The last two years involved a decline in his living pattern. He lost his rented accommodation and resorted to bed-and-breakfast accommodation and sleeping rough. Barbiturate dependency became the dominant feature of his drug taking and his health deteriorated significantly.

Six months ago, Robert attempted to arrest this decline by entering Phoenix House, a drug-free rehabilitation project. He stayed for three months and then discharged himself and resumed his lifestyle at the point he had left it. He made several visits to an advisory service for drug takers and a worker there suggested application to City Roads.

STUART

Stuart was adopted at a very early age, and does not know anything about his real parents. He spent most of his childhood in a council house in a Scottish city. He was one of two adopted children, and recalls that it was made clear to them at an early age that they had been adopted. His parents said that they had been 'chosen' because they were 'special'. His adoptive parents both worked, his father as a milkman and his mother in a chemist's shop. When they were all in the house together (which Stuart says was not very often) the atmosphere was usually tense. He remembers his father frequently shouting at his mother about her drinking habits and being out on her own a lot. Occasionally, his father would physically push his mother around, and the mother and children were always somewhat fearful of him. Stuart remembers several occasions before his teenage years when his mother left home and took the children with her to her sister's house, a short train journey away. Although he was only rarely beaten by his father, Stuart was aware of a very strict upbringing under his control.

By the age of 15 Stuart was receiving medication for depression and insomnia. He had been in trouble over truanting from school. Relations with his parents were very strained. At this point he left home and went to the North of England to stay with relatives with whom he had been during school holidays when younger. However, this situation lasted only six months, as these relatives expected him to be going out to work and since Stuart had not found work they were not prepared to support him. He was taken into a hostel for homeless boys, but again there was an expectation of work and Stuart left with another resident and arrived in London aged 16.

Stuart had already found it easy to obtain drugs from doctors for treatment of symptoms of depression and for insomnia. He continued to get drugs in this way and was taking Valium on a regular basis, although he was not involved in any drugs 'scene'. He moved into a children's home shortly after arrival in London and found himself in a warm and caring environment which he enjoyed very much. He still obtained tranquillizers and there was occasional use of cannabis, but no experimentation with opiates or barbiturates. He was given a lot of encouragement to train for a secure job and attended a work experience programme as a hairdresser. Jobs, however, were never held for long, and Stuart drifted through a range of jobs in hairdressing, catering, and shop work which lasted only a few months at a time. He admits that his rather drowsy state under the influence of tranquillizers probably had something to do with this job mobility. There was no criticism from staff at the home when he was not employed, and he felt 'at home' during the two years he was able to stay.

When he reached 18 years old he was obliged to leave the home. Stuart's life became seriously disorganized from this point. He drifted towards the West End and became involved in prostituting himself to older men who seemed willing to 'look after' him, but these relationships were always short-lived. When no one was offering him a place to stay, he used short-term accommodation such as Centrepoint and River-point. His drugs use escalated to regular use of barbiturates as well as Valium. Within the past year he was convicted of minor theft offences (shoplifting) and drunk and disorderly behaviour (when he was under the influence of barbiturates). His health began to deteriorate and he was overdosing on barbiturates and admitted to hospital about a dozen times in the past six months. Three months ago he started to inject barbiturates and developed abscesses on his arms which were treated at hospital A and E departments. His contact with helping agencies has been superficial: he had one interview with a hospital psychiatrist following one of his recent overdoses and has visited several of the West End advisory services but has had no consistent contact with any of them. It was following a barbiturate overdose that Stuart was admitted to City Roads from the Middlesex Hospital.

MARY

Mary is a 25-year-old woman whose upbringing is characterized by serious disruption and deprivation. She was born in a town close to London. Her father had been in the Merchant Navy for many years and when he was at home earned a living as a carpenter. He was a heavy drinker with a violent temper. Mary's mother was quite incapable of looking after her as she had long suffered from debilitating mental illness which frequently involved hospitalization and chronic mood-swings when at home. Her parents abused each other both verbally and physically and abused Mary (an only child) in the same way. Mary's home life with her parents was only intermittent as she was often taken into children's homes or handed to foster parents for several years at a time. Mary cannot recall anything but maltreatment wherever she was living. The children's homes were cold and disciplinarian and Mary's own behaviour was often very aggressive and disruptive. There was a similar pattern in the foster families. In one case, Mary refused to do household chores (she was about eight years old) and her aggressive response was punished by being deprived of food for two days. Whether she was in homes or with foster parents, Mary made continuous attempts to be with her mother and frequently ran away from these places. For short periods when her mother's condition appeared to be stable, she would be returned home (her father was rarely around), until her mother deteriorated again. Even during stable periods, her mother would treat Mary in a brutal fashion. Mary's view of this is that her mother 'couldn't help it'.

Because of the behavioural problems she presented, Mary went to approved school and left there with a very low level of educational attainment. She came to London at the age of 16 and got a living-in job in an hotel, which she held for around one year. Mary had experimented with cannabis and stimulants, but was not using drugs in any consistent way. However, she had been drinking regularly for several years and this habit escalated during her first two years in London. She moved around London, sharing flats or squats with friends and working occasionally. She was increasingly using drugs in the company of others, and began to spend more time in the Piccadilly area. By the time she was 20 years of age Mary was using opiates and barbiturates and was fully involved in the West End drugs 'scene'.

Mary had been in legal trouble once at the age of 15 when she had broken into an empty house, but she was now making a number of court appearances for public nuisance offences, theft from shops and causing a disturbance in a police station. She was also increasingly damaging her health through drug taking: she was hospitalized for hepatitis and was treated for several abscesses. Overdosing with barbiturates was a frequent occurrence, in some cases with very large quantities of drugs, and Mary herself was unsure whether or not she was making any serious attempt at suicide.

Mary made one attempt at drug-free living when she was 22 years old and went (with some firm encouragement from her probation officer) to stay at a small rehabilitation project for women in the South of England. Mary's own view of this place is that 'it was too nice to be true' but she left after around three months. She returned to London and was convicted almost immediately of several offences of robbery and was sent to Holloway prison.

She was released from prison after serving 15 months and was found after-care accommodation by her probation officer. For some months Mary's life had some degree of stability. However, she had become involved with a woman outside her own accommodation who was receiving a prescription from a hospital Drug Treatment Centre. (Mary had been involved in bisexual relationships since she came to London.) Mary moved in with her friend and resumed regular drug use. Within a few months the relationship broke down and Mary found herself homeless and dependent on drugs. She used hostel and emergency accommodation and sometimes stayed with friends. Her use of drugs became increasingly chaotic and barbiturate overdoses became frequent. Mary was in regular contact with her probation officer, who suggested City Roads as a chance for stabilization and Mary agreed to the referral.

COLIN

Colin is 30 years of age and was brought up in a working-class neighbourhood of a Northern city. His father worked as a machine operator in a factory and his mother was a canteen lady in the same factory. As far as Colin is concerned, his parents had normal 'ups and downs', but in general provided a good home for himself and his two brothers and sister (he was the eldest). His only serious conflict with his parents came in his early teens when his father tried to impose short hair and early nights when Colin wanted long hair and late nights. He had similar problems in rebellion against school rules and showed no interest in school work.

He took unskilled employment and in the main devoted his energy to group activities in the evenings and at weekends with his friends. He lived at home until he was 17 years old and then left home because he had been sacked from work and did not want to face the consequences from his father. He moved into a shared house with friends, although he continued to visit his parents' home and would sometimes stay overnight. He obtained work on a fairground in the summer, and decided to move on with it when it moved away from the area. For nine months, when he was 18 years old, he travelled around the country with the fairground, and has not returned to his area of upbringing since.

Colin had already displayed troublesome behaviour. He had truanted from school and at the age of 15 had broken into the school and been cautioned. He had been involved with his friends in heavy drinking and rowdy behaviour which attracted the attention of the police, and when he was 17 years old he was convicted of an offence of Actual Bodily Harm to a police officer and put on probation. Drug use was not a prominent feature of his behaviour. He had smoked cannabis with his friends and used stimulants to sustain his energy over the weekends. Drinking was a more serious habit, and was sometimes accompanied by sleeping tablets.

Colin continued to move around the country, basing himself mainly in London, and occasionally picking up short-term work. He developed no lasting personal relationships. He spent a considerable proportion of his twenties serving a number of prison sentences, mostly for crimes of burglary and robbery. Alcohol and, increasingly, drugs played a significant part in his life. He was 'dried out' in hospital on two occasions after heavy alcoholic binges. He tended to use stimulants in between bouts of heavy drinking, and this may be connected with his criminal activity. He has attempted to inject drugs on only two occasions and has not usually associated with other drug takers.

Colin's criminal activities have so far been separate from his drug use. He has one conviction for supplying drugs and none for possession of drugs. Two years ago after a prison sentence, he spent six months in a residential project for male drug takers who are ex-offenders. According to Colin, this was simply a way of securing accommodation. He was convicted again of petty theft and served another prison sentence and then went to live in a probation hostel. One feature of Colin's periods in prison is that he has taken up his education again, and has accumulated several qualifications over the six prison sentences he has served. After the last prison sentence, his involvement with drugs became more serious, and over the past 18 months he has been using barbiturates (together with alcohol). This resulted in admission to hospital A and E departments on two occasions following overdoses.

A few weeks before admission to City Roads, Colin was arrested and charged with receiving stolen goods (in fact, stolen from an off-licence). He had heard City Roads mentioned by one drug taker he knew, and referred himself to the project.

Conclusion

Having looked at the profile of the 308 people who went to City Roads over a three-year period, having studied in depth a representative sample of the case histories of 80 of them, and having spent three years getting to know the residents around the House, it might be hoped that we could come to some definite conclusions about why people misuse drugs. But unfortunately a complete answer still eludes us. First of all, we should say that we did not set out to try to explain drug misuse in terms of any particular theory: we did not test any predetermined hypotheses. The focus of our study was on service provision and what we found out about the clients was in a way incidental to this. However we should be able to offer some suggestions about why people misuse drugs from our knowledge of people who went to City Roads. We should emphasize that what we say may cast light only on a specific form of drug taking. In a society where drug taking is a major and organized part of daily life, there is nothing unusual about drug taking in itself. Nor are we even talking about problem drug taking or drug misuse in general. What we know about refers to a particular category of drug misuse, which is associated with being homeless, chronically unemployed, down and out, criminally active, and mixing principally with other drug misusers, that of the *junkies*, defined by Stimson. And even within this, we are talking very much about those who may be reaching the end of the road, those who are overdosing frequently, who have been in and out of prison, hospital, or rehabilitation projects, and who find themselves at City Roads.

Once they reach that stage, it is clear that drug taking has become for them their principal social and personal identity and the focus of their daily routine and network of social relationships. It is what they know about, it is where their friends are, it is what keeps them going. It is not surprising that they stay with it, in the same way that we all get stuck in a rut or set in our ways. Except that, for these people, they are not in control of things; drug taking, and all that is associated with it, is controlling them. They are subject to the vagaries of the availability of drugs on the street and the unpredictability of the activities of other people on whom they depend for supplies of drugs and for social contacts and income, and the unpredictability of the interventions of other agencies around the scene, especially of the police. The drugs themselves, although possibly taken as a form of self-medication to reduce anxiety or depression, are also unpredictable in their effects especially when obtained illicitly, and sometimes things go wrong, plans do not work out. All this is stressful, but it is also what makes it so exciting, and the search for excitement and adventure seems to be a strong one. Perhaps alternatives offered need to be as demanding if they are to be attractive. However for some, the excitement begins to pall or becomes too much when physical and mental strength begin to fade. It does seem though that with these people what is needed is not just treatment of drug dependence but also the offer of an alternative social identity, a way of being and living in the world, with a new set of associations and friendships.

These comments can be made with some confidence. But what about the question of how they came to be in that state? Why from all those who take drugs, from the large numbers who become dependent on drugs, do some people slip to becoming down-and-out junkies? What is important to note here is that we are attempting to explain not only drug dependence but also, and perhaps more importantly, homelessness, being a migrant, a drifter, becoming an outsider, even an outcast. The situation of the people at City Roads parallels that of other homeless and down-and-out people, such as those discussed by Leach and Wing (1980) and those in drinking-schools described so well by Peter Archard (1979). The particular form of deviance, problem drinking, drug misuse, even perhaps prostitution or criminality, may differ, but these groups share other social characteristics which may help to explain how they came to be 'beyond the pale'.

We have mentioned the idea that the central values in our society are home, family, and work. What is striking is that these people are much more likely to be outsiders in these terms: they have hardly a toe-hold on these structures, few associations or interests invested there. Here the fragile structure of their upbringing seems relevant. Their early lives were very often, but not always, characterized by disturbance, either through broken families, or through separation from parents, or by erratic and sometimes cruel treatment by their parents. This may have had some effect in producing more fragile characters, that panoply of behaviours which are variously referred to by writers and practitioners as 'inadequate personalities', associated with failures of socialization and parental control, low self-esteem, poor coping ability, and so on. Certainly there seems to be some support for Thorley's description of the behaviour of more extreme cases of drug misuse as indicating handicap in the social skills necessary to maintain close and meaningful interpersonal relationships and that they had experienced homes where there had been parental disturbance and family disruption (Thorley 1979: 283–84).

Another feature that may be as important here, as well as affecting personality and character development, is the poverty of these families as regards the resources with which to support their children when difficulties arise. They were much less likely than most people to have been brought up in a caring family. In adolescence, many children get into trouble, test out how far they can go, may get caught up with the police or into trouble at school; or may be difficult to deal with at home, especially where they start to experiment with drugs. But not all of them carry on and develop drug taking into a career. The backgrounds of the people seen at City Roads do seem to indicate that they were 'vulnerable' in that their families were less likely to have the resources to help them through difficulties, to help them over obstacles and, later, to be there to fall back on when serious trouble arose. They did seem less likely to have strong supportive and caring families so that although their behaviour might not be very different from that of other problem drug takers, the consequences were harsher because they were on their own.

The other disadvantage of becoming deeply involved in drug taking in adolescence that seems relevant is that that is the period when the other central identification in modern society, source of associations, sense of direction and supports, begins to be built up, i.e. that of occupation. Although for many working-class youngsters the world of work may be unexciting and increasingly harder to get into, it is still a prime source of support for most people. Where it is lacking, people feel socially isolated, cut off and adrift, as all the studies of unemployed people show. This social isolation is compounded for those who have no families to turn to and thus the social networks and culture of the Dilly scene and the junkie world are an understandably attractive alternative to being a nobody, not mattering.

The educational attainment of these drug misusers was low on the whole and few had any experience of rewarding work. As time went on, their deprivations accumulated. There was no necessity about this. We are not talking about causes but about an accumulation of deprivations, as the experience of one made the likelihood of the next more probable. By the time they reached City Roads they were locked into the world of drug misuse. The major forces that seem to have pressured them along that path have to do with early family life, the probability of material and emotional deprivation as a child, with experimentation with drugs after coming into contact with this in early teens, and associated with this, truanting, poor educational attainment, and getting into trouble with the law.

Leaving home, going to prison, treatment at hospital follow. Being homeless and unemployed, rootless in London, without a foothold in mainstream society, they find themselves on the Dilly, or squatting, involved in petty crime or prostitution, and using drugs in an increasingly undiscriminating way.

Drug use thus appears to mask other problems. And the previous careers of the people who came to City Roads had been long. Clearly one should not expect change to come about overnight or even after a few weeks' contact: this would be little short of miraculous. How then should services respond? Those working at City Roads and those supporting it decided not to abandon them, not to give up just because they were difficult cases. But the problem remained. How to react to the wide array of needs and problems presented at City Roads? In the next chapters, we shall see how attempts were made first of all to meet their basic, immediate needs and then to work beneath and beyond these to try to fathom the more deeply entrenched emotional difficulties, aiming at this point not to treat these difficulties, but to identify needs and recommend future courses of action.

5 Multi-disciplinary Team Work: A Professional Approach?

'To operate at a crisis-intervention level providing a warm, sheltered environment where nursing, medical, social and psychiatric support is readily available.'

Basic, immediate care

City Roads offered accommodation, food, and basic medical and nursing care. These were extremely important aspects of the service, since clients were often homeless, under-nourished, and suffering from physical ailments, the result mainly of drug misuse. Each new resident would spend two to three nights in the reception area where they could be closely observed. The medical officer examined each resident soon after being admitted. Medical problems treated ranged from infections resulting from injecting drugs (25 per cent of cases), nutritional deficiency (18 per cent), and injuries (13 per cent) to a number of other problems of the digestive, respiratory, and genito-urinary systems, and parasitic diseases (case history survey). Seventy per cent of cases received medication for at least one problem. In a typical month, two or three residents would be taken to hospital for tests (such as liver function or EEG), for X-ray or treatment of injuries. Local dental and optical services were also regularly consulted.

On admission, 7 per cent of residents were 'significantly intoxicated' with drugs and a further 28 per cent displayed some degree of intoxication. One third of residents were then described as 'anxious', while a quarter were said to be 'depressed' or 'sad'. Only 2 per cent were described as 'aggressive' on admission, an interesting contrast with drug misusers' reported behaviour in A and E departments.

After their stay at City Roads, most people were visibly stronger, cleaner, and more adequately dressed. Until November 1980, the majority of residents received a clothing grant from the DHSS. After changes in the Supplementary Benefit regulations, they had to make do with the choice of second-hand clothes held in stock at City Roads.

It might be argued that this basic care should be available elsewhere through GPs, A and E departments, or the Soho medical walk-in centre, and that accommodation was available in the form of hostels and reception centres. Yet these were clearly not being used effectively by these people, in that they had reached a point of exhaustion and general self-neglect after living on the streets.

The shortage of GP services in the London inner city areas forms the background here (Acheson Report 1981). Because of this, it is fair to conclude that access to the services of GPs was limited for this client group where they were moving around and without a fixed address. Other evidence indicated that where they did visit GPs, the treatment provided might be inappropriate. As we saw in Chapter 4, residents reported that very often their source of supply of drugs was a prescription from a GP. In addition, few GPs have the back-up services available at City Roads, nursing care, bathing facilities, and the time to give a complete check-up. The proportion of time devoted by the medical officer and nursing staff to stabilization, diagnosis, and health education was high, and indeed the medical officer appointed to City Roads, a local GP, has now built up considerable expertise in dealing with the medical care of drug misusers (Waller and Banks 1983).

A vital aspect of the City Roads service was that it offered a *drug-free* environment. People there did not have the option of further self-neglect through drug misuse or overdosing. 'Drug free' meant that the only drugs allowed were prescribed drugs: people on opiate scripts or other prescribed medication were allowed to take this under supervision. In addition, City Roads operated its own barbiturate detoxification programme. This regime was worked out by the medical staff and the Director. It was based on, but different from, other existing regimes. Residents were withdrawn over a period ranging from four to eight days, depending on their average daily use during the week previous to coming to City Roads. The drug used was phenobarbitone. One of the important functions of the nurses was to observe the residents closely during this period.

The details of the barbiturate detoxification regime were as follows: the maximum dose anyone was started on was 100mg phenobarbitone, three times daily. For someone starting on the maximum dose (calculated on the basis of drug use during the previous week), the regime was:

Days 1 and 2: 100mg 3 times daily
Days 3 and 4: 60mg 3 times daily
Days 5 and 6: 40mg 3 times daily
Days 7 and 8: 40mg twice daily.

Alternatively, people might start with 90mg or 80mg on days 1 and 2 instead of 100mg. If they started on 60mg, their regime would start, as it were, on day 3 and last only 6 days. Similarly, if they started on 40mg, they would be withdrawn over 4 days. (For example: a person who had been taking 8 Tuinal a day on average during the week before admission, would start on 90mg phenobarbitone three times daily. This was arrived at in the following way: 8 Tuinal = 800mg phenobarbitone. The dose prescribed would be one third of this per day, i.e. 270mg (= 90mg three times daily).)

On admission, 78 per cent reported current use of barbiturates. Most were using the drug regularly enough to have developed physical dependency. In the three years studied, 459 admissions (69 per cent) commenced the withdrawal regime. Sixty-two per cent of these completed the regime (44 per cent of all admissions). Thus City Roads treated 153 cases per annum through this withdrawal regime, a figure which compares favourably with the 132 cases discharged in a comparable year from Tooting Bec Hospital's detoxification unit.

As staff became aware of changing patterns of drug misuse, with the increased availability of opiates, they decided to introduce opiate detoxification, firstly on a limited experimental basis. During the three years studied, 1978–81, no one was actually admitted for opiate detoxification, but afterwards it became an important part of the City Roads service. By 1983, we were told that more residents were being withdrawn from opiates than from barbiturates.

Multi-disciplinary team work

It is now time to consider the people who actually delivered these services and the relations between them. The City Roads Operational Document states that

'An important and essential innovation of the unit will be its intention to adopt and develop a *multi-disciplinary* team response to ensure a comprehensive and more effective service to its residents . . . City Roads will employ *professionally qualified* and experienced staff with medical, nursing, psychiatric and social work skills . . . all staff will be expected to share their knowledge and experience with other members of the staff team . . . and be generally committed to the principle and practice of multi-disciplinary co-operation' (p. 2) (our italics).

Multi-disciplinary team work is often talked about, even attempted in the health and social services, but is rarely successful. Generally speaking, 'professional barriers' seem to be in the way: but what exactly does this mean? Alvin Gouldner in his classic study 'Cosmopolitans and Locals: Toward an Analysis of Latent Social Roles' provides some useful insights into the problem (Gouldner 1958). He looked at types of workers in bureaucratic organizations and pointed to an important distinction between 'Cosmopolitans' and 'Locals'. Cosmopolitans are those low on loyalty to the employing organization, high on commitment to specialized role skills, and likely to use an outer reference group orientation. Locals, on the other hand, are those high on loyalty to the employing organization, low on commitment to specialized role skills, and likely to use inner reference group orientation. The experts or professionals tend to be cosmopolitans, they identify with their profession more than the organization for which they work, because their continued standing as competent professionals often cannot be validated by members of their own organization, and they are therefore more likely to esteem the good opinion of their professional peers elsewhere. The reason why this is problematic, Gouldner points out, is that experts or professionals are no more necessary for organizational survival than other conditions, one of the most important of which is 'loyalty' to the organization. This distinction between cosmopolitans and locals usefully focuses attention on the tension between the modern organization's dual need for loyalty and expertise. We shall see later how City Roads dealt with this dilemma and how it might be appropriate to refer to the professional work there as a form of *local professionalism*, but let us look at the staffing and organization of work before moving on to consider the decision-making process.

STAFFING AND THE ORGANIZATION OF WORK

The staffing was as follows: the Director and Deputy Director were both social workers, although in principle the possibility of a nurse as Deputy Director was never excluded, and indeed the Deputy Director appointed in 1983 was a nurse who had worked previously at City Roads. We have already seen that when the unit opened in 1978 there were fifteen team workers, i.e. five social workers, five nurses, and five care assistants (later called second team members). These were organized into five teams, each with a social worker, a nurse, and a care assistant. They worked 12-hour shifts so that at any time there would always be at least one team on duty. After nearly two years, the DHSS granted money to appoint an extra nurse, because it was found difficult to provide 24-hour nursing cover with the existing establishment. Each team had a team leader, who would be either the social worker or the nurse, depending upon qualifications and experience. As time went by and some of the staff began to leave, team leader posts tended to become occupied through internal promotion. In addition to these staff, there were an administrator, a secretary, a cook, and a cleaner. On the medical side, were a part-time medical officer (a local GP who came in at least twice a week) and a consultant psychiatrist, who came in one morning a week for the weekly review meeting.

The structure of accountability was hierarchical: team members were immediately accountable to their team leader for implementation of House procedures in respect of residents. Team leaders were accountable to the Deputy Director, who in turn was accountable to the Director. The ultimate responsibility for the proper management of the unit lay with the Management Committee.

The position of the nurses was interesting. They were formally appointed by the then Camden and Islington Area Health Authority and as regards their nursing duties professionally accountable to the Divisional Nursing Officer, Community Services, Camden and Islington AHA. In practice, the Management Committee selected the nurses with the involvement of the Divisional Nursing Officer, who was a member of the Management Committee. Furthermore, in respect of their non-nursing duties, they were accountable to their team leader and the Deputy Director. This position of the nurses, one might have thought, could have led to some problems of role conflict, but it did not, as we shall show.

The medical staff were outside the City Roads hierarchy of accountability. The role of the medical officer was to provide general medical cover to the House, undertake clinical sessions, and be available to respond to medical emergencies. The consultant psychiatrist was not there primarily to see residents, but to advise the staff on the day-to-day management and treatment of residents where it was felt that there were underlying personal and psychological problems.

In order to be able to discuss the concept of multi-disciplinary team work, it is necessary briefly to look at the tasks that had to be done, how they were divided, and how decisions were made.

Five areas of work were covered in the daily routine:

Nursing tasks. Observing and supervising new residents, administering phenobarbitone, monitoring their condition as the dose was reduced, dressing abscesses, and dealing with emergencies such as withdrawal fits.

One-to-one sessions with residents. These constituted the core of the social work with the residents. Information was obtained (including taking case histories) and advice and counselling were given.

Administrative tasks. These included answering telephone calls, liaising with other agencies about residents (obtaining information, arranging onward referrals), writing in residents' files, and writing court reports.

General supervision of residents. This meant 'being around in the House' talking to the residents, keeping them occupied, and generally reassuring them.

Duties outside the House. These included 'assessments' of new referrals, escorting residents to DHSS and dental or hospital appointments, and organizing leisure activities.

All five areas were part of the daily routine, but the time devoted to each varied. The nursing tasks were essential and never neglected. Usually, however, they did not take up much time. The counselling sessions by contrast took up a great deal of time. As far as was possible, the workers attempted to have one 'session' a day with each resident, especially during the early part of their stay. Many of these sessions were done in the evenings by the night shift. Even so, the team workers often felt that they did not have enough time for sessions and they did not always manage to see each resident every day.

Much time was spent on administrative tasks which often demanded immediate attention. The Director and the Deputy Director did some of these as part of their routine, but certain tasks, like writing in residents' files, had to be done by those workers who had taken the counselling sessions. More general administrative tasks, like financial matters relating to residents as well as to the project in general, the purchasing of large items, arranging for repairs to be done, preparing budgets and accounts, were the work mainly of the administrator assisted by the secretary. The Director, having overall responsibility for the project, also did much administrative work. He also followed very closely the work done with the residents and was involved in review meetings. He shared the supervision of staff with the Deputy Director. The main bulk of his activities, however, involved liaising with agencies outside City Roads. The workload in this respect was particularly heavy because of the funding problems which were with the project from its inception.

As a rule, at least one worker was expected to be supervising the resident group. However, there were times when other tasks took priority. Towards the end of the day, when files and handover notes were being prepared, and during handover sessions, residents were often left to themselves. Duties outside the House were very time-consuming. Assessment of referrals as well as visits to the DHSS tied up workers for hours. These often had to take place at the cost of counselling sessions with residents. Whereas DHSS visits and court appearances were at that time unavoidable (although later, changes were introduced to try to overcome this problem), 'assessments' of new referrals were often postponed or cancelled because of a shortage of workers. The staff were often faced with the dilemma of having to choose between responding to referrals and responding to the demands of the residents. On most occasions, the resident group was considered more important than new referrals. This no doubt contributed to the fact that residents liked the place and that there were no major problems in containing the resident group: on the other hand, it seriously limited the extent to which the project was able to fulfil its 'crisis intervention' function. Outings of a more leisurely character were sometimes undertaken with residents but only when the workers had spare time.

The division of labour within the teams was practised as expected. Apart from the nursing tasks, all tasks were shared among team workers, although there were differences of emphasis, depending on position in the hierarchy. Team leaders tended to spend more time in the office, doing administrative duties and answering telephone calls. They spent less time on escort duties and on general supervision. These were done more by the new and inexperienced staff. The decision as to who would go out of the House (on 'assessments' and escort duties) was often made on practical grounds. For example, if the team consisted of a social work team leader, a nurse team member, and a second team member, the latter would be likely to go out because there had to be a nurse on the premises and it was also desirable for the team leader to be there. If going out involved driving the taxi, only those who possessed a driving-licence could go, which often did not leave much choice.

All the workers were involved in counselling residents (including taking case histories) after an initial training period. They all made notes in the residents' files, and they all contacted other agencies about residents. All the workers were clearly acting as 'social workers'. However, the specific nursing duties were performed exclusively by the qualified nurses, although medical notes were kept in the same file as the social work notes. All the workers were given some in-training about medical matters. They all had some knowledge about the various drugs and their effects and they were all equipped to help the nurses deal with emergencies.

Thorough medical examinations and issuing prescriptions were the duties of the medical officer. His notes were entered in the same file as used by other staff, and he often added notes on background information about residents. He came in regularly twice a week, but in addition, he was often called in or consulted by telephone when staff were in doubt about medical matters. He was highly committed to the project and put in more time than he was formally obliged to do. The consultant psychiatrist came in once a week. Apart from advising at review meetings, he saw the residents whom the workers thought might have a psychiatric problem. Like the medical officer, he entered his notes in the same file as all the other staff.

The Director and the Deputy Director did not take part in work with the residents to the same extent as did the team workers. They saw residents only under special circumstances, such as if they had broken the rules and needed to be 'confronted' and/or discharged. The Deputy Director co-ordinated the team work and discussed progress and plans for residents. He also liaised with other agencies, in particular probation officers. In addition to these tasks, the Deputy Director organized the rota system, a task which was not only time-consuming but also a source of constant concern and worry. He also organized the training of new staff and was involved with the Director in staff recruitment.

Shortly after the project opened, recruitment of volunteers was initiated and continued throughout the three-year period. On average there were about six volunteers available at any one time. Their degree of involvement varied: some came in to help once a month and others came in daily over a period of two to three months. They included students, nurses, housewives, and unemployed people. The volunteers were extremely useful in helping with general supervision and escort duties. However, there were costs involved in using volunteers. The recruitment and induction process itself took time. Since volunteers came in at irregular intervals, the staff had to spend quite a lot of time briefing them about residents. However they were useful in helping out at times of staff shortage, although they were not always available when they were most needed, such as during weekends. The volunteers' view was that City Roads did not offer the most rewarding kind of work, since with a constantly changing resident group, following up particular individuals was an even bigger problem for them than for the full-time workers.

City Roads became well established as a good and popular project for social work students on placement. It seemed to be used in this way for three reasons: first, it offered an alternative type of residential work; second, it was known as a place where students could learn counselling skills; and finally it offered students the chance to learn about the particular area of drug misuse. Although students used up staff resources in their training and supervision, most of them, especially those on long-term placements, were able to function as competent workers alongside the permanent staff. And, the income from student placements was a useful addition and was mainly spent on staff development and training.

DECISION-MAKING AND CO-ORDINATION

The team leader on duty was responsible for day-to-day routine decisions but normally involved other workers in decision-making. In cases of doubt and uncertainty, she or he consulted the Director or Deputy. The shift system required that work initiated by one team had to be continued by another. A range of 'mechanisms' thus grew up to provide continuity and to enhance communication between teams – especially holding regular meetings, and an elaborate record-keeping system.

Morning meetings

Each morning the team on duty had a meeting to discuss the progress of residents, to make decisions about their further 'treatment', and to plan the team work for the day. The Deputy Director participated in these meetings and provided crucial continuity and consistency between the teams. Because of his separation from the rota and involvement in morning meetings, he exercised much influence over decisions.

Handover meetings

Whenever there was a changeover of teams (8 a.m. and 8 p.m.), the team going off duty would stay for about half an hour – often even longer – to give a verbal account of the situation. This meant that the workers were usually on duty for at least twelve and a half hours. In the third year this extra work was recognized by the Management Committee, who granted the staff free meals when on duty as compensation.

Review meetings

Once a week the Director, Deputy Director, medical officer, consultant psychiatrist, and one or two team workers met to discuss selected cases in more depth. The extent to which definite decisions were taken varied from case to case. It depended partly on when a resident had been admitted in relation to the day of the review meeting, and partly on whether there was doubt and uncertainty about suitable plans. In cases of doubt, the review meeting became more important, and then the views of the Director or the consultant psychiatrist played the decisive role.

Staff meetings

Staff meetings for all City Roads staff were held every five weeks. The aim was to discuss general practical matters, policies, and staff issues. This was the only opportunity for the whole staff group to get together and debate matters. However, the turnout was low – on average, less than half the staff group would attend. One of the reasons was that the workers had to come in for this meeting during their spare time (unless they were the team on duty). In addition the agenda of the meetings did not seem to generate sufficient interest. Attempts were made to hold meetings at different times to encourage greater participation, but with little success. Much time at these meetings was spent sorting out rather tedious practical administrative matters. Discussions of policy were occasionally interesting, but in many cases the low attendance made such discussion appear less important. Whereas the interest of the workers in discussing policy matters was rather low for the first two years, this interest increased, however, during the third year. A number of policy matters were then raised by the team workers, which resulted in some fruitful debates. However, the low attendance continued to be a problem, so that issues relating to inconsistent practices between teams and matters requiring some decisive action to be taken, were not always dealt with satisfactorily. Some team workers expressed dissatisfaction with existing practices and decision-making procedures.

Residents' files

A file was kept on each resident, in which all information was recorded. A comment was entered in each resident's file at the end of each 12-hour shift. This was done by the worker who had had most contact with him or her during those twelve hours. When a new team came on duty, they could tell from the file how residents had behaved, whether they had had any sessions, and whether any plans had been made.

Review notes

The day before the review meeting, the team leader on duty wrote 'review notes' on those residents due to be reviewed. These notes contained a summary of the resident's background and an assessment of their problems.

Handover book

The handover book was used whenever a new team came on duty after having been off for several days (i.e. three times a week). The situation of each resident was summarized in this book. This was done as a joint team effort, although most of the notes tended to be written by the team leader.

Daybook

A daybook was kept in which events and messages were recorded, for example, who was on duty, who went out of the House on assessments, escort duties, and incidents involving residents breaking rules.

Telephone messages

The contents of, and response to, all incoming telephone calls, were recorded on separate message sheets. Although this was originally instituted at the request of the research team, telephone messages were found invaluable for a range of administrative purposes, not least for communication and provision of continuity between teams.

Supervision

Owing to pressure of time, the team leaders' supervision of their team members was less in the form of formal one-to-one sessions and more in the form of informal talks between the whole team. Whereas some team members felt that this informal system gave them sufficient and useful support, others would have liked to have had some direct feedback from the directorate in addition to seeing their team leader. The team leaders themselves also received less formal supervision than originally intended, but this was compensated for through meetings and informal discussions, which were ongoing.

It is clear that the formal supervision which took place at City Roads had more to do with giving general support than with actual training. The training which new staff members had when they first took up post (usually a three-week programme), was not followed up in any significant way. Most of them would have liked more training opportunities, but they all agreed that it was not possible to have much during working hours and they preferred to spend most of their spare time relaxing after a very exhausting time at work. However, through the system of continuous discussion and consultation, supervision and training were in fact exercised in day-to-day work. All the workers who had been at City Roads for some time said that they had widened their knowledge and experience immensely.

CITY ROADS PROFESSIONALISM: A COMMON TREATMENT
PHILOSOPHY

In most respects, the work at City Roads was real team work. Residents were not allocated to a particular worker, although within one shift each of the team workers would be allocated their particular residents. All workers on duty would take part in the discussion of the residents – at team meetings, handover meetings, and throughout the day whenever they felt a need to discuss a case. They all shared a common philosophy, upon which the casework was based. There was no friction between the social workers and the nurses, and no difference between the casework tasks of the social workers, nurses, and care assistants, once they had worked at the place for some time. From the very beginning, those appointed as social workers did not necessarily possess a formal CQSW, but were appointed because of their particular experience. This would most often, but by no means always, be in the field of drug addiction. The care assistants did not often have much social work experience; the majority of those appointed were young graduates. But through the induction programme and through the frequent discussions involved in the team approach they rapidly picked up what the counselling was all about. The term 'care assistant' was therefore soon abolished in favour of 'second team member'. When the expected staff turnover began towards the end of the first year, many of these second team members were promoted to first team members, and some of them eventually made it to team leader status. In other words, in professional terms, experience at City Roads counted more than anything else.

How was it possible, then, to develop and sustain this common philosophy around which all the staff were united? A number of different factors played a part. First, the recruitment process was important. The team workers were all young people both men and women, mainly in their twenties, who were particularly attracted to working with young, homeless clients with 'personal problems'. They were also attracted to what they saw as an informal setting (where the staff as well as the clients wore jeans). Perhaps most important of all, they were attracted to the idea of working in multi-disciplinary teams. The nurses recruited specifically wanted to get away from a medical setting and the nursing hierarchy, and also away from doing solely 'nursing tasks'. Some of them, but only a minority, had a psychiatric qualification (RMN) in addition to their SRN. An indication of their commitment and interest can be found by looking at the kind of jobs they went into after leaving City Roads. None of them went back to a permanent position in general hospital nursing. Some went on to do a CQSW, others an RMN, others again went into the community side of the NHS.

Second, the structure of the organization made the multi-disciplinary team work possible in a way which is mostly much more difficult in traditional NHS settings. In the day-to-day work, the administrator, the social workers, and the nurses were all accountable to the *same* person, the Director. Although the administration of drugs and the monitoring of their effects, doing dressings, etc. were important tasks, which could legally only be done by the nurses, they were seen by everybody, including the nurses, as secondary and not very time-consuming compared with counselling. The fact that nurses were accountable to the AHA in doing these duties was seen as a formality, which did not in any way affect their everyday work. The nurses, like the other staff, saw themselves as City Roads workers above all.

This situation is different from hospitals, where, for example, the treatment of one patient might involve doctors, nurses, social worker, physiotherapist, and occupational therapist, all of whom would have their own separate professional superiors to whom they would be accountable. Any practices which were not strictly defined within their job description, but which might represent innovations for the patient's benefit, could be blocked by their own profession. Doctors often complain that co-operation with nurses is inhibited by the nurses' superiors. This is especially the case in settings where doctors and nurses work side by side most of the time, for example A and E departments or health centres. Unlike an in-patient ward, where the Sister is clearly in charge and the doctors are more like visitors, these settings can often be the scene of a power struggle between the two disciplines. Doctors will tend to see the nurses as too rigid and uncooperative, and the nurses will see the doctors as too dominating. They are probably both right to some extent in their perceptions of each other. There is no doubt that nursing is characterized by an overcautious adherence to rules which is often paralysing and inhibits discretionary decision making and innovation (see Menzies 1960 and Lees 1980). On the other hand it is certainly also true that the medical profession operates in a culture of dominance; the doctor tends to see his or her relationship with the patient as exclusive and therefore sees other professionals like nurses or social workers as relating to him or her rather than to the patient. This problem has been well illustrated by June Huntington, who analysed the relationship between social workers and doctors in a general medical practice (Huntington 1981). She points out the reluctance of GPs to involve the social workers, because they feel this introduces a third party into the relationship with the patient.

A great deal, therefore, depends on the attitude of the doctor. This is illustrated by the positive example set by some of the Drug Treatment Centres, where the nurses, social workers, and Consultant are almost equally involved in the work with the patients. Thus at University College Hospital's DTC, there is a well-established practice of multi-disciplinary team work.

This brings us back to City Roads, because the consultant Psychiatrist here was in fact from UCH DTC. In other words, from the very start the unit had ensured the involvement of a doctor who subscribed to the concept of multi-disciplinary team work, who did not support a strictly medical model of drug addiction, and who had indeed years of experience in working with drug misusers, not only in a clinical setting, but through involvement with the Phoenix House rehabilitation project. He was a consultant in the true meaning of this word, i.e. an advisor to the staff, and on a part-time basis. The fact that City Roads was not structurally dominated by the medical profession accounted in a large part for the success of the multi-disciplinary team work. The medical officer also clearly saw his involvement as part time, and consequently did not see the residents as in any way 'his patients'. (He had 'his own patients' elsewhere, back in the general practice.) A bonus that no one could have predicted was that he developed a keen interest in the residents and in the non-medical aspects of their problems. He actively participated in the review meetings and fully supported the City Roads philosophy.

In what way then can this multi-disciplinary team work be said to be 'professional'? The term 'profession' is usually connected with a specific discipline and its body of knowledge. If social work, nursing, and medicine were integrated at City Roads and practised in a way that enabled even the non-professional care assistants to participate, could it then be said to be professional at all? The staff themselves often used the term professional, in fact increasingly so. (Indeed their reason for upgrading the care assistants was that they were as 'professional' as the rest of the staff.) It is our view that it *is* possible to talk about a professional approach at City Roads, but paradoxically (cf. Gouldner) it seems more appropriate to call it *local* professionalism. By this we mean that the system which operated was characterized by a specific area of expertise and skills, a particular body of knowledge, and a treatment philosophy centred on therapy. This expertise was embodied not in any one particular worker or discipline, but in the system of work.

The role of the Deputy Director was absolutely crucial in developing and maintaining this system. He did not usually see the residents himself, but he was the all-important link between the teams and was the guide for the workers. He organized training for newly appointed staff and he was always available to discuss residents with the workers. It was a system of mutual interdependence, of learning, teaching, and debating. This had the great advantage that no one felt isolated in their casework, and that any worker on duty could deal with any resident in the House. The cost, however, was the time spent in meetings and discussions, which, although highly beneficial to the staff, did not quite measure up as regards benefits to the clients. It is probably fair to say that the casework was dominated by the social work profession; the staff certainly saw City Roads as primarily a social work agency, and both the Director and the Deputy Director were social workers. However, it was the kind of social work which is not at all far removed from what is often also performed by psychiatrists and psychiatric nurses. (When the City Roads staff were talking about 'nursing duties' they were referring to quite a narrow meaning of this term, involving physical care only.)

In this respect the nurses were quite isolated, because legally only they could perform these duties. About half the nurses did not mind this, because they still kept some identification with their nursing profession; the other half, who wanted to get away from being nurses, were at times resentful of the situation and expressed their regret that the social workers could not, for example, hand out medicines. However, the problem never really grew into anything approaching a conflict, partly because nursing tasks took up only a fraction of their time, but also because the other workers showed an interest and took part in discussions about nursing aspects of the residents' problems. And as we have shown, there were no separate files for nurses (or doctors); nursing information was not in any way kept separate from other types of information. It seems to us that, given the legal position, as much as possible was done to integrate the disciplines.

Conclusion

The multi-disciplinary team work at City Roads functioned in a fully integrated way: the full-time workers were all in practice accountable to the Director and the different professionals and non-professionals were united through a common treatment philosophy which cohered around the role of the Deputy Director. Certain aspects of psychiatry, certain aspects of nursing, and certain aspects of social work all fitted into this model or ideology: the concepts used were not specific to any one of these disciplines. However, the approach was managed by social workers, since both the Director and the Deputy had social work backgrounds. Also, it was generally thought that the City Roads approach was dominated by social work. And, finally, it was clear that what they did, although ostensibly highly eclectic, was in fact based on a body of literature which relates to social work. In the next chapter, therefore, we shall not only consider in some detail what was actually entailed in the City Roads approach but shall attempt to discuss this in the light of the general debate surrounding the nature of social work.

6 Social Work at City Roads

'not to attempt to offer a complete treatment and rehabilitation programme under one roof but to see its function as making contact with multiple drug misusers and attempting to encourage them to accept longer-term help from existing treatment and rehabilitation services.'

The City Roads approach: crisis intervention?

City Roads claims by its name (City Roads (Crisis Intervention) Ltd) to offer a crisis intervention service. The concept of crisis intervention is well established in the social work vocabulary and is often referred to in the textbooks as one of several models of social work (see for example Butrym 1976). Its theoretical origin is to be found in the field of psychiatry where Caplan (1964) is often referred to as the father of modern crisis intervention (Smith 1978). Very briefly, the central arguments in crisis intervention theory are the following: people are in a crisis when they experience an imbalance between the problems they are faced with and the resources available to them to cope with these problems. Thus imbalance or disequilibrium are key concepts. This situation, according to the theory, presents both an opportunity for psychological growth and a danger of psychological deterioration. A person in a crisis is thought to be particularly vulnerable – hence the danger – but at the same time particularly open to help from others – hence the opportunity. Professional intervention at this stage is therefore thought to be particularly promising and fruitful, because the person is highly motivated; it may increase the person's capacity to cope with future problems and thus act as a preventive measure. Crisis intervention is supposed to concentrate on the here-and-now problems of the client, trying to alleviate the immediate impact of stressful events, and as Smith argues, it is therefore not an appropriate method for treatment of chronic problems such as problem drinking or schizo-phrenia (Smith 1978).

How closely does this model fit the City Roads approach? Rather little, we would argue, for basically two reasons. First, it is doubtful whether the clients' situation could be said to match exactly that envisaged in the model. Second, the work that actually went on at City Roads went beyond what can be described as crisis intervention. At one level, the clients who asked to come to City Roads could be said to be in a crisis in that they might have overdosed, have run out of their supply of drugs, or be due in court. Whatever the reason, it is fair to say that most of those asking for admission found themselves in a situation in which they were unable to cope with the pressures of life on the street. City Roads offered them some relief at this point. As a crisis intervention service which could respond quickly, it could patch-up people physically, so that when they went back to the street they would perhaps be better able to cope with sleeping rough, lack of regular meals, and so on. The other thing City Roads could do to help their coping mech-anisms was to put them in touch with hostels and street agencies. However, many clients would attempt readmission even within a day of leaving the House, or ring up regularly for help. Most of those who went back to the street from City Roads went back to a lifestyle characterized by a constant struggle to find accommodation or money for drugs, over-dosing and involvement in crime. The 'crisis' that caused them to seek help at City Roads was not a unique occurrence in their lives; rather, they lived from crisis to crisis or, as the City Roads workers put it, their lifestyle was generally 'chaotic'. Given this, it is not surprising that the City Roads workers did not see their inter-vention as the only and final solution to these clients' problems. Their problem was their lifestyle. If they wanted to avoid future crises, indeed if they wanted to survive, that would have to change, and this meant that they would have to stop misusing drugs. The City Roads staff did not for a moment think that a three-week stay would be sufficient to achieve this aim. They saw their role as providing the beginning of a long-term process, which would have to be continued elsewhere, most obviously in long-term rehabilitation projects. The role of City Roads would be twofold: to assess the long-term needs of the residents, and to build up their motivation to change. This was a process that went beyond what is strictly entailed in the model of crisis intervention. The significance of the crisis element in this connection was the motivational aspect. People who voluntarily came to City Roads because they felt they were somehow in a crisis were expected to show at least a minimal level of motivation, which could be used as a starting point for further work.

Assessment and motivation building

The City Roads model of 'treatment' is outlined in an inform-ation sheet ('Three-weekly timetable') used in training new staff. It operates through a number of stages:

1. *Admission and settling-in process.* Emphasis is on empathy, reassurance, and practical tasks, on information giving and initial information gathering.
2. *Information phase.* Continuation of information gathering, culminating in case history taking. Aim: to move away from immediate crisis to more general problems. From 'drug problems' to 'problem problems'.
3. *Agreeing the problem.* The aim is to agree (or to 'agree to disagree') what the main issues seem to be for someone.
4. *Beginning the debate.* This means the debate about what to do – clarifying needs before plans.
5. *Forward planning.*
6. *Discharge.* This covers the period from which plans are agreed and set in motion and the residents' eventual departure. It involves dealing with anxieties or undue optimism.

The basic and very important premise of the model was that the residents had some problems underlying their drug use ('problem problems' rather than 'drug problems'). These problems were seen to be very personal and individual, which could only be looked at in private one-to-one sessions. These sessions formed the central core of the social work; they were seen as absolutely necessary. Residents were encouraged to focus on themselves, not only in sessions, but also between sessions. Consequently entertainments during 'working hours' were discouraged because they might distract the residents from concentrating on themselves. Some activities did take place; residents were expected to involve themselves in the daily routine housework and in a daily meeting with the staff. This was important, because it was an attempt to teach them to live a structured life, helping other people and taking on responsibilities. Apart from routine duties, however, there were in the House, board games and such things as table tennis and pool, television, and a record player, and residents were taken out shopping and to play football and so on when there were staff available to accompany them. In the early spring of 1981, it was decided to appoint an art therapist to come in one afternoon a week to organize painting activities. However, it was made clear to her that those activities were to be 'art' rather than 'therapy', because it was not to interfere with the social work counselling offered by the staff.

The counselling sessions themselves took up only about an hour a day for each resident. The activities of the staff, how-ever, were very much centred round these sessions – planning them, discussing their outcome, and taking any appropriate action such as writing onward referral letters. The aims of counselling were to clarify *needs* and to build up the residents' *motivation* to do something about their needs. The assumption was that there were certain needs which should be 'dealt with' and that people were not necessarily totally willing to admit needs and/or do something about them. The first phase involved getting to know the resident, building up confidence and trust in City Roads. The very fact of sitting down and talking to a staff member who took an interest in one could in itself be fruitful. The resident started to feel that someone cared. This was for them a very positive experience, which many were not used to.

The next step was 'getting to the root of the problem', exploring personal strengths and weaknesses and their origin. City Roads did not work on the basis of an explicit theory, indicating exactly what type of problems people might have and why they had these problems. The approach was called *eclectic*, but there was no specification as to on what theories, ideas, or experiences one should draw. However, by looking at the actual practices, it is possible to form a picture of the set of assumptions underlying the City Roads approach. First of all, the needs or problems under investigation were seen as psychological ones. People were seen as being unable to take responsibility, unable to form relationships, depressed, bitter, angry, frustrated, and lacking in trust. The diagnoses of different residents varied in emphasis rather than type. There was little variation in the definition of their problems. Although they might behave in different ways – e.g. some were aggressive whereas others were passive and withdrawn – these different types of behaviour were seen as manifestations of the same kind of underlying problems. The causes of these problems were thought to lie in past experiences, most commonly in an emotionally unstable childhood characterized by lack of parental care, alcoholism in the home, and institutional upbringing, which were thought to have led to deprivation of warmth, care, and stability.

The case history, which was taken after the sixth day, marks the start of difficulties in managing the residents. At this stage, they were expected to begin to 'open up'. Some residents did and they often found it traumatic and felt anxious and 'wound up'. Others were resistant and, as the staff saw it, 'unco-operative', 'blocking off', 'not prepared to work seriously with themselves'. The atmosphere in the House was consequently often tense, and the staff spent much time trying to defuse this tension by talking to the residents or by being around with them.

Although the ideal was to define needs and plan onward referral within a three-week stay, in most cases, this was not reached in one admission. Almost a third of the residents spent less than two weeks in total at City Roads: perhaps the intensity of the approach did not appeal to them. Other people stayed on and/or came back repeatedly but without using the place in the way the staff would have liked them to (in accordance with the model). With these people, the major aim became that of motivation building, persuading them to 'start looking at themselves'. Yet over the three years, the staff increasingly came to realize that not all residents were willing, able, or ready to go through the City Roads programme. Less ambitious goals were set for them: for example, where people kept coming back without staying for more than a few days at a time, the aim became merely trying to make them stay longer the next time, and this would be put to them as a condition of readmission.

In principle, the definition of *needs* took place through talks with the resident, at team meetings and at review meetings. However, needs as such were not always spelled out explicitly in discussions or notes. Often, the debate was about what the resident wanted and about possible *plans*. The overall view was that the clients needed some kind of therapy, and the assessment process most often seemed to focus on the degree to which a resident was ready for rehabilitation. Broadly speaking, the existing network of rehabilitation projects for drug misusers ranged from supportive accommodation, places offering a structured setting (mostly Christian communities) to projects with a psychotherapeutic approach, most of which are known as concept houses. Of this latter group, Phoenix House was the largest and most accessible. The City Roads assessment approach whereby people were encouraged to 'open up', face their own weaknesses and 'increase their self-understanding', was very much geared towards testing people's suitability for therapeutic rehabilitation.

Case studies

In order to illustrate more fully what was entailed in the 'City Roads approach', i.e. the counselling work, we analysed a sample of the case files kept on each resident. A random sample of 20 (26 per cent) of the 76 individuals admitted between 8 July 1980 and 7 January 1981 was taken. Of these, 16 were new admissions. The remaining four had been admitted previously, one as early as February 1979. The distribution of the 20 residents according to number of admissions was: 11 had one admission only; four had two; two had three; two had four; and one had five. This distribution reflected the distribution of admissions in the resident population as a whole.

The aim of the analysis was to obtain some qualitative material relating to the social work aspects of treatment, to throw light on the following questions:

1. What criteria were used in admitting and readmitting a client?
2. How did the staff define the problems of the residents?
3. What did the staff see as the causes of these problems?
4. What problems did residents present for the staff in the House?
5. How did the staff deal with the residents' problems?
6. How were plans for the residents arrived at?

THE SHORT-STAY RESIDENTS

Four individuals stayed only one to two days. Two were discharged for bringing in drugs. The two others left of their own accord: one of them said he did not like the rules and had only wanted a bed for the night: 'you have to say anything to get a bed for the night', he told us. On admission (during the 'assessment') he had said that he wanted to go to Phoenix House. On the first day a staff member had attempted to talk to him about his relationship with his family, his 'hurt and resentment', but the resident had refused to talk about it, saying that all he wanted was a job.

The other person who left on the second day said he wanted

to go out and get drugs and that he felt that the residents were violent. This person left at 6 p.m. – he had not been seen by a staff member all day. The staff member who had admitted him had reported that he had seemed confused and insecure and had been told by the court to try to get to a rehabilitation project.

ASSESSMENT/ADMISSION PROCESS

What were the admission criteria used by the staff on initial assessment? ('Assessment' here refers to the interview conducted outside the House prior to admission. (It should be remembered in this connection that much information would have already been obtained over the phone before it was decided to go out on an 'assessment').)

In the cases studied here, high motivation did not seem to be essential in gaining admission. In five cases (25 per cent), nothing was mentioned about the client's possible reasons for coming to City Roads. In three cases (15 per cent) people appear to have been admitted despite the staff's suspicion that the request for admission had to do with pressure from the probation officer or family or need for accommodation. In the remaining 12 cases (60 per cent), some kind of positive motivation is mentioned, e.g. 'wanted to go to rehab.', 'wants space to think about his problem', 'wants to kick the habit'.

The main area covered in the files is that of general background information, about recent drug use, court cases pending, accommodation situation, and family background. Here, there was no specific mention of 'crisis' in any of the cases studied. In the case of first admission, then, no strict admission criteria as regards motivation or crisis were applied.

When it came to readmitting people, however, staff clearly felt the need to comment on the reasons why these people were readmitted. In the majority of cases, a typical entry would be – 'sounded genuine about really wanting to do something about himself' or 'seems determined to succeed'. In a number of cases, certain conditions were attached to readmission: 'his stay is to be about planning how to exist in the community'; 'agrees to look at what went wrong at "Life for the World".'

HOW DID THE STAFF DEFINE RESIDENTS' PROBLEMS?

In attempting to answer this question we looked for the key concepts most commonly used. It was evident from reading the files that certain concepts were used very commonly. In all cases (with the exception of those who stayed for a few days) at least one of the following concepts was used to describe the problem(s) of the residents.

	N	%
Bitter and full of hate	5	25
Anger	9	45
Loneliness	9	45
Difficulty in forming relationships	8	40
Low self-opinion	8	40
Inability to trust	8	40
Guilt	6	30
Blocking off feelings	6	30
Inability to take responsibility for him/herself	6	30
Depressed	4	20
Frustrated	4	20
Feeling of rejection	1	5

(The figures indicate the number of cases in which these concepts appeared in either the case history or the review sheets.) These concepts appeared in a variety of combinations. Here are a few illustrations of typical cases.

Val

The case history summary mentioned the following: 'anger and rebelliousness'; 'presents as shy and withdrawn, lonely, afraid of her emotions'; 'negative emotional material in her'.

The review sheet summarized her problem in the following way: 'lonely, depressed, difficulty in forming relationships, frightened of her emotions, particularly of her anger towards parents . . ., does not trust authority. Severe guilt feelings, sometimes leading to self-mutilation.'

Vince

The case history mentioned 'three themes': '(i) bitter and full of hate; (ii) feels a freak; (iii) feels rejected by society.' It adds: 'little experience of relating, lack of social skills . . . needs to come to terms with his feelings of worthlessness and hate for himself. To be accepted and liked so that he can learn to like himself.' (No review notes.)

The picture that emerged from the City Roads diagnoses was

one of a category of people with *psychological* problems of some kind, people who were not psychologically equipped to cope with life. Their problems concerned their attitudes, views, and feelings. Before looking at how City Roads dealt with these kinds of problems we shall briefly look at what they seemed to consider to be the *cause* of these problems.

WHAT DID THE STAFF SEE AS THE CAUSE OF THE RESIDENTS'
PROBLEMS?

The staff view on this matter emerged *indirectly* in that certain specific factors were emphasized in the case history summaries, the review sheets, and the routine entries. There is no doubt that the key factor was thought to be the emotionally unstable childhood of the residents. In 13 of 15 (86 per cent) cases where a case history had been taken, family background was mentioned as a significant factor.

The staff's view of a typical City Roads resident then was someone who took drugs in order to cope with or escape from certain problems. These problems had to do with an inability to relate to other people; distrust; lack of self-confidence; anger and frustration. They were angry and frustrated because they had experienced rejection or lack of care in childhood, and they had therefore never learned to trust or relate to other people. The drug-using aspect of residents' lives was considered to be a secondary problem, a symptom of some 'underlying problems'. As staff were told during their initial training: one of the important steps in the assessment process is 'to move away from "drug problems" to "problem problems" '.

CITY ROADS' RESPONSE TO THE RESIDENTS

We have seen that the City Roads model of treatment operated through a number of stages, from admission and settling in, to information-gathering, agreeing the problem, beginning the debate, and forward planning and discharge. Through the daily routine entries in the residents' files which recorded in great detail what the staff had been discussing with the residents, either in one-to-one sessions or in general conversations in the house, we can consider how far the City Roads model of treatment was followed in practice. Forward planning did not usually start until after day seven of a person's first admission. Up till then, sessions were clearly used to get to know residents, their backgrounds, and what they felt were their problems. The focus varied from resident to resident and seemed to be very much guided by the residents' behaviour in the House. If they threatened to discharge themselves, for example, effort concentrated on trying to persuade them to stay and to reassure them about how they could use City Roads. If they were negative and uncooperative, efforts were made to get them to change this behaviour, to try to teach them how to use City Roads. The model of treatment presupposes co-operation, a certain amount of willingness to talk and 'open up'. Some residents learnt to do this quite quickly, but some resisted and wanted either to discuss plans immediately or not at all. The model did not always operate fully in practice. 'Problem problems' were not always agreed upon and needs not always clearly established before the planning phase. However, this was hardly surprising. Staff did not expect new residents always to be able to use City Roads fully during their first stay. (Only one quarter of these cases left City Roads with a specific onward referral arranged after their first stay.) Not only was it expected that some residents would leave within a few days, but some were also expected to want to use City Roads merely for accommodation and basic care. In principle, and to some extent in practice, the staff did not accept City Roads being used *solely* at the level of basic immediate care. But in no case was the treatment model totally discarded: the staff would always attempt to practise the model by putting as much pressure on the residents as they thought suitable. In some cases, they did not succeed, but residents were not discharged for this reason. They might be refused readmission at a later stage on the basis of previous lack of co-operation, or certain specific conditions might be attached to readmission. But new residents were never asked to leave on the grounds that they had not co-operated during one-to-one sessions.

The staff observations on residents' behaviour entered in the file indicate the sort of problems they perceived in dealing with the residents. The following are some typical statements: 'playing sexual games . . . awful behaviour . . . winding others up . . . telling untrue stories'. 'Bossy, nasty, mean – had to be pulled up for behaviour.'

All these are examples of 'difficult behaviour', which the staff tried to 'deal with' in the sessions. However, residents were not always 'difficult' and some were more 'difficult' than others. Residents had 'good days' and 'bad days'. The feelings of the staff alternated between frustration and gratification, and the files are not lacking in positive comments like: 'making efforts in sessions . . . making progress – realizes problem of relating', 'subdued, good around the House', 'really good, friendly, chatty . . . more open', 'a star resident, honest about herself . . . in touch with her feelings and aware of the amount of work she has to do'.

Although some residents were generally 'better' and more co-operative than others in the eyes of the staff, it was much more often the case that the mood and attitude of the same resident varied. For example, one resident during his stay was characterized with the following words: 'playing around, being aggressive', 'emotional blocks', and a few days later 'coming out with something. Putting effort into looking at himself, looking more hopeful.' On leaving this person was said to be 'well motivated – wants to go to rehab.'.

The positive and negative statements refer to different aspects of the residents' behaviour and attitudes. The three most common areas referred to were:

1. Behaviour in House: from co-operative to aggressive/ provocative.
2. Behaviour in sessions: from honest/open/trusting to closed/blocking off.
3. Attitude towards change: from highly motivated to not motivated at all.

A 'good' resident would be defined by staff as someone who scored high on all three scales.

PLANNING

What was the process through which plans for onward referral were arrived at?

In 14 of the 20 cases (70 per cent) residents stayed long enough on their first admission for plans to be debated. Usually, plans, in the form of suggestions by the staff or the resident, did not occur until the end of the first week.

The ideas recorded initially ranged from specific rehabilitation projects to more general statements of needs, or things not wanted/needed. In six cases (30 per cent) specific rehabilitation projects were mentioned; in three cases (15 per cent) 'rehab.' or 'concept rehab.' was mentioned; in one case 'need for support' was suggested; and in two cases the statement referred to what was *not* desirable (e.g. 'not Christian community', 'not rehab.'). In two cases 'flat and job' were mentioned.

In eight of these fourteen cases the residents' expressed wishes were recorded. Let us see how staff dealt with these expressed wishes. In two of the eight cases where residents had expressed a specific wish, the staff disagreed with this. In one of these two cases, the resident wanted a job and flat – the staff views were that he would not be able to cope without first going through rehabilitation. The review meeting decided to 'explore his willingness to change' and on day 22 this resident agreed he needed 'rehab.'. On the following day he was discharged for breaking House rules, and no arrangements had been made by then. In the other case where the staff disagreed with the resident, he had wished to go to Coke Hole (his probation officer was already applying on his behalf). The staff considered this to be 'an easy option' and recommended a concept-type rehabilitation. Two days after this was put to the resident, he discharged himself. In the six other cases where the resident had expressed a specific wish, this was followed through by the staff: in two, the residents wanted to go to Phoenix House. Applications were made and interviews arranged, but both residents discharged themselves before they were due to go there. In three, residents wanted rehabilitation and specific places were agreed and two of them went off to these places after leaving City Roads, whereas one discharged himself after an application had been sent off. The last of these six was the resident who wanted a flat and a job. The staff did not attempt to arrange for rehabilitation for this person, because, as they said, 'she was not ready for rehab.'. They agreed with her that immediate rehabilitation plans were not realistic, although they did not agree that what she needed was a flat and a job.

In the remaining six of the fourteen cases, the staff initiated the first ideas. In three, the staff idea was pursued with the agreement of the resident. Of these residents two were referred directly on to a rehabilitation project; one left to wait for admission to a rehabilitation project which had a waiting-list. In one other case a rehabilitation project was agreed upon, and an interview arranged, but the resident discharged himself prematurely. In another, the resident agreed initially to go to rehabilitation but later changed his mind, saying he wanted to think about it and was eventually discharged to a hostel. In the last of these six cases, the resident did not wish to go to a concept house, which was what the staff had recommended. An alternative rehabilitation project was suggested by the staff, but the resident discharged himself after two weeks.

REASONS FOR PLANS

Were decisions about 'rehab. or not' and what type of rehabilitation explicitly based on a clear assessment of needs as the model suggests? It must be stressed that the files, although at times recording thoughts and feelings in great detail, did not necessarily record *all* discussions going on in the daily meetings, and often, when a particular suggestion was mentioned, the reason for it was not always recorded. However, the case file analysis does give some indication about the kind and extent of reasoning behind the planning. In six cases (30 per cent) the idea of concept-type rehabilitation (specified (i.e. mainly Phoenix House) or unspecified) was mentioned. Different reasons were recorded in different cases. In one case the reason given was 'to deal with anger', in another case 'he can handle groups', and yet another case 'to get in touch with feelings'. In another case, the consultant psychiatrist was asked and he recommended Phoenix House for a resident who had expressed an interest in this place. In the last two cases, no clear reasons were evident. In one case the resident was said to need concept, although 'not yet ready', and in the other case, Phoenix House was mentioned as a possibility together with 'Christian Community'. In a few cases a number of rehabilitation projects were considered simultaneously. Another example of this is a case where the staff rejected a resident's suggestion because 'the group there is far too strong' and instead suggested 'either a place which would require him to use his head (e.g. Suffolk House) or a place which would require less initiative but offer a structure (e.g. Life for the World)'. In this case the resident chose the latter option. As for the remaining 14 cases (70 per cent) reasons for plans were either not mentioned, or the reasons were to be found merely in the residents' stated wishes.

Where we have referred to 'staff' views, this can mean either the views of individual staff members or the views of the *review meeting* as expressed in the review sheet. The role of the review meeting varied from case to case. In some cases, concrete plans originated from review meetings, in others, ideas which had developed before the meeting were debated and supported. Yet in other cases the meeting recommended ways in which staff might approach the residents rather than concrete plans, for example the review meeting recommended staff to 'explore his willingness to change' (in the case of a resident who did not want rehabilitation) and it expressed 'scepticism about motivation . . . and the need to continue debate'. (This was a case of a resident who wanted a particular rehabilitation project because his probation officer had recommended it.)

READMISSIONS

In principle the approach to residents who were readmitted was the same as for first admissions, especially in cases where the residents left before plans were made. Then, the planning stage might commence earlier than on first admissions. In other cases people were readmitted after having been referred on to a rehabilitation project on their first admission. Here, the debate initially centred very much around the question of why the arrangement had broken down.

From all this, one can see that there is no obvious relationship between readmission, length of stay, and outcomes of stay. In 11 cases (55 per cent), where residents had only one admission, ten discharged themselves before the three weeks were up and one person was discharged to a rehabilitation project. The complexity of these patterns of stay and outcomes is clear if one looks at the nine cases where readmission occurred (45 per cent).

There was *no consistent pattern* whereby residents can be said to be working *towards* rehabilitation over a number of admissions. Thus although overall there was a tendency for readmission to relate to referral on to rehabilitation, the pattern was not one of a clear and uninterrupted progression. Any one individual might be readmitted several times and might be referred on to rehabilitation more than once. In four cases people were readmitted *after* having been discharged to a rehabilitation project. Most often, subsequent readmissions did not result in 'rehab. discharge', although in some cases, alternative rehabilitation plans were worked out. Sometimes, rehabilitation plans could not be put into practice immediately because of waiting lists, and residents had to be discharged without arrangements or to a hostel while they waited for a vacancy.

Another factor which might indicate something about the extent of 'progress' made over several admissions is length of stay on each admission. Again, no 'progression' in this sense was manifest. With the exception of one case, all the residents who were readmitted had stayed for at least two weeks (and in the majority of cases nearly three weeks) on their first admission. Often, subsequent stays were in fact shorter than the first stay.

What was the length of time between admissions? With the exception of four cases, where the period was between four and 18 months, readmissions usually occurred less than a month after the previous stay. The average number of days between each stay was 12. All the four cases where a much longer period elapsed before admission had spent some time in rehabilitation projects.

That then is an illustration of the way in which the clients' problems were perceived and dealt with by the workers. Clearly these staff operated with a rational model of assessment and planning in mind. In practice, however, they were faced with obstacles and frustrations because the residents did not always respond in the ideal way, and external forces, like the availability of rehabilitation places, were out of City Roads' control. One of the key problems which workers faced was the motivation of the residents. The case files offered plenty of evidence to suggest that the residents could not simply be divided into categories of more or less 'motivated'. Rather, the majority of cases were highly ambivalent: they were partly motivated to change, and receive help and advice, and partly attracted by their existing lifestyle. One day the motivation to change would be strong and they would 'open up' in sessions. The next day the desire for drugs or to meet friends might be stronger, so strong that they might discharge themselves, only to change their minds in the evening and ask for readmission. Under such circumstances, it is hardly surprising that goals were redefined and plans changed.

The City Roads workers had to come to terms with the clash of perspectives operating about needs and the preferred way of life and they had to think out their plans for dealing with the residents in a way which matched up to the strategies of their clients. They worked then like chess players, but to them the game they played was not a zero-sum game. If they were losing, unable to make progress and plans for the residents, they felt that the residents were losing as well. Hence the stress and frustration experienced in this kind of work. The way the staff coped with this was through lengthy meetings and discussions amongst themselves and to some extent by lowering their expectations over time. They began to accept that in some cases, all they could do was patch-up people temporarily, increasing their chances of surviving. However, this was seen only as an exceptional approach: in the majority of cases, they still hoped to achieve more long-lasting results.

City Roads and the concept of social work

The nature of social work has been the subject of much debate during the last couple of decades, in particular since the publication of the Seebohm Report in 1968. Social workers themselves as well as others, sometimes 'competing' professions, have been concerned with questions like: What *do* social workers do? What *should* social workers do? What *can* social workers do? Clearly, there has been much disagreement and confusion about the answers to these questions.

An attempt to clarify matters was made in 1980, when the National Institute for Social Work was approached by the then Secretary of State for Social Services, to undertake an enquiry into the role and tasks of social workers. The results of this enquiry were published in 1982 in what is known as the Barclay Report. This report is inconclusive and reflects the present state of the profession in two ways. First, it is extremely general in its attempt to specify the nature of social work, because, the introduction states, 'We have been warned . . . not to impose a blueprint on a scene which is very complex.' (National Institute for Social Work 1983: xi). Second, even at the level of generality at which the working party was operating there was not total agreement; hence two appendices, each of which express dissenting minority views within the Committee.

The main part of the report is based on the view that social work comprises two major strands – counselling and social care planning. Social care planning

> 'may be related directly to solving or ameliorating an existing social problem which an individual, family or group is experiencing. But social care planning also includes what we call indirect work, to prevent social problems arising by the development and strengthening of various kinds of community groups and associations, and to enable informal as well as formally organised resources to be brought to bear upon them when they do.' (National Institute for Social Work 1983: x)

The key recommendation of the report is that of 'community social work', i.e. 'a focus on individuals and families set in the context of all the networks of which they do, or might, form part' (National Institute for Social Work 1983: 217). This recommendation can be seen as an attempt – yet again – to widen the focus of social work by emphasizing that social work is more than one-to-one counselling, or case work, as it is often called.

We say 'yet again', because not only did the Seebohm Committee recommend a community approach, but throughout the seventies many social workers advocated a closer involvement in the community, in particular through 'radical social work' (see for example Corrigan and Leonard 1978). The radical movement within social work has remained a minority one, both in theory and in practice. However, the idea of a 'community approach' has never really been explicitly rejected, at least not at the theoretical or ideological level, although it may have been less visible at the practical level in the work of social services. The reason for this is obvious, because as Pinker has pointed out:

> 'It is one of the most stubbornly persistent illusions in social policy studies that eventually the concept of community – as a basis of shared values – will resolve all our policy dilemmas. The very fact that this notion is cherished from left to right across the political spectrum makes it highly suspect. There is no unitary definition of community because, like the concept of equity, it is open to various interpretations.' (National Institute for Social Work 1983: 241)

Pinker and others reject the notion of community work for several reasons. One reason is that they fear that involvement with the community – whatever that means – might lead to the politicization of social workers' activities. Linked to this is a fear of the de-professionalization of social work. Whether either of these possible consequences is necessarily 'bad', depends to some extent on one's political views. If one considers social problems to be consequences of the social structure as a whole, then any social work activities which go beyond an attempt to help individuals cope with their problems will almost certainly be political. However, ignoring this problem, the concept of community work is extremely vague, and it is difficult to translate this concept into practical action. The case of City Roads illustrates this very well. Among the aims of City Roads, the Operational Document says, 'As a *community-based* service the Unit will need to establish and to maintain close working relationships with all relevant statutory and voluntary agencies and *community groups*' (our italics). City Roads was seen to be a community service primarily because it was a small unit and not linked directly with large institutions like hospitals. But it was still an institution, albeit a small one. Another factor which is often mentioned in connection with community services is 'openness and easy access'. Although it was possible for clients to be admitted within hours, City Roads was hardly an open system with its closed door policy and selection procedures.

Finally, one of the assumptions underlying the community approach, which has caused many to question its feasibility, is that somehow the 'community' has its own resources that can be mobilized to sustain informal care. It is doubtful however whether a community spirit exists in many inner city areas. Certainly, drug misusers live in an environment which can hardly be described as a community of mutual support and care. Life on the street is a tough struggle, and although they may in some ways feel that they 'belong' to a street subculture, it is not one from which they derive the kind of support they would need to survive without drugs.

No wonder, therefore, that the core social work at City Roads, both as the workers themselves saw it and in terms of the amount of time spent, was the one-to-one counselling. In other words, the kind of social work done at City Roads comes under the heading of *casework*. Whereas the Barclay Report acknowledges casework as part of social work, Pinker sees casework as the essence of social work. He is of course not alone in taking this view. Throughout the 1950s and 60s social work was identified with casework (see for example Butrym 1976; Rees 1979; Yelloly 1980; Brewer and Lait 1980) and indeed despite the challenge from the radical left in the 1970s it widely remained so.

There exists a variety of definitions of casework, but the one given by Rees is typical of those found in the social work literature: 'casework refers to a social worker's art of trying to use his relationship with people whom he assumes to be under stress, in order to mobilize their capacities and resources in their environment to reduce or solve conditions leading to such stress' (Rees 1979:53). Rees further comments somewhat critically,

> 'Casework's popularity with educators and practitioners continues despite lack of evidence about its effectiveness . . ., despite criticism that all emphasis on understanding problems in interpersonal relationships is an inappropriate response to nationwide difficulties associated with poverty and unemployment.' (Rees 1979:53)

It is interesting that Rees refers to the activity as an 'art' rather than a science. This is a reflection of the practice of social casework rather than of its theoretical base. According to A. O.

Freed, for example, the theoretical base of casework is: ego psychology, communication theory, behaviour modification, transactional analysis, problem-solving theory, social role theory, family therapy, small groups theory, and crisis intervention theory (Freed 1977). Others point to the strong link between casework and psychoanalysis (Yelloly 1980). There seems to be no shortage of theoretical bases. However, in practice it is not at all unusual to find that the theoretical base of social casework is highly eclectic and/or unrecognized by the practitioners themselves. The very comprehensive examination of the task of the field workers in local authority social service departments headed by Stevenson and Parsloe came to exactly this conclusion:

'On the whole, our respondents' descriptions of their work with clients did not suggest that practice was drawn from specific theoretical perspectives . . . there was evidence that social workers used concepts from sociology, social and individual psychology to understand clients and their difficulties. But there was less evidence that these concepts had been assimilated into an integral system to guide practice.' (DHSS 1978: 134–35)

This quote applies equally well to the City Roads workers.

However, although not based on one coherent and explicit theoretical perspective, the counselling at City Roads was clearly practised on the basis of a common philosophy. The approach was said to be *holistic*, which, put simply, means looking at the whole person. This assumes an essential unity between mind and body. It also stresses the intrinsic link between the observer and the observed, between the practitioner and the client: the two cannot be separated. The main innovation here is to recognize the importance of the subjective, not to exclude everything but the objective, as conventional medicine has previously done. The idea is also that the benefits of treatment cannot be measured solely in terms of cure or effects on particular aspects or specific problems of bodily function. Rather, other benefits may be derived which have to do with the quality of life and the ability to cope. Other key elements of the City Roads philosophy were the value of establishing relationships with other people; the importance of opening up and talking about problems, here especially those underlying drug use; and the importance of facing aspects of oneself which might be consciously or unconsciously suppressed.

The most important question that the sceptical scientist might ask about the City Roads approach is whether it worked. It is difficult to answer this fairly since for these people the approach was applied at the end of the line. It is arguable that if it had been adopted at an earlier stage in life, perhaps even as a form of prevention, the results might have been better. However here we can say that the answer to the question, 'Did the City Roads approach work?', has to be, unfortunately, yes and no. There were clearly benefits but there were also dangers, especially given the intensity of the counselling, which increased over the three years. A 'good session', as the team workers would say at the handover time, was one in which the resident had broken down in tears, having talked openly about a traumatic experience in the past or what they saw as their own inadequacies. For some residents this was a salutary experience, and, more importantly, it was the beginning of an experience that they continued by going to a long-term rehabilitation project like Phoenix House. For others, though, it was traumatic, and at best the beginning of something which was left unfinished, and which did not necessarily equip them any better to cope with life on the street. It is doubtful therefore whether the costs in terms of the time and effort devoted to casework were balanced by the benefits to the residents. The approach was very much geared towards assessing people's suitability for long-term rehabilitation and preparing them for this, but only 19 per cent of all admissions resulted in onward referral to rehabilitation, although 36 per cent of residents were referred to rehabilitation at some time. Indeed, towards the end of the three-year period a staff member raised the question whether rehabilitation was the only answer, calling for alternatives such as protected work schemes and Community Service Volunteers. However, there was no response to this from the rest of the staff.

The approach as it had developed made sense to the workers for several reasons. First, it fitted the services most immediately available, especially Phoenix House, one of the places with the shortest waiting list. Second, by focusing so exclusively on individuals rather than groups, the staff had less difficulty in controlling the residents. They did not encourage group discussions and tried to limit leisure activities, which they thought would distract the residents too much from their 'real problems'. Finally, but not least importantly, it made the work at City Roads meaningful to the workers themselves; the one-to-one counselling provided them with a clear focus, and although it was at times frustrating, there was nothing as gratifying as a 'good session'. If the effect of the sessions on residents was limited, they were important for the staff in maintaining their morale and commitment to a task which was fraught with obstacles and frustrations. Without a relatively stable and committed staff group City Roads would not have been able to offer such a warm, friendly, and stable setting for its clients. And this was important. Most of the City Roads clientele were thoroughly disillusioned and pessimistic about their prospects in life; many of them really did lack the experience of being cared for. At City Roads they met people (i.e. the staff) who actually took an interest in them and seemed to care for them. This experience of care was of immense value to the residents. However, it was a rather costly way of working: some of the staff time could have been more usefully invested in activities geared towards encouraging the development of more general social skills and interests other than drugs.

7   Links with the Environment

'As a community service to establish and maintain close working relationships with all relevant statutory and voluntary agencies and community groups.'

One of the expectations very clearly attached to the setting up of City Roads was that it would have a beneficial effect on the existing services. Advice, co-ordination, and relief were key concepts here. Indeed, sending in extra troops for the relief of A and E departments was an urgent priority for the DHSS.

This chapter will consider what kind of agencies used City Roads; how they used it; how successful they were in their attempts to use it; and what they thought of the service. The whole question of access to the service is important here, from the point of view of agencies as well as of the clients themselves, since City Roads was supposed to be a service easily accessible to the community.

The use of City Roads by other agencies

The main channel of communication between City Roads and the outside world was the telephone. Before the unit started to admit any clients, staff made a number of visits to potential users, but once it started to operate, the work of the staff was concentrated at the House, except that they went out to 'assess' clients before admitting them. Also, the door of City Roads was kept locked. Clients were discouraged from turning up on the doorstep. If they did, staff would talk to them but never admit them. To be admitted they had to be seen by the staff away from the House, preferably at an A and E department. Non-clients, like workers from other agencies, were seen by appointment. Most of the communication that went on between the organization and the outside world can then be described by considering the telephone messages that recorded all incoming calls.

Every day, City Roads received telephone calls from either workers or clients asking for advice. The unit soon acquired a reputation for expertise in the drugs field, being able to inform people about drugs and their effects and of services available for drug users. However, by far the greatest number of telephone calls concerned referrals to City Roads. The referral figures give some indication of who tried to use City Roads, and how the use of City Roads changed over the first three years. During this period, City Roads had altogether 1,925 referrals, i.e. requests for admission. Many clients were referred or referred themselves several times during this period, and the 1,925 referrals represented 888 individuals, of whom 308 were admitted. Figure 2 (p. 136) shows the origin of these referrals and how it changed over time. The categories of referral sources used show first, to what extent other services made referrals compared with the extent of self-referrals; second, the proportion of referrals from the statutory sector compared with the voluntary agencies; and finally, the number of referrals from the health service compared with that from the social services, including referrals from the probation service. City Roads was expected to establish links with all these types of services, but the extent to which the various services would actually use City Roads was not known in advance. In the light of the interest taken by SCODA in the establishing of City Roads, it was expected that the voluntary agencies would refer clients. Likewise the DHSS expected that A and E departments would make referrals, indeed they insisted that City Roads accept referrals only from A and E departments during the first three months, partly because of the importance they attached to establishing close links with A and E departments and partly as a 'protection' for City Roads, to make sure that clients had been vetted medically before admission.

In the first year, hospitals made more referrals than any one of the other sources mentioned. However, during the following two years, their share of the number of referrals declined steadily, and instead the share of the voluntary agencies increased, although this fell again in the third year. Self-referrals increased dramatically and constituted the largest source of referrals in the third year. Probation and social services made more or less the same number of referrals throughout the period and the probation service accounted for the majority of these referrals.

The close links which developed with the probation service had not been anticipated. No formal links had been established

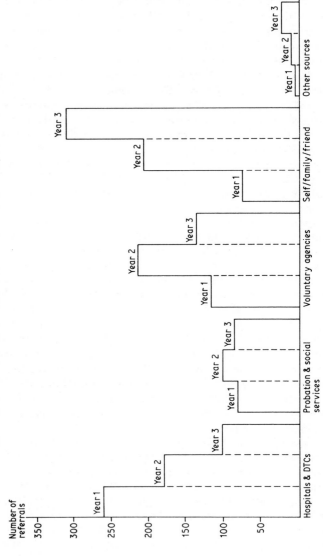

Figure 2   Pattern of referral sources in each of the three years

before City Roads opened. However, it turned out that criminality amongst the clients was extremely high, and many of them were on probation or had a Probation Officer involved with their case. City Roads was never at any times used as a bail hostel in the sense that the courts might use it as a direct alternative to prison. The staff were always very firm that they wanted to be able to discharge residents if necessary without having to send them to prison.

However, in effect City Roads did act as an alternative to prison in cases where the court was in doubt about whether to send them to prison. Sometimes if young offenders expressed a determination to 'do something about themselves', i.e. go to City Roads, the court might decide to give them a second chance. City Roads was clearly accepted as a reliable service within the system of treatment of young offenders. This function is worth bearing in mind in view of the debate about the prison system and how best to deal with young offenders. To those who did not see prison as the most suitable way of dealing with certain offenders, a service like City Roads offered one possible alternative. It is interesting in this connection to look at the attitude of the Home Office to City Roads. At the beginning of the life of the project, the Home Office was only marginally involved, mainly because of the drugs aspect of the service. The Drugs Inspectorate was represented on the Steering/Management Committee. The possibility of the Home Office actually contributing financially to City Roads was however not considered seriously at that stage; indeed the Home Office representatives made it clear that this was out of the question. After the first three years when the extent and range of criminality among clients had become obvious, the Home Office did become involved and eventually decided to take on a small part of the financial responsibility. Their contribution, though symbolically significant, is however still minor, and one wonders whether, from the point of view of relieving other services, their contribution should not be at least as high as that of the health service. (Note here the similarity between the number of referrals in the third year from A and E departments and from the probation service as shown in Figure 2.)

Success rate of referrals

When discussing the question whether City Roads can be said to have been a help to agencies, it is of course not enough to look at referral figures. To what extent were these referrals successful, i.e. did they result in admissions? *Table 11* shows the success rate of referrals from different sources. Clients were admitted from all sources, but some were more successful than others. Clients who referred themselves were most successful in obtaining admissions, and the voluntary agencies were more successful than hospitals and the probation and social services. These differences had nothing to do with any deliberate discrimination by City Roads. Rather, two factors decided the success rate of the referrals: the suitability of the clients, as regards the City Roads admission criteria, and their

Table 11   *'Success rate': percentage of referrals resulting in admission, May 1980–May 1981*

DTCs and hospitals	probation office & social services	voluntary agencies	self	other	total
27%	26%	39%	46%	18%	38%

Source: Telephone messages.

persistence in attempting admission. We shall consider the admission process below, but first the whole question of the impact of City Roads on other services deserves some further mention.

Throughout the life of City Roads, much attention was directed at referral and admission statistics to see 'whom City Roads was serving'. However, these figures are really of limited value in this respect. The most noticeable changes which took place during the three years were the increase in the proportion of self-referrals and consequent reduction in the proportion of agency referrals, and in particular the absolute decrease in referrals from A and E departments. As City Roads became more widely known on the drugs scene, clients referred themselves and to a large extent by-passed these other agencies. Seen in this light it could be argued that the burden on these other agencies had indeed been relieved. They did not even have to refer clients who would previously have come to them first. This is certainly true in the case of readmissions. Many residents who had first been referred to City Roads by another agency, referred themselves subsequently. Some new residents also referred themselves. Some of these would most certainly have gone to another agency for help, had they not known about City Roads: others might not have sought any help at all.

Effects on A and E departments

The position of the A and E departments deserves special mention in this connection, given the expectation on the part of the DHSS that City Roads would relieve the burden on them. If burden is measured purely in terms of work loads, that is, time spent on drug misusers in A and E departments, then the establishing of City Roads probably created more rather than less work for the staff in these departments. First of all, the service provided by A and E departments could not be done by City Roads. The vast majority of drug misusers are brought into hospital because they need resuscitation. At times they would behave violently when under the influence of the drugs. City Roads did not admit people who were too intoxicated to make a rational decision to come to the House, and in such cases they would ask the A and E staff to contact them when the person had sobered up. However, according to the A and E staff, once people were well enough to stand on their own two feet, most of them discharged themselves immediately. As one A and E nurse put it before City Roads opened, 'They can't get out of here soon enough. They stagger out as soon as they regain consciousness, and they don't want to talk to anyone. I don't think many of these people will want to go to City Roads.' It turned out that she was right. Judging from the records kept at the Middlesex Hospital, only a minority (20 per cent) of the drug misusers who went to this hospital had also used City Roads. Yet the existence of City Roads improved staff morale, because as one of them put it, 'At least we are now in the situation of being able to offer them *something* if they do ask for help.' As regards the overall workload in terms of numbers of drug-related cases seen, City Roads cannot be said to have had any noticeable effect on individual A and E departments, simply because of the relatively small number of people who could stay at City Roads compared with the total numbers going to A and E departments. And, of the people who did come to City Roads, the majority went back to the same lifestyle once they left the House.

In addition, City Roads, because of its admission procedure, actually created more work for the A and E departments in many instances. No client was admitted without first being seen by a staff member outside the House. This so-called 'assessment' process was a very important part of the City Roads regime. The staff wanted to make sure that the people referred were appropriate, so they wanted to ascertain for themselves, not only that the formal admission criteria were met but that the client was physically and mentally suited to come. They were anxious that the place should not become a dumping ground used by other agencies to get rid of clients. Also, and this is where the A and E departments come into the picture, they wanted people to have a physical check-up in advance, and because the City Roads doctor was not permanently on the premises, they often needed an A and E doctor to write up the initial dose of phenobarbitone for the barbiturate users. It therefore became practice from the very beginning that anyone referred by a non-medical agency would be directed to the nearest A and E department where a staff member would assess them before bringing them back in the yellow taxi.

For the DHSS it had from the beginning been seen as very important for City Roads to establish links with the hospitals. It is ironic that the insistence of the DHSS that City Roads should only accept referrals from A and E departments initially marked the beginning of an extra workload on these departments. When this policy was first proposed, both the City Roads staff and the street agencies protested, because they saw it as an exclusion of clients from the street agencies. However, in practice the problem was overcome simply by the street agencies directing their clients to an A and E department, so that on paper (i.e. in the monthly returns to the DHSS) all admissions came from A and E departments during the first three months. By this time, City Roads realized the advantages of admitting people through A and E departments and therefore continued the practice when they were officially permitted to take referrals from any agency. About 80 per cent of admissions involved 'assessment' at an A and E department which had not made the original referral. (This figure is approximate, since 'assessment' agency was not always recorded. It is based on a six-month sample (November 1980–May 1981) of 124 admissions.) This put a considerable burden on the A and E departments, in fact mainly on the Middlesex Hospital's A and E Department which was the one used in the vast majority of cases. The Middlesex staff were very co-operative and did not complain about City Roads using their department for assessments, although it clearly did give them more work to do. On the other hand the big advantage of this procedure was that the A and E staff were reminded of the existence of City Roads. Because of the staff turnover in A and E departments, there was a tendency to forget about City Roads and what it could do.

Admission barriers

Other agencies, in particular the street agencies, were not altogether happy with the use of A and E departments in the 'assessment' procedure, as will be shown below. They found it very cumbersome, and thought that in many cases the City Roads staff might as well collect the client from the referring agency. This whole admission procedure did create problems for the staff, who would often be tied up in A and E departments for hours and therefore could only go on 'assessments' when the staffing situation in the House was satisfactory. And it constituted a considerable barrier for the clients. It was certainly a test of their motivation to be told to go to an A and E department and wait for a City Roads staff to meet them. Quite a few clients (about 25 per cent) changed their minds and never came to City Roads (see *Table 12*). Some of these might have ended up at City Roads, had the process of intervention been more speedy.

Table 12   *Reasons for non-admission*

	May 1978–1980 %		May 1980–1981 %	
Client unsuitable without 'assessment'	42 ⎫		54 ⎫	
Client unsuitable after 'assessment'	3 ⎭	45	4 ⎭	58
Contact broken before 'assessment'	25 ⎫		26 ⎫	
Admission declined by client after 'assessment'	2 ⎭	27	1 ⎭	27
No vacancies/unable to assess	28	28	15	15
	100	100	100	100
Total number of referrals not resulting in admission		853		412

It must be said that many of the so-called referrals were more like enquiries made by social workers or others on behalf of clients who were themselves not really sure whether they wanted to come to City Roads at all. Some of those with whom contact was broken might probably never have been persuaded to come to City Roads, but others might, had they met a staff member at the right time. The mood and aspirations, and therefore the level of 'motivation', of this client group was forever changing. Their behaviour in the House showed this clearly. One day they would be determined to come off drugs, to change their lifestyle, to go to a rehabilitation centre; the next day they felt drawn back to drugs and life on the street. Given that their level of motivation was not a constant factor, and since for most residents even a short spell of contact with City Roads was a positive experience, it is likely that City Roads missed out a considerable number of people whose level of motivation at a particular time was insufficient to break the admission barriers.

Over the three years, 580 individuals were referred but never admitted. About half of these were deemed unsuitable (especially since, at that time, predominantly opiate users were not admitted), but the other half were not known to be unsuitable. They were either turned down because City Roads was unable to admit people at the time, or they lost contact. Ninety-one per cent of these 580 individuals made no further attempt to be admitted, so they were clearly not a very persistent group. City Roads kept a card index of all individuals referred, recording some basic information about them. This index was analysed, and it was found that the age and sex distribution was similar to that of those admitted, as was the pattern of drug use, although at the time of referral, mention of opiate use seemed to be one of the major obstacles to admission. (The detailed results of this analysis can be found in Jamieson, Glanz, and MacGregor 1981.) At the time the first Steering Committee was constituted, the then chairman, talking about the plan for the unit to have a taxi, painted a picture of the staff driving round the streets of London picking up people directly from the street. This idea, expressed somewhat jokingly, was never seriously considered by the staff appointed to City Roads. They always insisted that the service would not function properly unless a certain level of motivation was present in the residents. They were probably right that an attempt to reach those most outside the network of services would not have been a very gratifying task and it might have been very difficult to recruit suitable people to work under these conditions. Nevertheless, one should not ignore the fact that there were a large number of people whom City Roads never reached, but who might have benefited from some form of intervention.

Table 12 (p. 141) shows that almost half the referrals were thought to be unsuitable. To be admitted, people had to meet certain basic criteria. They had to be staying in the Greater London area; in fact very few referrals came from outside London. They had to be aged between 16 and 30 years, although some flexibility was exercised regarding the upper age limit. About 6 per cent of unsuitable referrals were rejected on the basis of age. Pattern of drug misuse constituted a significant reason for non-admission. City Roads was set up to provide for multiple drug misusers and in that connection to offer barbiturate detoxification, but not opiate detoxification, for which it was thought that there were adequate existing facilities. Consequently the policy during the first two and a half years was to reject referrals of people who at the time of referral were considered in need of opiate detoxification, whether or not they were also using other drugs like barbiturates. About a third of the unsuitable referrals were made by or on behalf of opiate users. However, it became clear that a large number of multiple drug users took opiates among other drugs and that therefore people who were using opiates at the time of admission were not necessarily any different from those who were not. The type of drugs used depended very much on their availability and price. By then, heroin and a range of opiates and opioids were becoming more widely available. Recognizing this the staff and management decided early in 1981 to introduce opiate detoxification on a limited, experimental basis. The aim was to offer it to ex-residents, who were known to fulfil other admission criteria. By May 1981, however, no one had been admitted for opiate detoxification; the admission criteria were clearly as yet too cautious.

As mentioned above, City Roads did not admit people as a condition of bail. If is difficult to estimate precisely how many were turned down because of legal complications. Many of those with whom contact was broken had legal problems, for instance a court case coming up on the day of referral. Such people would be asked to ring back after their case had been heard, and in many cases these people seemed to have changed their minds about coming to City Roads, or perhaps they received a prison sentence. It is worth noting in this connection that the so-called voluntary nature of a City Roads admission must be taken with some qualification. As we saw in Chapter 4, a prime motivation which drove many clients to City Roads was fear of being sent to prison, and to these people coming to City Roads was only a choice in so far as prison might have been the only other alternative.

The refusal on the part of City Roads to take clients directly on bail was closely connected with the admission criteria which had to do with their physical, psychological, and social conditions. Basically the staff wanted the residents to know and accept the working philosophy and rules of the House before being admitted. If they were highly intoxicated they would not be admitted. They had to show a certain degree of 'motivation'. The interpretation of this varied. There were cases when a staff member would refuse a client admission because 'he did not say that he wanted to come off drugs'. However, in most cases it was (rightly) agreed that the most they could ask for was for people to accept not to use their own drugs on the premises and a willingness to 'think about their situation' and talk to the staff about their problems. In other words, the staff wanted to make sure that they could contain the residents and that there was a reasonable chance that they would be able to 'work with them'.

More than a third of 'unsuitable' referrals were made by or on behalf of ex-residents. The referral rate for ex-residents was generally much higher than for others, and this accounts for their high number in the category of unsuitable referrals. As a whole they had a higher 'success rate' as regards admission, because they were generally more determined and persistent in their attempts to be admitted. Special criteria applied in the cases of ex-residents. First of all, there was a general rule to the effect that no one was readmitted within one week of leaving. This rule was established shortly after the unit opened, in the light of the experience that people would leave the House to get drugs and soon afterwards attempt readmission. Accepting them back immediately would have made the House programme meaningless, since City Roads operated a 'closed system' (whereby residents were expected only to take prescribed drugs and not to leave the House unescorted). Residents who were dismissed for breaking a rule, like bringing in drugs, would not be allowed readmission until after three weeks – not so much as a punishment, but so that the House would be occupied by a new set of residents who would not have witnessed the rule-breaking incident. Apart from these rules, the motivation, progress, and needs of each individual ex-resident would be scrutinized closely before re-admission was agreed. The readmission criteria had the effect that ex-residents often attempted readmission many times over a period of weeks or months before they were finally readmit-ted. This was not the result of a deliberate programme of torture on the part of City Roads. Certainly, they would have argued quite the contrary, that they were trying not to make people too dependent on City Roads but instead to encourage them to try to cope on their own. The staff were always willing to talk to ex-residents on the telephone, and much time was spent on this 'telephone counselling'. However, with time the staff began to reconsider their readmission criteria, because they realized that there was a certain category of ex-residents who were probably at such high risk that if City Roads did not admit them regularly to give them some general care, they would be likely to die. In fact, the research team raised this issue after the death of Penny, an ex-resident, who had been refused readmission to City Roads. It was gradually acknowledged that there were some people – a small minority – from whom 'progress' in terms of increased motivation to change or come off drugs could not be expected but who needed City Roads simply to survive.

There was finally one more admission barrier, which had nothing to do with the clients but with the situation in the House. Between 15 per cent and 28 per cent of referrals were turned down because of the 'house situation' (see *Table 12*). Some of these cases represent occasions when the House was actually fully occupied. However, this was not often the case, as Figure 3 shows. On less than 10 per cent of all days were there 12 residents in the House. The average rate of occupancy was never more than nine in any one year. Most of the referrals here were turned down because they felt unable to send a staff member off to assess a referral at the time the referral was made. The procedure whereby prospective residents had to be 'assessed' outside the House, preferably at an A and E depart-ment, was very time consuming, so if they were short of staff or in the middle of a team meeting or a handover session, staff were likely to ask people to ring back later. Those who were determined to gain admission would persist and keep ringing, sometimes for days, until they could be 'assessed'. These were most often ex-residents, who knew the system, whereas those who had never had contact with City Roads and who were perhaps unsure about wanting to come, would tend to give up after this first attempt.

The work in the House, that is, the work with those already

resident rather than those who wanted to become resident, was always given first priority. There were times when they had empty beds and plenty of staff, when they might still refuse

Figure 3   Numbers of days when house occupied by specified number of residents (year 2 compared with year 3)

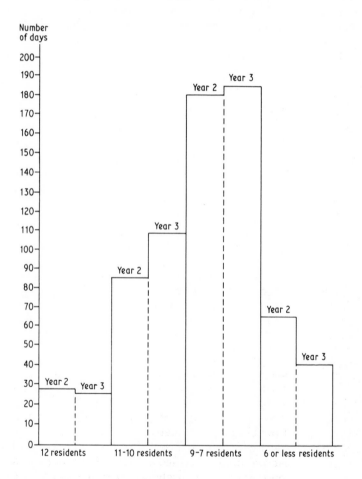

admission of new residents. These were times when the atmosphere in the House was thought to be 'unsettled' or 'tense', and when therefore the introduction of new elements into the system was thought to threaten the work with the residents.

The views of other agencies

To assess the extent and nature of the impact of City Roads on other services, a questionnaire survey was conducted. In April 1981 questionnaires were sent to all agencies which had referred clients to City Roads at least once during the preceding six months. These 50 agencies comprised 13 probation offices; 11 voluntary street agencies/day centres/night shelters; 19 hospital A and E departments; and seven Drug Treatment Centres. Of the agencies contacted, 52 per cent replied. The highest response rate came from the street agencies (64 per cent) and DTCs (57 per cent); 46 per cent of probation offices replied, but only 26 per cent of the A and E departments; in addition 8 per cent of agencies returned the forms without completing them. The reasons given for returning the blank forms were the following: one probation office felt that the office had not used City Roads sufficiently for them to be able to give an opinion; two A and E departments were unable to identify any staff members who had made referrals. One A and E department claimed never to use City Roads, saying that they had a Drug Treatment Centre and one A and E department referred the questionnaire to their DTC for answers.

It is not surprising that the response rate was higher for street agencies and DTCs than for the probation service and A and E departments. The former group of agencies is smaller and includes those agencies which deal specifically with drug misusers and which used City Roads most frequently. The probation service, on the other hand, although as a whole accounting for a considerable proportion of the City Roads referrals, was divided into numerous offices, each with a large number of staff members, some of whom might have only one or two drug misusers on their list of clients. Likewise, most of the individual A and E departments made only very occasional referrals. And the shift system and high staff turnover there seem to have contributed to their low response rate.

Agencies were asked what were the most common needs and problems of the people they referred to City Roads. The most frequent answer was 'drug misuse' (mentioned in 62 per cent of replies), most commonly specified as 'multiple' or 'barbiturate' misuse. Second, workers themselves were said to need advice, support, and help with assessment (42 per cent of replies). Homelessness or an unstable home situation was mentioned by 35 per cent, and 23 per cent mentioned the need for detoxification. Other problems mentioned were overdosing and 'crisis'.

The agencies were asked why they considered City Roads to be an appropriate service for the people they had referred. The reason given by 46 per cent of agencies replying was that City Roads was the only service readily available for immediate detoxification and crisis intervention. In 38 per cent of replies the *specialist* service and approach of City Roads was stressed. Other reasons mentioned were the special knowledge of and links with City Roads that these agencies had built up.

The agencies were asked what, if any, had been the main benefits of City Roads for their clients. In the large majority of cases, the short-term benefits were most heavily emphasized. Thus 35 per cent of replies stressed the chance for assessment and test of motivation as one of the main benefits. Immediate relief and breathing-space was mentioned by 27 per cent. Other benefits mentioned were detoxification, and improved health, and some commented that the experience of being at City Roads (the caring staff) was in itself a benefit. One agency said accommodation was the main benefit. Long-term benefits, i.e. onward referral to rehabilitation, were mentioned by 19 per cent of agencies replying. Three agencies felt uncertain about the benefits because they said they had received no feedback or had not been able to follow up the clients sufficiently.

Agencies were also asked in what ways, if at all, had City Roads been useful to their organization. By far the most common answer to this question (69 per cent of replies) was that City Roads was a place to send clients whom no one else would accept. The DTCs stressed that City Roads was useful by taking barbiturate users. The 24-hour service, that is, the ability of City Roads to admit people in the evening, was specifically mentioned by two agencies. Five agencies mentioned advice and information and one praised the City Roads court reports. One agency was critical: this agency said it had not benefited from City Roads recently.

Since the City Roads system relied heavily on referrals from other agencies and, as discussed above, large numbers of people referred were not successful in gaining admission to the House, the agencies were asked whether they had experienced any difficulties in getting clients admitted to City Roads. Of those replying, 42 per cent said they had not, but another 42 per cent said that they had. Of those answering yes, the most common difficulty reported was 'no vacancies' (38 per cent of agencies replying had encountered this obstacle). Two agencies specifically mentioned the lengthy admission procedure and in 35 per cent of replies, the agency had been told that the client referred was considered unsuitable. One agency had not been told the reason for the client's unsuitability. However in the rest of the cases, the reasons given to them were to do either with the motivation of the client, opiate use or that they were ex-residents whom City Roads considered unsuitable at the time.

Following from this, agencies were then asked whether there were any changes they would like to suggest in connection with City Roads' admission policies and procedures. Eight agencies (31 per cent of replies) had suggestions to make. Three agencies found the assessment procedure, whereby clients had to present at A and E departments, extremely cumbersome and would like assessments to take place at the referral agency. Two agencies wanted opiates to be included in the term 'multiple drug misusers'. One agency suggested that the age limit be put up; one agency thought that the demands made on residents were too 'intense' as regards the level of motivation and commitment to the City Roads approach. These key referring agencies were also asked to comment on whether, in their opinion, there were any ways in which the services at City Roads could be improved. Twenty-seven per cent had no suggestions for changes. Four agencies said they wished that City Roads had more beds available. Suggestions for changes included: extension of the three-week limit on residents' stay (suggested by three agencies); two agencies wanted City Roads to explore the possibilities and suitability of supportive accommodation, rather than just rehabilitation projects for their clients; one agency wanted City Roads to provide 'full-time medical cover' so that clients in very poor condition and needing opiate detoxification could be admitted. One agency pointed out that it was difficult to refer 'new' users into a well-established network of 'old users'. One suggested that City Roads undertake counselling on a non-residential basis.

These agencies were asked to what extent, in addition to referring clients to City Roads, they used it as an advisory service. Fifteen per cent said they never did; 50 per cent that they did so occasionally, and 19 per cent that they did so regularly. What kind of advice did they most often seek from City Roads? Forty-two per cent sought advice about resources available for drug misusers in general; 23 per cent mentioned advice related to knowledge about drugs and treatment of drug addiction; 19 per cent consulted City Roads about specific clients.

Agencies were also asked what kind of service (other than

City Roads) they had referred drug misusers to in the past year. The other services utilized by these agencies in order of mention were: hospitals, mentioned by 65 per cent; street agencies, mentioned by 58 per cent; DTCs by 50 per cent; rehabilitation projects by 46 per cent; and sheltered accommodation by 38 per cent. It was clear then that other services besides City Roads were being used, especially hospitals, including DTCs. All the different categories of agency were referring people to these other services, although relatively few referrals from A and E departments were made to the non-medical services. This complements the picture built up from the information on residents at City Roads, of a stage army composed of the population of drug misusers which moves through this network of interconnected services. However, movement into and out of these agencies was not easy. Agencies were asked if they had experienced any difficulties in referring their clients to any of these services. Sixty-nine per cent answered yes and only 15 per cent answered no. The difficulties mentioned all had to do with difficulty in gaining admission. An additional problem mentioned was that of inadequate information about which service was appropriate.

Following from this, agencies were asked to comment on the provision of health and social services for the drug misusers seen by their organization. None expressed satisfaction with the existing provision of services. Four agencies found the provision poor but did not go into more detail. One agency thought that the provisions in the statutory sector were insufficient. Five agencies pointed to short-term residential facilities as being in particularly short supply, as were facilities which would offer general supportive accommodation rather than specific attempts at 'rehabilitation'. As one agency characterized the range of existing residential projects: 'It's either God or Therapy.'

Agencies were invited to comment further on City Roads. Most of those who had further comments confined themselves to general praise of City Roads, stressing the need for the project to become established as a permanent service with secure funding. One agency thought City Roads has improved by not insisting that clients should want rehabilitation in order to be admitted (thus implying that this used to be the case). Three A and E departments expressed the need for some more information about City Roads, and one other agency repeated the need for further discussion between City Roads and its referral agencies.

One of the problems of drawing conclusions from this survey derives from the extremely heterogeneous nature of the population of referral agencies. There was a small core of agencies and individual workers who, because of their frequent contact with drug misusers, used City Roads regularly, had built up close links with the project and knew in great detail how it operated. Outside this core there was a large number of agencies that made only occasional use of City Roads and whose knowledge of it was thus patchy. Some of these agencies declined to comment on the services at City Roads, because they said they did not know enough to be able to give an opinion on this. It is very clear that knowledge about City Roads amongst A and E staff left a great deal to be desired. It is particularly interesting that two of the agencies which expressed a wish for more information about City Roads were from the group of seven A and E departments originally designated as the main referral sources. The problem of communication with A and E departments was clearly immense.

It did seem clear, however, that there was an obvious demand for a service like City Roads. There was a demand from the agencies for somewhere they could send clients immediately – clients who wanted instant support and accommodation. The short-term benefits, for the clients as well as the agencies, were stresssed as the most important ones. The need for services in general, as expressed by the agencies surveyed, was for more supportive accommodation rather than more therapeutic rehabilitative settings. There was some evidence of pressure on City Roads to extend this aspect of their service (for example, the wish for the three-week limit to be extended) and to put more emphasis on this in their assessment and onward referral procedures.

Conclusion

Both the way City Roads was established and the way in which it developed over time were rather different from the conception of an appropriate service outlined by Ghodse in 1977. He had concluded that the A and E departments were left to cope with people whose needs went beyond the physical complications of drug dependence, which were dealt with medically in these departments. He had recommended social intervention at this stage of crisis, when the patient might be more receptive to help than at other times. However, the City Roads workers concluded that the moment of overdosing was *not* the moment of crisis in which a patient might be more receptive to help than at other times. In fact, because of the confused state of these clients due to intoxication, they might then be less receptive and would also not be fully aware of what was expected of them at City Roads. In practice, other 'crises' like pressure from the courts and police, lack of accommodation, sickness, and loss of contact with drug supplies proved to be more influential forces encouraging people to reappraise their situation. Staff at A and E departments agreed with City Roads in this, and the reason why they did not refer many people, they said, was that they were 'not motivated', or 'they did not want to come off drugs'. However, the residents of City Roads *were* the client group to which Ghodse had referred. If the social intervention practised at City Roads did take some people out of the system, and thus directed them away from a pattern of life which involved over-dosing, to that extent the service relieved the burden on other agencies. Another aspect of the situation had to do with the demoralization of staff at A and E departments who felt that they had nothing to offer patients after patching them up following an overdose. The existence of City Roads alleviated this feeling.

By giving advice and information over the telephone, City Roads did at least help other agencies function more efficiently and supported them in their work. Since only 12 people would be resident at City Roads at any one time, the overall impact of the service in terms of numbers could only be small, although the provision of any extra service is bound to relieve the burden on other agencies to some extent. On the other hand, by putting people in contact with other agencies, the existence of City Roads increased their work, in particular the A and E departments which were used for 'assessment' of clients they had not referred themselves.

The response of the agencies which used City Roads most and therefore knew something about the place was on the whole very positive. However, their enthusiasm was qualified in one respect, which is linked very much to the internal operation of the unit and its benefits to the clients: many agencies would have liked more easy access to City Roads and would have liked City Roads to have been less stringent in its demands of the residents as regards therapy. We must there-fore conclude by questioning again the benefits of the time devoted to casework at City Roads, which tended to make the place very inward looking and less accessible, and therefore less of a help to other agencies than it might otherwise have been.

8 An Assessment of City Roads

In the previous four chapters (Chapters 4–7), we have been assessing City Roads in terms of its main objectives, its 'banner goals'. City Roads was unusual, perhaps, in having such clearly defined and carefully worked-out objectives, as it was relatively unusual in having a detailed Operational Document covering practices and management. Credit should go to DHSS who insisted that this be worked out in advance and to the Director, Deputy Director, and Administrator of City Roads in post in early 1978, at the start of the project. In addition, City Roads formulated a clear model of treatment, which was discussed in Chapter 6. In these ways, this 'experimental innovation' encapsulated all that was best in the 'rational planning' approach to the development of services.

In looking at City Roads' performance in terms of its main, stated objectives, we have presented a detailed description of what happened. Description is not a simple matter but needs care, thought, and sensitive awareness in the construction of categories and recording of information. The particular kind of description we preferred looked at processes and aimed at clarification rather than relying on a few crude indicators, wrenched out of context. In this, we were deliberately taking a position opposed to the positivistic model of social care research, where the client is viewed as the object of an experimental method more appropriate to the laboratory sciences. Social research cannot work in this way. Rather, we wanted to focus on the interaction between the client and the services, which may at best be a partnership but may also be a battle of wills and interests. In this way, the service is not seen as the means and the client as the object but their joint endeavours are both means and ends.

It may be more helpful to consider the experimental innovation at City Roads from the perspective of policy studies. Rather than focus on the outcomes of that service, simply viewed in terms of changes in the clients' behaviour, as a vulgar form of the 'medical model' might do, we should consider the distribution of resources through the service and related agencies and the distribution of benefit, especially here the relative benefit derived by staff, clients, and other agencies.

What we are looking at are, basically, the problems posed by attempts to enact policy, that is, the study of policy implementation (see Webb and Wistow 1982). In this case, the policies were fairly explicitly stated and we gave an account of the hopes and expectations for City Roads in Chapter 2. Now we should try to assess the impact of this innovation. What modifications or changes took place? We are back to considering the issues of the appropriateness and the effectiveness of the change in policy and practice experimentally tried out through the City Roads venture. These have been the themes of Chapters 4–7, which considered the relevance of the approach adopted to the problems of the clients (Chapter 4), and the difficulties faced by staff in trying to put into effect their model of treatment, and how they dealt with those difficulties (Chapter 6). In Chapters 3 and 5, we saw something of the immediate effects of the service on the clients and staff and in Chapter 7 the effects on other related services, hospital A and E departments, the probation service, and street agencies in particular.

In looking at what happened through the City Roads innovation, we looked not at outcomes in the narrow sense of one or two pre-selected changes in clients' behaviour patterns but first asked the question, what were the *outputs* of that service? Since this was an experimental, innovatory project, it was an open question what would be produced. Having seen what were the outputs, we could then try to explain how they were produced. To do this, an analysis of the system as a whole was required. These outputs could then be compared with the stated goals of the unit and thus began the process of assessment, weighing up, judging the unit's performance overall. This 'understanding' approach begins by setting up an idealtype or model of the service (as shown in Chapters 2 and 6) and then compares the reality with this. There will always be, by definition, a gap between the model and the reality, and our task then is to explain the difference, and for practitioners and managers, perhaps, to consider whether further modifications could be introduced that might narrow the gap. It may be, however, that elements in the model were inappropriate, so that the model rather than the practice should be changed to bring the two closer together. This then is the role of 'illuminative' research, to help the participants to make informed decisions, set out the issues, and provide the information relevant to making decisions regarding policy and practice. (From a number of such studies, it might be possible to move further to produce some general criteria on which services could be assessed, an issue of increasing importance in an era of low growth in social expenditure.)

Anthony Thorley (DHSS Seminar 1980) has suggested that to justify the provision of any new treatment in the area of homelessness and addiction, five questions need to be asked of that service:

1. Is it acceptable to patients or community groups?
2. Does it have a higher success rate than previous methods?
3. Is it cheaper than previous methods?
4. Does the service meet the special needs of certain drug-taking sub-groups?
5. Is it more adaptable and experimental than present approaches?

We might go beyond this and add in a further list of questions:

6. Is the occupancy rate high (does it operate at full capacity)?
7. Are many people of the specified client group asking to use the service?
8. Are the staff of high quality, in terms of relevant experience and qualifications?
9. Do the staff come and go in smooth rotation, moving on mainly to further their career development?
10. Is the level of activity high; is there a positive and happy atmosphere?
11. Is the service held in high regard by all who have contact with it and real knowledge of how it works, especially the clients and other agencies who make use of it?
12. Is the service clear about its objectives and does it engage in open discussion about these and the best way of achieving them?
13. Are resources distributed evenly through the system?
14. Do all participants (clients, staff, and agencies) benefit to some degree; is benefit evenly shared between staff, clients and other agencies; and especially is benefit distributed towards people who previously received less and were in greater need?
15. Do all participants (clients, staff, and agencies) improve and benefit in their own terms?

16. Most importantly, does the service achieve its prime, high priority objectives; does it do what it set out to do, what it claims to be doing?

A service which answered yes to all these questions would indeed be distinguished, a shining example to others. Most would not attain this standard of excellence but would fall down on some points.

Often one will find that resources are under-utilized; beds and places are standing empty. Resources may be unevenly distributed, so that perhaps a lot of attention is given to new admissions and less to readmissions, or time and labour may be expended on staff's problems to the neglect of those of the clients. The service may be achieving good results in terms of its goals but the people who come may not be of the specified client group, particularly where more 'promising' cases are preferred to difficult ones (in some services this might be a major criticism, in others it might not matter). The staff may be deriving a great deal of benefit, say, high take-home pay, good working conditions, positive learning experiences, while the clients receive little. Activities may be standardized and routine, not innovatory. The staff may constantly be faced with obstacles or difficulties in trying to implement their aims. This may be because the plans and programmes are not well worked out, but it may often reflect the very fact that the service represents a radical innovation. There may be confusion in the unit or it may be careless about its objectives, unsure what it is supposed to be doing. The staff and the clients may find what goes on there irrelevant and meaningless, they may say they cannot see the point of it all. Total abject failure in a service, calling for radical reform or closure (in addition to cases where normal health and safety standards were not met), would certainly occur where no clients would use the service voluntarily, staff refused to work there, and the resources provided were used to decorate the Director's house or fund his holiday abroad. Such examples are happily only rarely found.

If we consider City Roads on these criteria, we see that it was a service acceptable to most residents. Other agencies expressed favourable comment and referrals remained buoyant. By offering a detoxification service to barbiturate users, and later an opiate detoxification service, by providing a package of services in one place, especially basic medical and nursing care, warmth, and shelter, and operating a system which coped satisfactorily with the 'difficult' and 'chaotic' among drug misusers, City Roads offered a particular service to a particular client group. It was experimental and adaptable to changes in the drug scene as reported by the street agencies and by its own clients. It was especially innovative and experimental in attempting to implement a pattern of care designed on multi-disciplinary lines, and one which did not involve the prescribing of alternative forms of drugs and which saw rehabilitation as the desired route for its clients.

Staff were well qualified, with relevant experience and, during the three years studied, there was a smooth rate of staff turnover. On all these criteria, then, City Roads approached the excellent.

Its performance on other criteria pulled it down from this, however. The occupancy rate was not as high as was hoped for, particularly given that it was a crisis-intervention unit. Admission barriers and arrangements regarding staffing and 'assessment' procedures contributed to this. The level of activity of the staff was very high but that of the clients for most of the day was low. Residents complained of being bored. This also links to the way in which resources were distributed in the system, here to some extent they were over-concentrated on one-to-one counselling sessions and on staff communication, which contributed to staff satisfaction but also had very much to do with the complications produced by the shift system, as shown in the discussion in Chapter 5. Not all clients benefited to the same degree from the service. Those who stayed longer and were readmitted appeared to benefit most, and less benefit was derived by those who came once only and/or stayed for only a few days. Again this reflected the distribution of resources, with more time and labour being directed to the intensive counselling sessions and relatively less to the basic immediate care or to explorations of a wider range of agencies as referral-on outlets.

To a considerable extent, however, City Roads adhered closely to its stated objectives, it came close to doing what it set out to do, what it claimed to be doing. This is very important because in the discussions which surrounded the issue of future funding, which we shall look at in more detail in Chapter 9, there were attempts to assess City Roads on quite different criteria. The main argument tended to be that City Roads did not 'cure' people, or enough people, and thus did not merit support from the health service. As has been pointed out, if one were to apply these criteria widely, large areas of the NHS would be decimated. Apart from that, it is a clever but quite unjust criticism, to argue that a service does not do something it was never intended to do. At no point do the objectives of City Roads – *to provide for the immediate needs of young drug misusers, to operate at a crisis intervention level, providing a warm, sheltered environment* and *to act as a multi-disciplinary service*, and as stated precisely, *not to attempt to offer a complete treatment and rehabilitation programme under one roof but simply to try to encourage clients to accept longer-term help from existing treatment and rehabilitation agencies*, and *to work closely with other agencies in this*, – at no point do they mention the word 'cure', and treatment and rehabilitation are specifically *excluded* as the goals of the service itself.

However, since the issue has been raised and since so far we have considered mainly the immediate and intermediate outcomes of the City Roads work (Chapters 3 and 5), we shall include here what we know of what happened to the clients in the longer term, as a result of our follow-up enquiries.

Follow-up studies

Of the 308 people who became residents of City Roads between 1978 and 1981, 155 were admitted once only. For the 153 who were readmitted at some point to City Roads, we know something of what they were doing in between admissions. On being readmitted, almost half (49 per cent) reported at least one incident of overdosing in the intervening period. Although the two groups cannot be strictly compared, since the half who were not readmitted differ in important respects from those who were readmitted (those who used City Roads most tending to be younger and to be more chaotic, less stable, as defined by being homeless and out of touch with their families, chronically unemployed, on probation and referred by a street agency), one may note that in an equivalent period, the three months prior to first admission, 41 per cent of all first admissions had overdosed on at least one occasion. Given that the more promising clients, those with better prognoses, tended to have been selected out from the readmission category, the incidence of overdosing can be said to have remained roughly the same. Thirty-two per cent had spent some of the time between admissions in hospital; 10 per cent had been in prison; and 26 per cent had spent some time between admissions in a rehabilitation project.

Fifty-six residents, admitted during May to October 1978 (inclusive), were followed up at intervals up to the end of April

1981 (a two and a half year follow-up period). As one might expect from the foregoing, half (52 per cent) were readmitted to City Roads at least once. Interestingly, however, of those not readmitted, 37 per cent attempted to be readmitted and a further 26 per cent had some form of contact with the service in this two and a half year period. Of this cohort of 56 people, 57 per cent spent some time as a resident of a rehabilitation project after being at City Roads. One third (32 per cent) lived for some time in some form of permanent accommodation. About one half of residents experienced for a time some positive improvement, either by being at rehabilitation or living for a period in settled accommodation after leaving City Roads (although how much City Roads contributed to this is not always clear).

On the negative side, however, 38 per cent were convicted of a criminal offence at some time during these two and a half years. Thirteen per cent had died. (This mortality rate of 5.2 per cent per annum is considerably higher than found in other studies of drug users, for example, 6.2 per cent of a sample of heroin addicts died over a 3.5–4-year follow-up period, 1.6 per cent per annum (Ogborne and Stimson 1975). Most disturbing is the finding that of the total of 12 of all residents (4 per cent) who were known to have died by May 1981, seven were women. Since women were overall one third of this population, this is clearly a much higher incidence than one would expect.)

In addition during this period, 45 per cent of the cohort of 56 were known to have overdosed, 56 per cent were known to have been 'of no fixed abode' at some time, and 93 per cent were known to have misused drugs at some time after leaving City Roads.

However, there did appear to be some stabilization among some of these drug misusers over time. In April 1981, two and a half to three years after first admission to City Roads, 27 per cent were known to be abstinent at that time (this excludes those who were in prison, whose abstinence might not be voluntary); 11 per cent were known to be both drug-free and employed.

As regards outcomes, then, it appears that little change in clients' overt behaviour is evidenced dramatically in the months after admission to City Roads. The pattern continues of misusing drugs, overdosing, going to prison, being admitted to hospital, and contacting street agencies. City Roads becomes another agency to which they can turn, as indeed the vast majority do, for some support and help, even for readmission.

Over a longer period of time, a proportion do seem to begin to change, and two and a half years later, over a quarter are abstinent. However, relapses can always be expected. It is also impossible to isolate City Roads' contribution to this from that of other services and agencies, since the process is complex and the time period long. However, one can focus to some extent on City Roads' particular contribution by looking at those people who were referred on to a rehabilitation project directly from City Roads.

Between May 1978 and October 1980 inclusive, 108 people were referred on to rehabilitation by City Roads (40 per cent of all individuals admitted during that period). As regards the third objective, then, City Roads appears to have had considerable success in encouraging people to go on to further treatment and rehabilitation. However, this should be tempered by noting that of these, 39 per cent had already had some experience of rehabilitation prior to admission to City Roads. Of these 108 people referred on to rehabilitation directly by City Roads, 54 per cent were referred after their first admission, 30 per cent after their second, 9 per cent after their third, 6 per cent after their fourth, and 1 per cent after their fifth admission to City Roads. Thus most success in terms of referral to rehabilitation seems to occur after the first and second admission, which fits with what was reported in Chapter 6, where staff found that they had to begin to lower their expectations and work out other goals for their 'regular' or 'chronic attenders'.

When followed up in April 1981, the mean length of stay in rehabilitation for these people was three months. Twenty-seven per cent had stayed for 20 weeks or more at the rehabilitation project (30 people): 13 of these people were still at the rehabilitation project to which they had been referred. Of the 95 who had left, three had left after successful completion of the appropriate rehabilitation period; 18 had been discharged for breaking the rules; 72 had chosen to leave; and two had died while resident at the rehabilitation project.

Fifty of these people (46 per cent of those referred to rehabilitation) were subsequently readmitted to City Roads after leaving the rehabilitation project. In 21 cases, a further referral to rehabilitation was made by City Roads. Re-referral does not appear to be any more effective; the average length of stay on re-referral to rehabilitation was 2.2 months. Nine of these 21, who were referred a second time by City Roads, were again readmitted to City Roads after leaving the rehabilitation project.

At the time of follow-up (April 1981), in addition to the 13 people who were still at their rehabilitation project after being referred by City Roads, a further seven of the original 108 had gained admission to a rehabilitation project by being referred by another agency and a further 18 cases of these 108 had spent some time at a rehabilitation project after leaving City Roads, although not referred on that occasion by City Roads itself. Thus, almost one quarter of these residents, who had been referred once to rehabilitation by City Roads, were admitted on another occasion to rehabilitation after referral by another agency or sometimes as a result of their own unaided effort.

Of this cohort of 108 referred by City Roads to rehabilitation, 34 per cent were, in April 1981, known to be voluntarily drug free (19 per cent in a rehabilitation project; 15 per cent outside). This 34 per cent is higher than the proportion (27 per cent) found among the cohort of the first 56 residents, partly because they were people who had been referred to rehabilitation and might thus be more 'promising' but mainly because 19 per cent were still at their rehabilitation project. On the negative side, however, 37 per cent of these 'rehabilitation referrals' were known to be currently misusing drugs; 13 per cent were in institutions (two were patients in psychiatric hospitals, not rehabilitation units, and 12 were in prison). Seventeen per cent of this cohort of those referred to rehabilitation had been in prison after leaving City Roads.

These results can be compared with those of follow-up studies on opiate addicts. In one study of 108 addicts first seen between 1963 and 1965, there was a trend toward abstinence, 9 per cent at one year, 17 per cent at three years, and 23 per cent at six years (Chapple, Somekh, and Taylor 1972). Most studies indicate that the less chronic groups are more likely to become abstinent. A follow-up of 128 subjects receiving opiates from London drug clinics found that at the one-year stage, 77 per cent were attending the clinics, 21 per cent were not attending, and 2 per cent were dead. Over the years there was a consistent trend and at the six-year follow-up, 51 per cent were attending and nearly all receiving opiates, 40 per cent were not attending, and 9 per cent were dead. The 40 per cent not attending a clinic were reliably found not to be using opiates. At ten-year follow-up, 38 per cent were still attending clinics and 15 per cent were dead (Thorley, Oppenheimer, and Stimson 1977; Wille 1981).

Inputs

Those were some of the longer-term results of the City Roads project. Before coming to any conclusions about City Roads overall, we should consider the other major component in the equation: so far we have been looking at the question of output; we should also look at the inputs.

The total allowable expenditure of City Roads in 1980–81 and approved for 1981–82 was £192,746 (this included an estimated £58,000 medical and nursing costs). In addition there were running-up costs prior to opening in 1978 and further funds were raised to allow purchase of the House in 1981. Less tangible but nonetheless crucial factors are those of the time and effort devoted by all those concerned with the establishment and operation of City Roads before and during the three years of the experimental period.

The basic measure of input is the cost of a bed per week. In 1980–81, based on 12 beds, this was £309. (An assessment

Table 13   *Range of costs in various agencies per week 1980–81*

Cost of a bed per week	£
resettlement units and shelters	24.50
	26.74
	28.00
residential projects offering support and/or rehabilitation	68.95
	70.70
	75.00
	76.57
	84.07
	109.09
psychiatric hospitals (including long-stay)	115.50
	156.80
	200.00
City Roads (short-stay)	309.00
general hospitals (short-stay)	318.50
	420.00
teaching hospital (short-stay)	455.00
	595.00
local maternity hospital	595.00
private hospital – psychiatric	630.00
NHS pay bed	669.00
private hospital – psychiatric	840.00
élite private general hospital	900.00

assuming 15 beds would produce a cost of £247 per bed per week and one assuming nine beds would be £411 per week.) In 1982–83, the cost of a bed per week at City Roads, assuming 12 beds, was £341. (This compares with £97 in the same year for a place in a Metropolitan police cell overnight (i.e. £679 per week).)

However, as we have seen, the City Roads service was not only concentrated on those residents living in the house: contact was maintained with ex-residents, and advice and information was given to other community services dealing with this client group. Assuming a total resident group of 103 persons per annum, the cost per head per annum of providing a service for that group was then in 1981, £1,871 per annum or £36 per week.

These different costs at different levels of use demonstrate the obvious point that the relative cost of a service decreases the more people receive the benefit of that service, and the more a service reaches out to a greater proportion of the client group, the more effective it appears to be. The implication of this is that a reduction of costs could be produced if more individuals were contacted by the service in a given year, especially if their contact with City Roads involved a period of residence followed by contact being maintained over the rest of the year through telephone conversations, visits, letters, and even some form of outreach or detached work. Obviously a reduction of costs per bed is arrived at by increasing the occupancy of the House at any one time. For illustrative purposes, *Table 13* provides a comparison of a range of costs in other agencies and services in 1981.

The views of the clients

Before coming to a final assessment of City Roads' performance, we should pay particular attention to an area which is sometimes neglected in studies of outcomes but which may be the most revealing of all: that of the clients' own perceptions of the service.

This section is based on a series of in-depth interviews with a sample of clients in the final stages of residence at City Roads (early leavers are thus not included). The restrictions imposed on residents were generally accepted as necessary for the stable operation of the unit. No one objected to the ban on drugs and alcohol but several residents had complaints about certain rules in the House. One individual was irritated because he could not use his bedroom before the 'official' bed time: 'I was feeling tired, so I went up to bed at 8 o'clock. Then someone came and told me to get up and come downstairs. What's the point of that? They should leave you alone.'

The most common complaint had to do with restrictions on going out of the House for visits or walks. Because outings depended on staff or project volunteers being available to accompany them, residents might not leave the House for several days at a time: 'I was in all week – they said there was a "staff shortage". I told them I was really fed up, and they went into a huddle and then took me out. But it's frustrating that you can't just go up the road to buy a packet of fags.' Many of this client group are accustomed to a free-floating street life and younger residents in particular found the constraints difficult to accept. There was also some dissatisfaction expressed about the limited range of indoor activities.

Staff adopted an informal approach in appearance and language; there was little overt distance between staff and residents. Residents liked City Roads' non-institutional character: 'It's not like a mental home. It's like a hostel, not a hospital – there's no uniform and it's informal. You can just talk to people. It's a relaxed atmosphere, good for getting yourself together.' They were impressed by the fact that the staff ate with the residents and 'chipped in' with domestic work around the House. One man who, like the woman quoted above, had a background of psychiatric treatment, was pleasantly surprised by the informality: 'I thought it would be a tight security place. I didn't expect communal living'.

Despite this, the boundaries between the staff and residents were clearly recognized. Almost all the residents interviewed distinguished between 'us and them'. There were numerous expressions of admiration and even affection for individual staff members, and the ex-drug users on the staff were highly valued. Nevertheless, it was widely felt, as one man put it, that 'When it comes down to it, they're not one of us.'

There was some dissatisfaction about difficulty in building up a continuing relationship with a staff member or team: 'Staff change over too fast. People get used to a team and then they go. A week at a time for a team would be better. People could build up trust.' However, there were no complaints about receiving conflicting treatment from different staff members.

The staff group as a whole was seen as very 'accessible': 'you can talk to them day or night'; 'they don't show authority, you can talk to them easily'; 'they respond well to everyone's mood'. There were only very few cases where clients felt they had not received enough attention: 'There could have been more contact. I didn't really think anyone wanted to talk to me. They could have been a bit more sensitive to me and what I was thinking.' Such views were not at all widely held, and the general feeling was that staff were available and attentive.

But some residents found staff *too* attentive. One of the dilemmas which clearly emerged was how far the project should, on the one hand, apply pressure to residents with a view to achieving significant changes in their lifestyle or, on the other hand, avoid alienating residents through such a demanding approach and instead offer largely supportive and basic care which might produce only very limited results in terms of personal change.

A mixture of feelings were expressed on this. Some residents felt that they were being subjected to unreasonable pressure, particularly about going on to rehabilitation: 'I came here because I thought it was a place to stay and think for three weeks. I didn't realize I'd have to go on to rehabilitation.' 'I think there's too much pressure. Every day they're asking me what I want. Heavy talking freaks people out.' The casework demands of staff were too strong for some residents: 'They want you to talk all the time. I sometimes don't feel like talking, so they say, "What are you doing here if you don't talk?".' 'I feel under lots of pressure sometimes. Some of the staff keep you talking all day. It's really heavy and you can't get away.' Another feature of the style of work which some residents were unhappy about was the channelling of encouragement towards rehabilitation along a single path: 'Phoenix House was the only thing that was offered to me'; 'They decided early on that Phoenix was the place for me, and the rest of the time it was a question of manoeuvring to get me to accept that.' 'Phoenix was the only place mentioned. They continually went on about it. I might have picked Phoenix anyway if I'd wanted rehab.' This sort of pressure was not, however, everyone's experience: 'There was a mutual discussion, no pressure. I was told about different rehabs.' 'I didn't know much at all. Different types of rehab. were explained. If I objected, they offered alternatives.' On balance, it does seem that residents experienced consider- able pressure to accept rehabilitation – particularly the more rigorous programme offered by Phoenix House. From the residents' point of view, the prospect of such a sharp change in lifestyle was threatening. Their situation seemed to offer only a stark alternative – 'What choice have you got? It's rehab. or the streets.' This limited choice puts on the pressure and the need for City Roads itself adds to it. 'Even if you don't want to talk, you talk because you don't want to leave.' Being confronted at City Roads with the limited choices open to them was clearly an experience which many found difficult to accept.

However, many felt that they could see things more clearly now: 'Things are definitely clearer – that's the major thing, here.' But clarification may be disturbing as well as enlightening: 'I certainly feel clearer, but until my case history was done, I didn't realize I had so many problems.' 'I'm beginning to understand myself, beginning to see things more clearly. I learned from what staff said.' 'I'm a little bit wiser, more open. I learned how to handle myself without drugs.' 'I could talk about problems constructively, and I learned a lot about myself.' Along with this sense of clarification and insight, residents commonly experienced a mood change: 'I feel better, less depressed.' 'I feel clearer and more positive.' 'Staff put positive points to me, and pulled me out of my depression.' 'I have the feeling that I can go on to better things.' Such improvements in mental state are connected with the opportunity to talk about themselves and their problems: 'The best thing about City Roads is being able to talk to someone, to get some problems off your back.' 'Talking does help to clarify things, otherwise they just go round and round in your head.'

It is interesting to compare these responses with those found among other social work clients. Rees and Wallace, in their review of studies of social work clients' views, found that it was of 'immense importance' for people seeking help with interpersonal problems to attain 'the emotional relief of having someone to talk to and on whom they can unburden their troubles'. Such emotional unburdening, they report, 'can improve feelings of dissatisfaction, helplessness, of being alone or overwhelmed and confused by events' (Rees and Wallace 1982: 62). This experience is echoed at City Roads. One man put it in these terms: 'There has been progress. I'm starting to see that there is a future. Now I feel that the whole thing is manageable.'

For the clients with few sources of social support and emotions muted by drugs (no doubt deliberately in many cases), the opportunity to receive attention from people who seem interested and concerned and to ventilate their feelings in a secure setting, has a highly positive significance. However, a sense of wellbeing or personal enlightenment often coexisted with considerable dissatisfaction about the practical outcome of residence. The man quoted above, who felt 'wiser, more open' and so on, also stated that because no onward arrangements had been made for the end of his stay, he was 'back to square one'. Several residents were unhappy that they were being placed in interim hostel accommodation, either because there was no vacancy at the rehabilitation project chosen, or because there had not been time while at City Roads for their application to be processed. A number of residents referred on to rehabilitation projects (particularly Phoenix House), felt they were accepting only under pressure and because of lack of alternatives.

It seems then that residents valued highly those elements of the service which were directly under the control of City Roads itself – the atmosphere of the setting, the approach of the staff, and the quality of the counselling. But for this client group, brief gains at the level of emotional development are soon dissipated when after a brief two- or three-week stay they return to the streets because of lack of alternative supportive accommodation.

Conclusion

City Roads is an interesting example of an attempt to offer an alternative approach to the treatment of drug misuse – alternative, that is, to the 'British system' as embodied in the treatment clinics.

There are five features of this alternative. The approach adopted is based on social work rather than being dominated by medical orientations. The practice at City Roads rests on the view that drug misuse is a reflection of 'problems in living' rather than a symptom of disease (a 'craving' or 'compulsion' of physical or pharmacological origin). The emphasis is on abstinence, self-help, and self-responsibility. Drug misusers are seen as capable of exercising control over their lives: they are not classed as passive 'victims'. Being 'professional' is an important feature of the workers' attitudes. This implies aiming to maintain a high standard of care. This professional approach should however be combined with a 'closeness', a similarity of style and status between the workers and the clients. There is an implied contrast here with the wide gap existing between highly paid, high status consultants and 'junkies' as found in the conventional system.

In setting up this alternative, special service, it was hoped also to find out what were the specific needs of 'chaotic' drug misusers and respond accordingly. Although ultimately one might hope that they would respond to treatment, that they would be cured of their problem of dependence on drugs, more realistically, in the short term, it was hoped to reduce the pressure on A and E departments caused by this group and to be seen to be doing something to meet the needs of homeless drug misusers, neglect of which might give rise to scandals.

These hopes reflected an awareness that the existing system of treatment and rehabilitation was not effective in treating all the patients it dealt with. The existence of 'chronic' cases presented a problem for these services especially once disillusion with maintenance prescribing became more general.

Ghodse's articles had also indicated that the young drug misusers at A and E departments were presently out of contact with existing services. The hope was that faced with the crisis of overdosing they might be more receptive to changing their lives and could be deterred from joining the ranks of chronic drug misusers.

Those who worked in the street agencies and others familiar with the question of drug misuse were less sanguine in their expectations. The possibility of cure in the short term was not expected. For them, the emphasis was on a service which could act *quickly* at moments of severe stress and could deal with immediate needs. The needs of clients were seen as for sheltered care, community social work, and basic medical attention, including detoxification – in short, support and encouragement, which might lead on to change in those who were receptive, would reroute those who had become accidentally caught up in drug misuse (but were relatively new to the scene), but would act principally to keep people alive, supporting them until they eventually 'matured' out of drugs misuse. In addition, the service would be able to treat those misusing a variety of drugs, especially barbiturates, since, being more flexible and not tied to the fixed concepts explicit in the Misuse of Drugs Act and the historical period in which the clinics were created, it could deal with the problems as they appeared on the scene.

Those who put forward the latter view saw the function of a crisis intervention unit as part of a much wider network of services, which would include a range of supportive accommodation and day centres, and some sheltered workshops, as well as the rehabilitation projects, DTCs, psychiatric units, and prisons which were, and are, the main services and institutions dealing with this population.

City Roads clearly filled one gap in the existing provision, being a short-stay, crisis-intervention unit, with particular interest in multiple drug misusers, in which barbiturate misuse played a part. But necessarily and predictably, there were difficulties for a service trying to operate within a system characterized by a shortage of places to which to refer people. The emphasis on a service which would act immediately, assess the needs of clients, and refer them to appropriate services, assumed that it could work effectively by rerouting people found in inappropriate services, such as A and E departments, and sending them off to other more appropriate services. Access to services could thus be improved for clients, using the special expertise of professional staff. However, in the event, City Roads had to act largely alone. Its effects were therefore severely limited since its function was to be part of a wider system of interrelated services, which would include day centres, supportive accommodation, and a greater variety of rehabilitation projects. It would therefore be unfair to judge its effectiveness as an alternative model in these terms, since without the other elements in the proposed system it could not be expected to function in the way originally conceived.

We have seen that the clients who used City Roads are people who use other services and have used other services for many years. Some began their career as a 'client' of the social services in childhood, when they were put into care or sent to approved schools. City Roads staff soon concluded that they did not have 'special needs', characteristic of a sub-sub-group – 'the chaotic, homeless, multiple drug misuser especially prone to overdose and use barbiturates and go to A and E departments'. On the contrary, their drug misuse was a form of secondary deviance or secondary handicap, which had been acquired as a result of primary problems in living, which were very similar to the problems of many other people with whom practitioners in the health and social services are familiar (see Lemert 1967; Leach and Wing 1980). They did not need any special attention specific to drug misusers other than that their career as a drug misuser had lasted for many years and had thus by that time become an integral part of their social and personal identity. Change could not be expected to come about overnight.

Given the lack of facilities to which to refer people, and given the assumption that these clients were basically inadequate in coping with problems of living, the project soon came to place great emphasis on encouraging people to go on to rehabilitation. Within the rehabilitation projects, Phoenix House was the one with which they built up very close links, and clients who went there seemed to do better than those referred elsewhere. The emphasis then became one of adapting the clients to the services available. They were encouraged to change, to fit themselves into the mould appropriate to referral to a concept-type rehabilitation programme. The model of care developed at City Roads, which formed a crucial part of the training of new staff and of the philosophy of the House (one on which City Roads' own co-ordination and sense of identity came to depend), was seen as appropriate to *all* clients using the project. In practice, it could not be applied rigorously because clients themselves injected resistance and unpredictable elements into the interaction and because not all staff were equally consistent in sticking to it. But the goal was there and a crucial part of the programme. This worked for those who could conform to the programme, especially for those on whom *other pressures* to conform were much greater, like pressure from the courts, pressure due to lack of alternative accommodation, or their physical condition. Others who did not or would not fit into the model or on whom pressures to change were less, left early, came only once or at most twice.

However as we have seen, during the second part of the three-year experimental period, staff began to realize that rehabilitation was not the sole answer. Since the average length of stay in rehabilitation for their ex-residents was about three months, they began to find their 'best customers' or 'star residents' (the ones who had fitted into the mould and had gone on to rehabilitation) coming back, after failing to stay at the rehabilitation project to which they had been referred. Policy and practice changed so that City Roads itself began to 'treat' people through offering more intensive counselling.

Over time, then, there had been a shift away from the original focus on basic care and offering an immediate response. Instead of providing a warm, supporting environment, a more intense atmosphere had been created. Meetings and discussions about how to treat people and the counselling sessions took priority at times over the response to requests for admission. The emphasis on therapy rather than care united the staff and co-ordinated the disciplines working there but was not entirely consistent with the original aims. The vast majority of the clients used the place only once or twice and stayed for relatively short periods of time. This might imply that City Roads was acting as an acute unit for cases of severe distress, but this was often not the case. People who were very confused, especially if they were intoxicated, because they were felt not to be in a fit state to use the service properly, were turned away. The same pattern of use might on the other hand seem consistent with the work of an 'observation and assessment unit', where the emphasis would be on the *differential* assessment of needs. But we have already seen that, partly due to the lack of variety in outlet points and strategies, the project was acting more as a persuasion than an assessment unit. Using City Roads began to be conditional on a willingness to talk about change and accept the idea of rehabilitation.

The City Roads project can then be seen to have moved through three phases in which the emphasis in practice changed in response to the problems with which it was faced. First, the main orientation was towards assessing the needs of residents and referring them on to appropriate services. This was soon discarded as the lack of a variety of services was realized. The second phase concentrated on applying a programme or model of care to residents. Those who got through the three-week stay would go on to rehabilitation suitably prepared. The third phase involved an attempt to treat people at City Roads itself. There was an increase in the intensity of counselling sessions, the aim being not to refer on after one or two stays at City Roads but, eventually and gradually, to bring about sufficient change in clients that they would be ready to accept the need to change and would go on to rehabilitation and stay there. Criticisms were voiced of this kind of development, especially where it influenced the selection of residents for admission to City Roads, and was the view of the research report written at the end of the three-year experimental period. The criticisms coincided with a period of reassessment and reflection which went on within the project, culminating in the resignation of the Director. (There were a number of other issues involved at this time as well as that of the drift away from the original goals, such as the insecurity brought on by lack of confirmed future funding, styles of leadership, staff turnover, the departure of the original Deputy Director and then of his replacement, and the end of the research exercise.) With the crisis that followed, the opportunity was taken to 'return to basics' to give more emphasis to the goals of basic care and to institute other changes in the House, such as the expanded role of the activities worker. With the arrival of a fresh contingent of new staff, the project then entered a fourth phase where it now is.

PART THREE
Barriers to Policy Implementation

9 Managing an Innovation

In spite of these attempts at 'rational planning' and 'rational assessment', what matters in the end are the crucial decisions taken about management and finance. And there, other forces come into play.

Management is about decision making at a number of levels: day-to-day operational management, which involves managing those who deliver the care and raises the question of leadership; management in the sense of managing a budget – the issues of accountability and executive responsibility; and management as the planning and co-ordinating of services, in which the question of innovation and change figures. The problems of managing innovation are not, of course, peculiar to the voluntary sector. Indeed, the obstacles to change in the statutory sector are often enormous. In the NHS, for example, professional self-interest and lack of clearly defined management responsibilities can inhibit change and innovation. No wonder then that often the only hope for some experimentation is seen to lie in initiatives from the voluntary sector. But even in the voluntary sector, as we have seen, attempts to innovate are fraught with obstacles. In the case of City Roads, as in so many other cases, the problems were not confined to the process of getting the experiment off the ground. The survival problems were equally serious. In taking up these issues, we shall deal with the management of City Roads at all levels.

Day-to-day operational management

The Director and his Deputy were responsible for the day-to-day operational management at City Roads. We have already seen in Chapters 5 and 6 the crucial role played by the Deputy Director in developing the treatment philosophy, in providing continuity of care and in moulding the attitude and behaviour of new staff. He did this with the support and partial involvement of the first Director. These two clearly saw themselves as managers of both the staff and the delivery of care. The Director was quite explicit that a project like City Roads, under constant pressure from clients and others, needed strong leadership, and the structure, being clearly hierarchical, allowed for such leadership to be practised. However, the formal structure, as outlined in the Operational Document, did not specify how this leadership should be practised.

The style of leadership adopted by the first Director and his Deputy showed an awareness of two crucial aspects of their managerial role: the first, which we have already shown they performed admirably, was that of guiding the staff; the second and equally important aspect was that of offering *support*. Right from the beginning, they were acutely aware that the staff would need constant support and supervision, and supervision here did not mean control but supportive counselling. This supervision was done in formal one-to-one sessions, although it was sometimes felt that these did not take place often enough. However, the informal support and advice which the Director and his Deputy offered constantly in the day-to-day work was at least as important. They were always keeping an eye on the workers and ready to offer help if needed. They succeeded in combining the caring and controlling aspects of their managerial role in a way which enabled workers to perform well, making them feel secure, and at the same time enabled the organization to survive. This is remarkable simply because, in all too many cases, in both the statutory and the voluntary sectors, one of these two aspects of management is missing. In voluntary organizations, there is a tendency to be 'anti-authoritarian' and subscribe to collective or no leadership. In this, no doubt well meaning, attempt to be democratic, such organizations often find themselves unable to cope with crises and may end up offering neither guidance nor support to their workers. In the statutory sector, certainly in the NHS, the problem is in a way the opposite, although often with the same effects. Managers in the health service, be they administrators, nurses, or doctors, often tend to neglect the supportive aspect of their role and over-emphasize their controlling function, leaving little opportunity for their subordinates to discuss their problems or develop their own ideas.

As already mentioned, towards the end of the three-year period, problems began to emerge at City Roads. These problems were not a direct effect of changes in leadership but were more to do with increasing competition for promotion as a result of staff turnover. However, these problems might have been solved, had the leadership remained the same. The new Director had a lot of work to do in getting to know the organization. In addition, he was faced with the problem of securing future funding. It is not surprising that the pressures on him spread to the rest of the staff group who began to show signs of uneasiness and dissatisfaction. Problems did not really surface during the three-year period of the research, because of the continuity provided by the Deputy Director, who did not leave until the end of this period. It would be unfair to discuss the process that went on after the research had finished, because we were not there to analyse it. On the other hand, we should note that in the following two years the organization went through several changes in leadership, at the Director as well as Deputy Director levels. City Roads experienced its own crises which indicated that whoever are the leaders of this unit, it is important that they see themselves as managers in the sense we have been discussing.

Over the three years, changes took place which may or may not be interpreted as to do with increasing 'professionalization'. There were two types of changes: formalization of the structure and procedures; and increasingly trade unionist behaviour. In many ways, City Roads merely went through a process which most new organizations go through. When it first opened, all the staff, directorate included, were new, and everybody felt equally uncertain as to what would happen once the doors were opened to clients. To some extent they were in a trial-and-error situation; procedures developed gradually and everybody learned them at the same time. Although the first year was one of uncertainty, it was also one of stability as regards the staff group. The turnover of staff turned out to be less than expected. On average, the team workers stayed for 16 months, and it was only during the second year that a considerable proportion of the team workers were new. It was at this stage that procedures began to be written down as guidelines to newcomers, although the real turning-point did not come until the Director was replaced. This happened towards the end of the second year, in February 1980. Clearly, the new Director needed comprehensive knowledge about what was going on. He needed to clarify the rules and regulations, many of which had been more or less unspecified, unwritten norms. One example of this was the role of the senior nurse. From the beginning, one of the nurses had been designated senior nurse. She was supposed to be the link between the City

Roads' nurses and the AHA. However this link was considered a formality which did not affect the everyday work. When the first senior nurse left, shortly before the new Director took up his post, she told the research team that she did not see her role as in any way different from that of the other nurses and that really there was no need for a senior nurse. However what happened was that a role was found for the new senior nurse, her duties were specified in writing and included, apart from things like checking and ordering equipment, involvement in the interviewing of candidates for new posts. This fact became an issue of contention towards the end of the third year, when the social work team workers demanded that they too be represented on the interviewing panel for appointment of new staff. The Director maintained that the social work element was sufficiently represented through the directorate, and that the senior nurse was involved because the Director as well as the Deputy Director were social workers. Had the Deputy Director been a nurse, this would not have become an issue.

The demand for representation on the interviewing panel was only one example of the changing attitudes and behaviour of the team workers. During the first 18 months or so, the atmosphere was characterized by goodwill and co-operation based on what was seen as a general consensus of interests. The style of leadership was an important factor. The Director was an exceedingly popular figure. He was friendly and caring, and the staff did not mind following him, which is what they did. The possibility of joining a trade union was mentioned by one of the team workers at an early stage, but the idea was strongly rejected by the Director and everybody forgot about it. They got on with their work and often worked extra time without pay. Attendance at the monthly staff meetings, which were supposed to be the forum for discussion of policies, was extremely low and interest in the affairs of the management committee was so poor that it was not always possible to find a staff representative to attend their meetings. But this spirit of complacency and consensus began to fade as the organization changed. The processes of formalization and change of leadership have already been mentioned as contributory factors but, added to this, the staff turnover gave opportunities for internal promotion. This had the effect of introducing a strong element of competition among the staff, which in turn increased the pressure of work and level of anxiety. Under such circumstances, it is not surprising that the staff became trade unionist. They joined a trade union and started to make demands, for example for compensation for working overtime and for more say in a number of areas.

This process was really only in its initial stages by the time the research was ending, but what was interesting about it, in relation to our discussion in Chapter 5, is that the term 'professional' was being used increasingly by the staff in connection with making their various demands. A typical example can be found in the following statement made by one of the social work team leaders: 'We must emphasize that this is a professional service; we can't be messed about without having a proper say in things or work hard without being properly rewarded for it.' When, in our earlier discussion, we raised the question of whether the City Roads approach could be said to be professional, we were primarily considering whether there was a particular body of knowledge or skills behind their work. The question of which occupations 'qualify' as professions has been much debated by sociologists, as well as by the professions themselves or those who claim to be professions (see for example Carr-Saunders 1928; Etzioni 1969). Much of this debate, in our view, is rather fruitless because, as Johnson has pointed out, professionalism is a piece of ideology which is often used to promote the interests of the professionals themselves (Johnson 1972). It is used by occupations to obtain or preserve independence and influence and to prevent outsiders from making judgments about them. This is, perhaps, most clear in the cases of nurses and social workers, whose status as professionals is constantly being challenged.

At City Roads, the term professional was originally used in the sense of offering specialist, expert care to a particular client group. As time went by, however, the concept became increasingly to be used in a way which seemed to have the interests of the workers in mind, tending to leave the clients outside the discussion.

The role of the management committee

As mentioned in Chapter 2, the actual initiative to formulate a proposal and enter negotiations came from SCODA, and most of the interested parties at that time came from the voluntary agencies. The majority of the members of the Steering Committee were from the voluntary sector, although for strategic reasons a number of people were there as representatives of statutory bodies, like the DHSS, LBA, and Home Office.

Until 1977, the Steering Committee met at irregular intervals and not very frequently. The meetings were informal gatherings, mainly to discuss progress in relation to premises and funding negotiations. By the middle of 1977, the realization of the project had become a distinct possibility and meetings became regular and formalized in the sense that officers were elected and meetings were minuted. At this time, the composition of the Steering Committee also began to change. Gradually, some of the voluntary workers withdrew and more members were recruited from the statutory sector. By the time City Roads opened, when the Committee became a Management Committee, there were three representatives from the voluntary sector, including the SCODA member, and nine representatives from the statutory sector: four from the NHS, the Divisional Nursing Officer, Community, Camden and Islington AHA, the consultant in charge of UCH A and E Department, a social worker from UCH DTC, and the nursing officer from the Middlesex Hospital's A and E Department; one from the probation service, one from the social services and three observers, one each from the DHSS, the Home Office, and the LBA. In addition to this, the staff (the consultant psychiatrist and visiting medical officer plus two staff members elected by the team workers), and the research team were represented, and the treasurer and the solicitor were also members.

There were political as well as practical reasons for this change in the composition of the Committee. The AHA had to be involved, because the nurses at City Roads were formally appointed by this authority. More significantly though, City Roads was keen to establish itself as a service widely accepted in the statutory field. The unit was expected to be working with a range of statutory as well as voluntary agencies and, indeed, to try to improve links between the two sectors. Also, there was the problem of future funding to be considered. At the end of the three-year experimental period, others had to take over the bill from the DHSS: the groundwork for this was already being prepared in the form of recruitment to the Management Committee.

This key function of the Committee was clearly reflected in its composition. The concern was overwhelmingly with financial and fund-raising issues, with the continued survival of City Roads rather than operational matters. Towards the end of the second year there was a short spell of rising concern with operational issues; some members felt that not enough attention was paid to these. Consequently, three additional members were recruited: a social worker with special expertise in the area of supervision and two representatives from rehabilitation projects. However one of these withdrew shortly afterwards, because he left his post in the rehabilitation project he was representing, and he was not replaced. The social work adviser resigned from the Committee after a year, expressing his disillusionment with the work of the Committee. He felt that its preoccupation was predominantly with funding problems, and that in any case the staff were not particularly interested in discussing operational policy matters with the Management Committee.

So the preoccupations of the Steering Committee had been mainly with raising funds and finding premises rather than with any detailed operational policies, the specification of which they preferred to leave to the staff. And after City Roads opened, the Management Committee continued to focus the main part of its attention on the 'survival' aspect. Negotiating the extension of the lease and raising the money for the purchase of the house took much time and effort. Also, whereas, before City Roads opened, the policy had been to 'keep a low profile' regarding publicity, once the project was established and running smoothly, the Committee embarked on a publicity campaign, bearing in mind that they needed all the friends they could get if City Roads was to survive beyond the three years. The funding issue was never off the agenda for two reasons. First, negotiations with the DHSS about adjustments in the budget were ongoing throughout almost the entire period. Salary increases had to be negotiated, as did an increase in the nursing establishment, whereby the DHSS agreed to fund an additional nurse. During the third year, the posts of care assistants or second team members, as they came to be called, were upgraded to social work status. Again, this meant raising more money from the DHSS. Second, the funding issue came increasingly important as time went by and the future of City Roads was still uncertain. Because so many different bodies were involved as potential contributors, the process of negotiation was slow and time-consuming.

Throughout this period, certain members of the Committee were regularly involved in the process of staff recruitment. It was through their involvement that contacts with the staff were most closely maintained. Indeed, when eventually conflicts within the staff group surfaced and the Management Committee did become involved in internal affairs, one of the main issues of conflict was in fact the process of staff recruitment.

Operational policy matters were not totally ignored, however. As already mentioned, certain new members were recruited to remedy what the Management Committee felt had been neglected. A Practice Sub-Committee was formed to discuss policies and practices. For a short period, this Committee was quite active, debating some formalization of the nursing structure and the introduction of opiate detoxification. Finally, the Committee held one meeting, attended by a few of its members and a majority of the staff, to consider the recommendations of the Interim Report produced by the research team. There was very little discussion of the report. The Director went through the recommendations and informed the Committee that some of them were in the process of being implemented, others were to be considered by the staff, and others had been rejected as inappropriate. After this the meetings became very infrequent, and in effect the Practice Sub-Committee ceased to function. It was difficult to get the members to meet, and the senior staff felt no need to involve the Management Committee in operational matters. In fact, the Director preferred to be left alone to get on with the day-to-day work. He interpreted any interest shown in the details of the internal affairs of the unit as undue interference.

Did the Management Committee fail to fulfil its role, or was the somewhat unsuccessful attempt to look at practices within the unit 'undue interference'? What is the model of management in a case like City Roads?

Formally, the Management Committee was ultimately responsible for 'the proper management of the project' and members should be concerned to see the proper development of the work of the project (Operational Document). How this responsibility might be exercised is of course open to interpretation. It could be argued that a Committee of people whose involvement is very part-time should leave detailed operational issues to the full-time, paid professional staff. If City Roads had been part of the NHS, for example part of the district community services, there would have been a number of professional line managers to whom the City Roads staff would have been accountable and who would have been exercising their responsibility on behalf of the health authority, whose members are part-timers in the same way as the City Roads Management Committee. One of the functions of professional managers above the operational level in the NHS is to co-ordinate a range of services. City Roads, being financially independent, was strictly speaking not formally part of any overall service provision in the same way as, for example, a hospital is part of the health care provision of a district or region as a whole. Yet the project was not working in isolation. It was very much part of a network of services and aimed to improve these services by relieving them, advising them, and co-operating in work with individual clients. The Management Committee, by being able to have representatives from various relevant services, was the body through which this coordination of services could at least have been attempted. The Committee, however, never really became involved in this aspect of the work, partly because it lacked representation from practitioners in other key services and partly because financial issues took up so much of the time of the active members that they never really had enough time to concentrate on operational matters.

The first Director of City Roads resigned at the end of 1979. Although he had private, family reasons for leaving, he did indicate that he would have liked the Management Committee to have shown more interest in the operation of the project and offer him more support, but that this had not been possible because of the continuous struggle for the survival of the project, and the time spent on funding issues. There was for example never much time to discuss the Director's report, which was usually the last item on the agenda. His successor seemed less worried about this and preferred the Management to concentrate on financial issues and the survival of City Roads.

It was perhaps inevitable that the Management would be preoccupied with securing the future of the project. The new Director, who himself put a lot of time and effort into this, had an enormous amount of support from the Committee. It was understandable that operational matters became secondary. The project seemed to be running smoothly; clients came and went, and the staff seemed content. The effort to take an interest in the operation of the project by setting up a Practice Sub-Committee failed mainly because Management Committee members were not well enough informed about matters to be able to contribute to a fruitful discussion. It was not that information was not available: meetings were held on the premises, so members had plenty of opportunity to talk to the staff and clients and look at the records; and after the second year, a detailed interim research report was available. But most of the members did not really see it as their role to get involved with the running of the project. However, as mentioned, towards the end of the three-year period disagreements within the staff group became manifest. By the fourth year tensions in the staff group were so strong that the Management Committee had to become involved. It may well be that an earlier involvement by the Management Committee on a more routine basis might have prevented events from developing so far that the Director handed in his resignation.

Future funding

Although City Roads gained the praise and approval of clients, other agencies, eminent specialists in drug dependence and accident and emergency care, the LBA Working Party on Addictions, the research report, DHSS Homelessness and Addictions 'client-group', and many others, these came cheaply compared to gaining approval for grant applications for future funding.

It is striking how much of an uphill task it was to get the short-stay, crisis-intervention service opened in the first place in spite of the continuing and indeed growing extent of drug misuse and the clear evidence of the lack of such a service. Once established as a three-year 'pump-priming' exercise by the DHSS in collaboration with the LBA, the project was continually harassed by financial problems. As we have seen, because of the delay in opening, the lease on the house came up for renewal during the experimental period and only heroic efforts by the Management Committee and the second Director eventually succeeded in attracting sufficient funds (£77,000) from charitable foundations to buy the house. But there was no time for rejoicing, as the next obstacle was to secure the future funding of the project once the experimental period finished in May 1981. Constant lobbying and pressure, using the media at times, together with special efforts expended by civil servants in the DHSS to win over Permanent Secretaries and Secretaries of State, elicited short-term extensions of funding but without a final commitment being forthcoming from the main potential funders.

A basic problem was that the provision of services for this client group became a political football between local and national authorities, principally between local government and central government and between Alexander Fleming House (central DHSS) and the regional and district health authorities. Because the issue coincided with the imposition of cuts in local authorities and a squeeze on expenditure in the health service and coincided with the reorganization of the NHS during which the middle level of area health authorities was abolished, there was a general unwillingness to accept responsibility for extra expenditure and a good deal of confusion as to where responsibility should fall.

City Roads was an innovation set very much within the parameters of existing health and social care provision. It was not going to rock the boat too much. It was a moderate innovation, guided by 'new orthodox' views in professional social work and psychiatry regarding the treatment and care of problem drug takers. This professional input and the great care exercised in ensuring responsible management and financial control (the product largely of the work of the co-ordinator of SCODA) ensured the build-up of a high degree of respect and trust from all quarters for the project. Yet it was still very difficult to secure a commitment to future funding. With so much in its favour, City Roads still had to fight for survival. How much harder then it must be for more unorthodox ventures to succeed.

The main difficulties had to do with the underlying problem of providing services for 'special needs' especially where the client group does not fall neatly into a particular administrative catchment area. A project offering a package of services designed to cater to a number of needs could not be seen as totally the responsibility of any one state administrative structure. Was City Roads mainly health care or social work or housing? Were the residents mainly Londoners or migrants? If Londoners, were they from south of the River, or north? Which borough or district could be seen as their 'parish of settlement' to take responsibility for these modern paupers of the 1980s? Few local politicians interested in winning votes would be prepared to advocate expenditure on such an unpopular cause.

The solution was to view City Roads as a joint responsibility. The bargaining centred on the relative contributions of the various authorities involved. Central government was inter-ested in securing a commitment, even a token one, to the principle of joint funding and joint responsibility at the local level. They recognized that the times were unpropitious, but that in the current political climate some recognition of the principle of local funding is a necessary, non-negotiable starting-point in discussions. The local levels would have liked to resist this, seeing it as the thin end of the wedge. They hoped, however, to exchange a paper commitment to local funding for some real concessions on central financial support, even if this was earmarked or tabbed in some way at first.

One factor seemed crucial in ensuring that negotiations about City Roads would be taken seriously by the officials in the health authorities. This was critical in lifting City Roads over the major hurdle from being yet one more noisy pressure group, hammering on the doors of the committee meetings, to actually sitting down at the table with the officials and having the issue of City Roads' funding placed high on the agenda for discussion. We refer to the sponsorship of the LBA and the DHSS. The LBA had participated in the funding of the experimental project from the start and had maintained its commitment from year to year in spite of cuts elsewhere. However in addition, key figures in the administrative and representative structure took a particular interest in City Roads and promoted consideration of the project actively. Theirs was an especially useful intervention in calling and arranging a meeting of the potential funders who ranged from the Home Office to the GLC to the LBA to the DHSS and the four Thames Regional Health Authorities. There seems to have been an element of good fortune here in the active concern of the chairman of the LBA Working Party on Drug Addiction and Alcoholism and the support he received from the administrators advising on grants and social services, one of whom had previously been on the City Roads management committee. A similar input came from the other party to the original funding of the experimental project, civil servants at the DHSS. They succeeded in pressing successive Secretaries of State to take a special interest in this area. Both Sir George Young and his successor Geoffrey Finsberg were won over to support for the project in principle. The main impetus for future funding continued to lie with the sponsorship of the original financiers of the project, the LBA and the DHSS, rallying at the last minute, so it seemed to the distressed City Roads Management Committee. These officials needed of course to vindicate a venture to which they had already committed considerable public funds and attention.

Geoffrey Finsberg, while impressed by these arguments, decided to ask for the independent advice of a man he had known for some years and whose abilities he respected, a retired Director of Finance in a London Borough. The research report had said a lot about the project but it was written by academic sociologists, and it did not deal with the precise issue of 'value for money', the current shibboleth in state administration.

Once in contact with City Roads, the adviser too became impressed with the work that went on there. His report came down in favour of the project, although recommending some changes in management, and was particularly influential, in that it gave a 'seal of approval' from a respected administrator and expert in the finance and management of state services. His private view was that the project should be a statutory responsibility. There was, he felt, no justification for leaving it to the voluntary sector where it had continually to spend time begging for money.

The purpose of his surveillance of the project was, in the words of his remit from the DHSS, to help the management committee of City Roads 'to satisfy the potential future funders as to the financial control of the project and that all reasonable economies which may be necessary to ensure their support have been fully examined and where practicable are being put into effect'. The key problem for City Roads was thus highlighted: its relative expense compared to other services for this disadvantaged and low-status group. Was it really necessary to have a 24-hour, round-the-clock service? Was it really necessary to have three staff on each team, would not two be enough, at least during the night? These were the sort of questions that concerned the potential funders, as they had bothered DHSS during the experimental period. Gradually, however, it was accepted that the service did require a relatively high level of resources if it was to be a good and useful innovation. If it were run on the cheap, it would cease to be 'City Roads' and become more like a night shelter or a long-stay psychiatric ward.

The adviser was enthusiastic about City Roads. He praised the 'calibre of the management and senior Directing staff and the general approach to the whole area of finance'. Although food costs seemed high, this was understandable because of the need to provide 'compensatory diets' for 'undernourished' people. He commented on the shabbiness of the house. (Indeed the change in the appearance of the house over three years was marked as the residents stamped their impression on the house and furniture and little attention was devoted to upkeep – due partly, but not entirely, to lack of cash.) He also commented on the overcrowding in the office.

In the summer of 1982, City Roads could envisage 47 per cent of its future funding being relatively secure, coming from the LBA (17 per cent), Supplementary Benefits (12 per cent), the GLC (10 per cent), and the Home Office (8 per cent). The missing 53 per cent had to be secured from the local health authorities. South East Thames RHA continually refused to

agree to participation. Their view was that they already provided a reasonable measure of local services comparable with
that at City Roads. Here they referred especially to provision at
Tooting Bec Hospital, Bexley Hospital, and Bethlem Royal
Hospital for detoxification and rehabilitation and to the
existence of the Maudsley Hospital and its offshoots in their
catchment area. They were not convinced by the research
report. Although they found it methodologically sound and
useful in helping the process of coming to policy decisions,
they added mysteriously that it did not deal with the issues in
NHS terms (see Appendix A). Many of these criticisms were
probably devices to explain away a fundamental unwillingness
to become involved with funding a service for an unpopular
client group who did not seem to have close ties with the
geographical area covered by South East Thames RHA.

Similarly, North West Thames RHA were at first reluctant to
participate in funding City Roads, although they had less
justification than South East Thames in that more of the
residents and agencies helped by City Roads were located in
their geographical area.

A key suggestion from the adviser, which was later implemented, largely following the initiative of the LBA, was for a
funders committee to be set up, representing the LBA, health
authorities, the Home Office, and the GLC. This funders committee would have to give approval to the budget in total and
settle the appropriate split of costs. He proposed too that OSM
practitioners should be asked to review the shift system and
that experienced finance professionals should be asked to sit on
the management committee. This suggestion indicates the
current concern about financial accountability in state services,
as much as any expectation that such members could actually
reduce the costs of the project. Authorities find it reassuring to
know that finance professionals are overseeing a project, sometimes together with social researchers, and such expertise
would relieve the burden on other Management Committee
members. Throughout the experimental period, this burden
had fallen mainly on the shoulders of the SCODA co-ordinator,
who was the key person ensuring the financial viability of the
project (supported by an honorary treasurer and the director
and administrator of the project).

So the adviser was satisfied with the budgetary and expenditure control of the project and with the security of these public
funds. The DHSS welcomed his report but stressed that their
responsibility was for pump-priming funding and that they

could not become involved in long-term funding, which was the responsibility of local levels. However, exceptionally, in this case, they were prepared to make a further contribution dependent on expressions of good will and cash support from other funders. This underpinning would be temporary only and the DHSS hoped to be able to withdraw gracefully within a specified time.

A contrary view expressed by SCODA was that there should be a continuing national component from the DHSS, since City Roads acted partly as an advisory service and since its contribution to the drugs field extended beyond simply providing a London service, by aiding other services nationally through training and advice. Others in the RHAs supported this view and pointed out that London as a metropolitan area was a magnet for problems produced elsewhere. This issue should not be overemphasized however: as we showed in Chapter 6, the client group at City Roads were not recent migrants to the capital.

It was generally recognized that City Roads had, through its experimental role, contributed to understanding of the drugs problem and to thinking about different ways of delivering services to drug misusers. This had been, and was, of benefit nationally. It was indeed because of this that the DHSS had continued to underpin support for City Roads well beyond the three-year experimental period. The RHAs had delayed discussion of City Roads partly because their time was dominated by questions of cutting expenditure (the Thames RHAs being particularly affected by government 'cuts') and because there was an internal game going on as to whether the issue should be discussed at regional or district level. One major explanation for the differences in the attitudes of the different regions relates to the attitude of the respective regional medical officers. Where these were favourable and involved, as in South West Thames RHA, where the RMO was himself a member of the Advisory Council on the Misuse of Drugs, decisions were positive and made relatively quickly.

Some overt, positive backing for City Roads in 1982–83 (North East Thames RHA offering £25,000 and South West Thames RHA suddenly coming up with £35,000) brought about a definite shift in the proceedings. It was much harder for the others to drag their feet. The DHSS, encouraged by these signs of commitment, felt able to promise funds for the years up to 1985. The GLC were steadily increasing their contribution, including contributions to capital expenditure to improve the

house, and the Home Office increased its contribution (to
£14,000 at the time of writing). The DHSS felt then that City
Roads had a real prospect of becoming viable and so felt able to
allocate £85,000 in 1982–83 reducing to two-thirds of this,
£56,000 in 1983–84 and to one-third of this, £28,000 in 1984–85.

However, for 1983/4, a deficit of £52,000 remained on medical
costs previously channelled through the budget of the AHA. At
a later funders committee meeting, the GLC Health Panel
agreed to make a recommendation to the GLC Grants Sub-
Committee for £25,000 and the DHSS and the Home Office
would contribute the remaining £27,000. For 1984/5, the North
West Thames RHA agreed to grant £25,000, the South West
Thames RHA to increase its grant to £36,000, and North East
Thames RHA to increase its contribution to £30,000. The GLC
Grants Sub-Committee would continue to fund and might
increase the £25,000 they gave in 1983/4 and in addition, the
LBA, GLC Housing, and the Home Office were increasing their
grants by an inflation-linked amount.

For City Roads, however, the future continues to be uncertain, as over each of the coming years it has to persuade the
local health and social welfare authorities to increase their
contributions substantially to make up the difference as central
government withdraws its support. This has been made even
more difficult by further squeezes on the expenditure of the
four Thames RHAs, the intentions of central government to
abolish the GLC and the breaking away from the LBA of Labour
boroughs to form the Association of London Authorities.
Given the continuing concern about the increase in drug
misuse, City Roads is even more relevant today than when it
opened in 1978 but, as more services go to the wall, its situation
remains precarious.

The doubts that concern the funding authorities, are its
relatively high cost; whether the benefits derived by the clients
can be classified as to do mainly with health or with social
welfare; and the residential qualifications of the clients, which
is their 'parish of origin'? No doubt these arguments will
continue to structure the debate about funding, as each
authority tries to reduce its expenditure and decide on
priorities within its total allocation. The struggle to persuade
will get harder each year. In the end decisions will be made
through the exercise of power. For success, sufficient
influential and powerful people would have to be won over to
the support of City Roads, especially within the administrative
structures, since much of the debate goes on in committee

rooms and behind closed doors, where officials in effect dispense public funds of great size as they judge fit. The support of professionals, experts and influential figures will continue to be much more important than any hard evidence that City Roads might be able to accrue. Information and knowledge play a part but certainly not the sole nor even major one. Building up trust, respect, good will, and active support are the essential ingredients for success, where a project chooses to look for its main revenue to the patronage of the state administration. City Roads, as a client of the state, finds itself ironically subject to similar pressures to conform to expectations and modify its behaviour to the demands of the situation as it places on its own clients.

10   Social Responses to the Drugs Problem

'When dealing with drug use and dependency, one always seems to be behind the times.' (A. Hamid Ghodse)

Introduction

We began this account of the City Roads project by posing some questions which that experiment might be able to answer: How best to provide services for the 'chaotic' problem drug taker? Why is the improvement of services such an uphill task? What should be the role of the voluntary sector? What should be the role of social work? We have shown that the answers to these questions are complex and there is no point in our repeating here what has been dealt with at length in the preceding chapters. However in the detailed experience of City Roads are contained some lessons for the national debate about an appropriate social response to the current drugs problem. And here it is important to note that 'chaotic' problem drug takers are not a distinct species, but perhaps only exhibit in greater concentration characteristics shared with other problem drug takers and with drug takers as a whole, to which category most people in modern Britain belong.

Some guidelines for policy and practice have emerged. In providing services for problem drug takers, ease of access is of paramount importance. Services are needed which respond quickly and immediately to a request for care and which are prepared to keep trying, to keep taking people back. That is, services which do not erect barriers to entry, requiring qualifications for treatment, such as 'residents' permits' or other such tokens. We need services which aim to care for and treat the whole person, using the skills of a wide range of disciplines.

To tackle the problem, crisis management alone is insufficient. A crisis such as that facing Britain today, produced by an imbalance between the size of the problem and the resources available, can provide an opportunity for radical change, or for just patching up, or can be neglected and avoided, leading to further deterioration. Treating the drug problem alone is not enough. It is necessary to go beyond the drug problem to get at the social, economic, cultural, and psychological problems that lie beneath.

Improving services or initiating new developments in the welfare field is at present an uphill task simply because resistance from entrenched interests is encountered. To make any gain at all requires dedication, commitment, and guile. Fundamental change could only be effected quickly if supported by those with power. But social reform is not even on the agenda in the present circumstances of retrenchment, cuts in the public sector, and a dominant ideology which praises individualism and inequality. Fortunately for some perhaps, drug taking, particularly of heroin, tends to produce passivity. However, where gangs and international traders muscle in, there is a threat to social order. An increase in such crime might lead to an increase in expenditure on police and prisons, but at the highest level of policy making there is little interest in providing more services for care and treatment and no interest in prevention, which requires more fundamental social and economic reforms.

In a welfare society, the voluntary sector would have the role of experimenting, initiating new developments, suggesting new ideas. Increasingly, however, the voluntary sector is being called upon to fulfil functions given up by the state, simply trying to fill the gaps caused by cuts in the public sector. And yet in doing this it has to spend an inordinate amount of time fighting for survival and trying to attract funds, generally, ironically, from central and local government budgets. The skills of expensively trained professionals are being squandered and the commitment of concerned people exploited.

Social work has a role to play, particularly where it does not simply mimic the medical profession but tries to implement wider-ranging and longer-term plans for the care and support of people who find it difficult to cope with the stresses of modern life. But City Roads learned that such people have a variety of needs, that no single approach can be satisfactory: it is necessary for people from a range of disciplines and with different qualities to work together.

Current issues

As in the detailed discussions about City Roads, the national debate is concerned primarily with three issues: whether funding and provision of services should be a central or local responsibility; the relative contribution of the statutory and voluntary sectors; and the relative contribution of social work versus medicine and specialist professionals versus general practice and community work.

The problem of funding, endemic at City Roads, is also found in the clinics, where they have to compete for local funds with other branches of medicine within their local health authorities. With the 'cuts', vacancies are frozen and posts in clinics given low priority. 'Nearly two out of three area health authorities have no special facilities for the treatment of addicts' concluded Stimson and Oppenheimer 1982: 222). The problem is at its worst out of London. Ghodse says there are probably not more than 12 consultants in the UK who spend six or more sessions per week in drug dependence (Ghodse 1983).

Concern about what is happening to the 'British system' has been growing in recent years and various solutions have been proposed. A *Times* leader in 1980, for example, commented 'the present machinery of drug addiction clinics, registration of addicts, maintenance dosage and drug replacement is not, for some reason, competing adequately in the eyes of many customers with the market' and urged a re-examination of 'the effectiveness of our containment policy towards hard drugs' (*The Times*, Wednesday 13 August, 1980: 13).

In early 1981, a conference was convened of representatives from the clinics and from the non-statutory sector – social work, advice, counselling and rehabilitation agencies – which culminated in a joint letter being sent to *The Times* (23 January 1981). The letter referred to the marked increase in the number of people seeking help for problems caused by drugs in the previous two years and pointed out that GPs were once again undertaking the care of opiate addicts. They noted also the long wait involved in gaining admission to detoxification units. The signatories agreed that the present trend to devolving the funding of services, both statutory and non-statutory, for drug abusers must be reversed. Central government should accept the financial responsibility for provision of the core costs of specialist drug services. It is inappropriate to depend on local funds in a field of care inextricably linked with national factors and having international ramifications. 'The effect of local funding, where competition with more attractive client groups is unavoidably direct, is to exclude many drug addicts from specialist care. . . . Increasingly, local funding has come to mean the withdrawal of support from resources and personnel' at a time when numbers are rising. The letter also advocated change in the law, extending licensing arrangements to cover methadone, dihiydrocodeine, dipipanone, and similar drugs. GPs involved in maintenance prescribing might be granted a licence but on condition that there be close consultation or supervision from a nearby appropriate specialist facility. There was also an urgent need for detoxification to be more readily available.

A controversial book by Arnold Trebach argued recently, however, that the essence of the 'British system', allowing the prescribing of heroin to addicts by medical practitioners, is still the correct solution to the problem. Attempts to restrict this right by limiting it to the clinics or licenced doctors encourages the involvement of organized crime in meeting the demand. If this continues, Britain will find itself in a situation similar to that in the USA. By forcing addicts out of legal medical practice into the arms of the black market, criminals have been enticed in (Trebach 1982).

Ghodse, however, puts the opposite view. He argued that in the clinics, among those best informed about the nature of drug misuse, the belief has disappeared completely 'that it is possible to undercut the black market by legal prescription. Instead there is general consensus that the black market is and always will be endemic, supplied in part by an overspill of legally supplied drugs. Frugal prescription of oral methadone mixture is recommended to keep such overspill to a minimum' (Ghodse 1983: 639). He commented, however, that some addicts are opting out of the clinic system in favour of consulting private, independent doctors who, after notifying the addicts to the Home Office, will prescribe injectable opiates, usually methadone. Similar concern about the role of private prescribing in the problem has been voiced by another eminent specialist in drug dependence who commented that a practitioner who takes on 20 such addicts privately 'would earn £500 a week from this group alone' (Bewley 1980: 497–98). Private doctors are also more likely to prescribe dipipanone and methylphenidate to addicts. They rationalize that a legal prescription for the addicts' drug of choice 'saves' them from the black market but this ignores the fact that, to pay for the private consultation and prescription, the addicts usually have to sell some of their drugs in the same black market. 'It seems as if in 20 years, the wheel has come full circle and that private doctors are again playing a substantial role in the drug scene' (Ghodse 1983: 639).

Echoes of this debate can be heard in the report *Treatment and Rehabilitation*, a Report of the Advisory Council on the Misuse of Drugs, published by the DHSS in 1982. Attention in this report concentrated on the 'problem drug taker'. There should be a move away from a substance- or diagnosis-centred approach towards a problem-orientated approach, adopting the term 'problem drug taker' to define the appropriate patient or client group. This would contain people who experience social, psychological, physical, or legal problems related to intoxication and/or regular excessive consumption and/or dependence as a consequence of their own use of drugs or other chemical substances (excluding alcohol and tobacco). The intention behind this very broad and all-embracing definition appears to have been to shift the concern from delivering services solely on the basis of the skills available to the medical profession to one which would be more responsive to a person's needs and this would involve a 'multi-disciplinary approach'.

However, in the report as a whole there was little attempt to discuss the provision of services for such a widely defined group and no attempt to deal with the wider problem of drug taking in society at large, legal or illegal. The report tended to focus in its recommendations on the more extreme cases. So although the use of the term 'problem drug taker' was in a sense a breakthrough for the conception of drug dependence as reflecting problems in living rather than a craving produced by particular substances, the general tenor of the report was towards a more narrow view. The Advisory Council in coming to its conclusions was in effect overtaken by the rapid emergence of the new heroin problem which crushed the more broad-based problem drug taker view. The need was re-asserted for a framework of services, although multi-disciplinary, to be set on the backs of an existing medical animal.

In the section on a 'framework of services for the future', the committee's ambivalence on the issue of local versus central funding was very clear. The report recognized that problem drug takers are accorded a low priority in service provision in many areas. They admitted that 'the majority of those who have given evidence have argued cogently that adequate services could best be achieved by a strong central body with the backing of sufficient funds and with power to take initiatives in individual areas'. However, they conceded lamely,

> 'such a course of action would . . . run counter to existing government policy which is to encourage the development of health and social services on the basis of local priorities, . . . even if there were to be central funding the prime responsibility for responding to these problems should be at local rather than national level where the needs of both the potential clients and of those caring for them can be assessed.' (Advisory Council on the Misuse of Drugs 1982: 37)

The problems caused by injudicious prescribing by GPs and private doctors and the licensing issue were handled diplomatically in the report. It referred to 'profound differences in professional opinion on the prescribing of opioids' (ACMD 1982: 25, para 4. 20) and noted that 'the lack of widely known guidelines on the forms that medical treatment of drug misusers should take has meant that dubious practices have escaped the censure they merit' (ACMD 1982: 57, para 7.22). They concluded, however, by expressing particular concern at the involvement of GPs (both NHS and private) and other forms of private practice in the treatment of problem drug takers. 'There may be a role for some of these doctors . . . "but" there is also a need to ensure that this role is consistent with good medical practice' (ACMD 1982: 82, para 11.7).

The conclusions of the report were that the existing services are now less able than ever to cope with the problems of drug misuse. There were growing difficulties in finding adequate funds to maintain existing services both statutory and non-statutory. And they questioned the practice of prescribing controlled drugs to addicts on a long-term maintenance basis.

The main recommendation was to establish regional or district drug advisory committees which would bring together representatives of a range of services. There should be more training and more research. An adequate response would require additional funding both at local level and from central government.

In the end, therefore, the ACMD Report on Treatment and Rehabilitation dodged the crucial funding issue. And, although starting to talk about problem drug takers and demedicalization, when it came to talking about services it fell back on the old medically dominated system, what Roger Lewis described as 'clinics with knobs on' (Lewis 1982: 425). These ambiguities reflect divisions within the ACMD itself and the need for compromise if a report is to be produced. Given the realities of the problems of funding in the health and social services in the present climate, new services cannot be created out of thin air and so the established structures tend to dominate. Theoretically, the existing community-based services could have provided a framework but the advocates of these are outnumbered and outclassed at these political levels by the medical profession. There is in effect an in-built dilemma or contradiction in present policy and practice about drug misuse: that between prevention and early intervention on the one hand and on the other, crisis management and cure. What is being attempted is to develop services which are based on a model of early intervention and the broader concept of problem drug taking but the context in which this model is to be applied is one concerned with heroin addiction and crisis management in a situation of depleted health, social service, and other resources.

Some of the voluntary agencies, such as the Blenheim Project and Release, criticized the proposal to limit prescribing to the clinics and related doctors. They would prefer an increase in the involvement of GPs in treatment. They argue that this would offer the addict a wider range of treatment possibilities. The introduction of further restrictions without the development of supporting facilities, a likely outcome in the present harsh climate, would be detrimental. Further restrictions would encourage more illicit manufacture and the black market, and it should be remembered that the consequences of participating in this market are much more dangerous and frightening for the user than contact with a benign GP. The power of the medical profession as a whole should however be reduced, preferably to a level where it would be supportive of a regime constructed and operated by social workers and nurses, and here they refer to City Roads as a model. Lifeline and the Hungerford (two other voluntary agencies) also considered that the dominance of the medical model had had a negative effect but that there should not be any increase in restrictions on prescribing by GPs. Nevertheless, the immediate problem for the services at present in the view of these agencies, remains the lack of treatment facilities available at short notice, including detoxification.

The other major response to the current drugs problem was that of the 'New Initiatives' launched by the government. This was less a response to the ACMD Report and the debate going on among the relatively small group of concerned voluntary bodies and experts than to the 'heroin horror' headlines and pressure from backbench MPs. The government had to be seen to be doing something. The fact that Norman Fowler (the then Secretary of State for Social Services) took a special interest in the subject and the view that drug addiction affects all classes probably had some influence too.

For the year 1983/84, the Secretary of State made available £2 million to encourage the development of projects. A further £2 million would be made available in each of the following two years, in total a £6m central funding initiative. The objective would be, through pump-priming grants, to encourage and support initiatives by health authorities, separately or jointly with local authorities, and by voluntary organizations, to strengthen and improve the help provided for people with health or social problems related to their misuse of drugs. The aim was to encourage local assessment of the nature and spread of drug misuse problems, to improve levels of professional awareness and ability to help people with drug-related problems, to improve links between hospital-based treatment services and the communities they serve, and (of course) to help improve the effectiveness of services provided and obtain value for money. Eligibility would depend on a number of criteria, including that schemes should have regard for securing value for money; details of efficiency gains to be made should be given where appropriate and provision should be made for evaluation of all schemes designed to improve the effectiveness of existing services or to test alternative methods of providing services. The main deficiencies to be remedied were with regard to staffing in DTCs; lack of specialist health service provision in parts of the country where drug misuse problems are growing; and under-subscribed and insufficient rehabilitation facilities. Appointment of new staff might be of community psychiatric nurses, clinical assistants in DTCs, ex-addicts as counsellors, or social researchers. New provision might be of half-way houses/hostels, rehabilitation houses or hostels, day centres, day hospitals, street agencies/walk-in centres, telephone information and advisory services, and training programmes.

The 'new initiative', despite its name, was not, however, a well-planned response to the problem but a hasty, *ad hoc* 'throwing money at the problem'. £6 million was placed on the table and it was hoped that services would materialize in response. But the old problems of pump-priming operations remained. Who would take over after three years? The administration of the initiative was at first predictably chaotic. The DHSS, who had little experience in these matters, were asked to administer a relatively large venture at the same time as their staff were being cut. Rather than developing services of a new kind, inevitably money tended to go to where the knowledge and interest already were, with those who knew how to apply for money. As yet, it is unclear whether money has been directed successfully to the major problems. Without a strong central strategic planning body to overview the situation this too was inevitable (and not necessarily a bad thing).

The extent to which these new initiatives will be proved to be 'value for money' or effective is doubtful. Some basic monitoring was supposed to be built in but in general the evaluation will turn out to be a farce. It has been left to each small-scale project to monitor itself. The reports produced will tend to be justificatory and an opportunity for comparative research has been lost.

Conclusion

A planned response to the present drugs problem would focus on the treatment and rehabilitation of the problem drug taker, adopting a multi-disciplinary approach and utilizing a wide range of hospital *and* community services. Treatment and re-habilitation would be one part of a two-pronged attack. The other would be prevention. Prevention is sometimes taken to mean early intervention. This too would be a part of the correct response, but more wide-ranging reforms are also required in structures other than simply the health and social services. Control over the supply of drugs would be required through licensing, customs and excise, and police activities, but more important would be an attack on the social and cultural conditions which make some people vulnerable to drug dependence. At the widest level, it needs to be recognized that the culture of our society is weighted heavily towards drug taking as the solution for what are seen as private and individual problems, through prescribed tranquillizers, alcohol, aspirin, tobacco, and so on. It is illogical to attack one form of drug taking only and not to try to tackle the cultural and commercial pressures encouraging people to deal with stress through such palliatives.

More generally, the translation of private troubles into public issues needs to be made over and over again. To recognize that vulnerability to drug dependence is in many cases caused by social conditions over which the individual has little control, especially unemployment and social deprivation. That the responsibility for dealing with individual 'inadequacies' and alienation is a social not an individual one. That emotional difficulties, while at present seemingly endemic in personal relationships, can be helped by care and therapy, but that present policies and practices actually tend either to neglect the struggles of children, young persons and adults in families and communities or even make things worse by the form of intervention practised. That people have been damaged and continue to be damaged by the way in which others treat them, sometimes by the harshness of their families towards them and sometimes by the failure of others to help those families cope with the pressures they have to face. The lack of services *in general* inevitably produces more people in *special need*. The promotion of health and social services and of wide-ranging egalitarian policies is in itself a preventive measure.

But for the present generation, for whom preventive policies would be too late, the main need is to keep on trying, to provide ready access to firm, patient and tolerant services, as City Roads did for Chris:

'At first, I desperately needed just a place to go, to recover. That was the first thing. But the counselling at City Roads was important – it made me face up to the choice I had to make. After that though, I think City Roads really saved my life. They kept taking me back. They showed faith in me and care for me as a person. Maybe it would have taken me longer to get here if I hadn't been nicked, but City Roads has prepared me for being here. It's still hard for me but if I mess up I will use City Roads again – as the only place I know where I could get the sort of help I'd need.'

Appendix A
Performance Indicators in the NHS

It is possible that what was being referred to in the comment from South East Thames RHA were the 'performance indicators' being applied within the DHSS to try to assess differences in performance standards between districts within regions and between regions. These are:

1. Average total cost per in-patient case.
2. Average cost of direct treatment services and supplies per in-patient case.
3. Average cost of medical and paramedical support services per in-patient case.
4. Average cost of general (non-clinical) services per in-patient day.
5. Proportion of all admissions classified as immediate admissions.
6. Proportion of all admissions classified as urgent involving a delay of more than one month before admission.
7. Proportion of all admissions classified as non-urgent involving a delay of more than one year before admission.
8. Average length of stay for hospital in-patients.
9. Average in-patient cases per bed over the year.
10. Proportion of all in-patients and day patients treated as day cases.
11. Average number of out-patients seen in each clinic session.
12. Ratio between new and returning out-patients.
13. Number of health visitors and district nurses per head of the population.
14. Number of NHS administrative and clerical staff per head of the population.
    (Social Services Committee 1982)

These data were in fact available in the form of the research report and the financial statements submitted by the management committee in their proposals. Clearly a predictable concern of these indicators is with costs and another is with the intensity of use. Least-cost forms of treatment are preferred and adequacy of treatment is judged in terms of waiting lists and waiting times.

Appendix B
Common Drugs of Use and Abuse

A drug is any substance that may be absorbed into the body and then affects its functioning. This includes a wide range of substances which are taken without a legal prescription.

A psycho-active drug is one which at least in part acts directly on the brain or central nervous system to produce an alteration of brain functioning.

Drugs that are abused are not necessarily 'illegal', many preparations are readily available over the chemist's counter and are used for their euphoric or sedative effects.

Few drug users use only one type of drug. Most drug users are multiple (or poly) drug users. Often 'illicit' drug use is supplemented or substituted with excessive alcohol use.

Many of the drugs commonly abused are addictive. This means that the body grows increasingly to depend upon their presence in order to function and that removal of the drug causes withdrawal symptoms which may vary from minor anxiety and feeling unwell through to major psychotic states and grand mal fits. Apart from the physical effects of addiction, the user also builds up an emotional and psychological dependence upon the use of drugs which complements the physical states. Withdrawal from most drug habits should be medically supervised if at all possible.

Apart from the physical effects caused by the drugs themselves, many drug users also suffer from a number of ailments and conditions caused by their administration or from physical debility, following prolonged use. Often people will have abscesses and ulcerated sites caused by injecting substances such as barbiturates or Diconal tablets which are themselves irritants. Although these abscesses are usually initially sterile they may become secondarily infected. Drug users are also prone to diseases such as hepatitis and septicaemia and to a range of digestive and alimentary tract disturbances. Access to medical aid should be sought to deal with these problems.

For our purposes, commonly used and abused drugs may best be divided into the following categories:

1. Central nervous system stimulants (CNS Uppers) – drugs which have an overall stimulant effect.
2. Central nervous system depressants (CNS Downers) – drugs which have an overall depressant or sedative effect.
3. Psychedelics – drugs which produce a profound alteration of consciousness, auditory and visual hallucinations.

CNS stimulants (Uppers)

Principal amongst this range of drugs are:

(a) AMPHETAMINES

These drugs were commonly prescribed during the last war to combat physical fatigue and in the 1950s and 60s as anti-depressants and slimming pills. They have a highly stimulant effect, graphically described as 'speeding'. Amphetamines are addictive and cessation can cause withdrawals ranging from mild sleepiness and hunger for about three days to a sudden onset of extreme somnolence. Prolonged amphetamine use, causing lack of sleep and hyperactivity for long periods, together with an associated lack of food, leads to rapid physical debility. Paranoid states are common in amphetamine users (amphetamine psychosis). Amphetamines are frequently used in conjunction with 'downers' to help people end a period of 'speeding'. (See cautions under barbiturates.)

Illicitly produced amphetamines, which are the most commonly available form, often do not contain pure amphetamine and may include other substances.

Commonly used amphetamines include:

Ritalin (methylphenidate) – popular because it can be injected
Dexedrine
Methedrine
Durophet
'sulphate' (illicitly produced)

Amphetamines are also combined with barbiturates to produce the following drugs:

Drinamyl
Durophet M
(This range of drugs is commonly known as 'blues'.)

(b) COCAINE

Produced from the leaf of the coca plant, principally in South America, it is thought to produce both physical and psychological dependence. Frequently 'snorted' through the nose, it can damage the nasal septum and in chronic users perforations are often observable.

(c) CAFFEINE

The most commonly used stimulant drug, readily found in small quantities in coffee, tea, chocolate and cola drinks. Physical dependence is rare but high consumption of caffeine is common in drug users.

(d) EPHEDRINE AND PSEUDO-EPHEDRINE

Both of these are common stimulants found in many medicines that can be obtained in any chemist.

(e) NICOTINE

The most commonly consumed dangerous stimulant drug. Causes chronic medical problems including bronchitis, hypertension, coronary disease, and lung and other cancers. Readily available in unrestricted quantities. Produces mild stimulant and euphoric effects.

CNS depressants (Downers)

Principal amongst this group of drugs are the following:

(a) BARBITURATES

Based on barbituric acid and used extensively up to the early 1970s as sleeping pills and anti-epileptic medications. Barbiturates are still readily available on the black market and through a few less cautious general practitioners. They are very addictive and may present severe problems on sudden withdrawal, which should only be done under medical supervision. There is a low margin of safety with these drugs and drug users frequently overdose – sometimes fatally. Taken with alcohol the effects of barbiturates are accentuated. Barbiturates also cause uninhibited behaviour, as does alcohol, which often causes people to be short of patience and can lead to abusive, aggressive, or violent behaviour.

Commonly used barbiturates are:

Tuinal
Nembutal
Seconal

(b) OTHER SEDATIVES/HYPNOTICS

The 'benzodiazepines' were thought to be the safe alternative to the barbiturates and have been very widely prescribed since the 1960s. Valium is now the most commonly prescribed drug in the country. More recent research has suggested that they have strong addictive potential and that cessation can lead to withdrawal symptoms such as anxiety states, perceptual disturbances, and possibly fits.

Commonly used benzodiazepines are:

Valium
Librium
Mogadon

Other common sedatives are:

chloral hydrate
glutethimide (Doriden)
chlormethizole (Heminevrin)

(c) ALCOHOL

The most commonly available and abused depressant drug. Although at first it produces feelings of elation and sociability, it can lead to depressive mood states. Alcohol is addictive and can also enhance the effects of other drugs. In severe cases sudden withdrawal can lead to psychotic states.

(d) INHALANTS

Recent publicity has caused much alarm about the use of solvents, particularly glue, by young people. Solvents have been abused since Victorian times (achieving respectability with ether and chloroform parties). The method of use, particularly inhalation using plastic bags over the head and in confined spaces, can lead to suffocation and death. Little physical harm has so far been detected from glue sniffing.

However, inhaling solvents found in cleaning fluid, fire extinguishers, and aerosols can lead to severe physical damage to the lungs and sometimes other parts of the body. Death has been known to occur.

(e) OPIOIDS

They are perhaps the best-known 'illicit' drugs, certainly the most publicized, and have been a very popularly used drug for hundreds of years. They are medically used to control acute pain (e.g. post-operative) and some chronic pain (e.g. terminal cancer). Opioid drugs include the naturally occurring opiates, which are derived from the opium poppy, and all their synthetic analogues. Opioid drugs are addictive and can cause withdrawal symptoms on cessation.

Commonly used opiate drugs are:

morphine
heroin
codeine

Synthetic derivatives (opioids) include:

methadone (Physeptone)
pethidine
Fortral
Diconal
DF 118

(f) CANNABIS

This drug does not easily fit into this category. Although it is a CNS depressant it is normally used to heighten perception. Usually smoked, but can also be eaten, it comes in the form of chopped leaves, blocks of resin, or refined oil. Users are rarely addicted, although this has been known to occur very occasionally. It produces mild intoxication and an elated mood. Some users also experience hallucinations.

Psychedelics

LSD, Mescalin, Peyote, STP, DMT, and Psilocybin. These drugs produce profound alteration of consciousness, auditory and visual hallucinations, confusion, and accentuation of sensory experience. Very few 'organic' hallucinogens (Mescalin, Peyote) are available on the black market though there is a growing interest in some mushrooms which contain small amounts of hallucinogens. Caution must be used as some mushrooms are poisonous. These drugs are non-addictive, but may produce neurotic and possibly psychotic states due to the severity of sensory disorientation.

Source: Drug Resource Pack available from City Roads (Crisis Intervention) Ltd 01-837 2772.

References

Acheson Report (1981) *Family Health Care in London*. London: HMSO.

Advisory Council on the Misuse of Drugs (ACMD) (1977) Treatment and Rehabilitation Working Group: Advisory Council on the Misuse of Drugs, *First Interim Report*.

ACMD (1980) Report of a working party, *Report on Drug Dependants within the Prison System in England and Wales*. London: Home Office.

ACMD (1982) Report of the Advisory Council on the Misuse of Drugs, *Treatment and Rehabilitation*. London: HMSO.

Archard, Peter (1979) *Vagrancy, Alcoholism and Social Control*. London: Macmillan.

Ashton, Mike (1980) 'Theory and Practice in the New British System'. *Druglink* ISDD **16**: 1–5.

Barnes, Jack and Connelly, Naomi (eds) (1978) *Social Care Research*. London: Bedford Square Press.

Berger, Peter L. (1966) *Invitation to Sociology. A Humanistic Perspective*. London: Pelican.

Berridge, Virginia and Edwards, Griffith (1981) *Opium and the People*. London: Allen Lane.

Bewley, T. H. (1980) Prescribing Psycho-active Drugs to Addicts'. *British Medical Journal* **281** (6238): 497–98.

Blakebrough, Eric (1983) Choosing the Wrong Vein. *The Guardian* Wednesday 6 April: 11.

Blumberg, H. H. (1976) British Users of Opiate-type Drugs: a Follow-up Study'. *British Journal of Addiction* **71**: 65–77.

Blumberg, H. H. (1981) The Characteristics of People Coming to Treatment. In Griffith Edwards and Carol Busch (eds), *Drug Problems in Britain. A Review of Ten Years*. London: Academic Press.

Blumberg, H. H., Cohen, S. D., Dronfield, B. E., Mordecai, E. A., Roberts, J. C., and Hawks, D. (1974) British Opiate Users: People Approaching London Drug Treatment Centres. *International Journal of Addictions* **9**: 1–23.

Brewer, Colin and Lait, June (1980) *Can Social Work Survive?* London: Temple Smith.

Bulmer, Martin (ed.) (1978) *Social Policy Research*. London: Macmillan.

Butrym, Zofia (1976) *The Nature of Social Work*. London: Macmillan.

Caplan, Gerald (1964) *Principles of Preventive Psychiatry*. New York: Basic Books.

Carr-Saunders, A. M. (1928) *Professions: Their Organisation and Place in Society*. Oxford: Clarendon Press.

Central Office of Information (1978) *The Prevention and Treatment of Drug Misuse in Britain*. London: HMSO.

Chapple, P. A. L., Somekh, D. E., and Taylor, M. E. (1972) A Five-Year Follow Up of 108 Cases of Opiate Addiction. *British Journal of Addiction* **67**: 33–8.

Chein, Isador (1966) Psychological, Social and Epidemiological Factors in Drug Addiction. In *Rehabilitating the Narcotic Addict*. Fort Worth, Tex.: Institute on New Developments in the Rehabilitation of the Narcotic Addict.

City Roads (Crisis Intervention) Ltd (with Phoenix House) (1983) *Drug Resource Pack*. London: City Roads (Crisis Intervention) Ltd.

Clark, David (1981) Heroin Horror in Our Midst. *The Observer* Sunday 4 January.

Committee on Local Authority and Allied Personal Social Services (Seebohm Report) (1968). *Report*, Cmnd. 3703. London: HMSO.

Coombs, Robert H., (1981) Drug Abuse as Career. *Journal of Drug Issues* (Fall): 369–87.

Corrigan, Paul and Leonard, Peter (1978) *Social Work Practice Under Capitalism*. London: Macmillan.

Departmental Committee (Rolleston Committee) (1926) *Report of the Departmental Committee on Drug Dependence*. London: HMSO.

Department of Health and Social Security (1978) *Social Work Teams: The Practitioners' View*. London: HMSO.

Dorn, N. (1983) *Alcohol, Youth and the State: Drinking Practices, Controls and Health Education*. London: Croom Helm.

Edwards, G. (1969) The British Approach to the Treatment of Heroin Addiction. *Lancet* **i**: 768–72.

Edwards, G. (1979) British Policies on Opiate Addiction: Ten Years Working of the Revised Response and Options for the Future. *British Journal of Psychiatry* **134**: 1–13.

Edwards, Griffith and Busch, Carol (eds) (1981) *Drug Problems in Britain: A Review of Ten Years*. London: Academic Press.

Essen, Juliet and Wedge, Peter (1982) *Continuities in Childhood Disadvantage*. London: Heinemann.

Etzioni, Amitai (1969) *The Semi-Professions and Their Organization*. New York: Free Press.

Etzioni, Amitai (1970) A Basis for Comparative Analysis of Complex Organisations. In A. Etzioni (ed.) *A Sociological Reader on Complex Organisations*. London: Holt, Rinehart & Winston.

Finigarette, Herbert and Finigarette Hasse, Anne (1978) *Mental Disabilities and Criminal Responsibility*. Berkeley, Calif.: University of California Press.

Fogelman, Ken (ed.) (1976) Preliminary Findings from the Third Follow-up of the National Child Development Study. *Britain's Sixteen-Year Olds*. London: National Children's Bureau.

Fogelman, Ken (ed.) (1983) Papers from the National Child Development Study. *Growing Up in Great Britain*. London: Macmillan.

Freed, Anna O. (1977) Social Casework: More than a Modality. *Social Casework* April.

Ghodse, A. H. (1976) Drug Problems Dealt with by 62 London Casualty Departments. *British Journal of Preventive and Social Medicine* **30:** 251–56.

Ghodse, A. H. (1977a) Drug Dependent Individuals Dealt With by London Casualty Departments. *British Journal of Psychiatry* **131:** 273–80.

Ghodse, A. H. (1977b) Casualty Departments and the Monitoring of Drug Dependence. *British Medical Journal* **1:** 1381–382.

Ghodse, A. H. (1979) Recommendations by Accident and Emergency Staff about Drug-Overdose Patients. *Social Science and Medicine* **13A:** 169–73.

Ghodse, A. H. (1983) Treatment of Drug Addiction in London. *The Lancet* 19 March: 636–39.

Ghodse, A. H., and Rawson, Nigel S. (1978) Distribution of Drug-Related Problems Among London Casualty Departments. *British Journal of Psychiatry* **132:** 467–72.

Ghodse, A. H. and Rawson, Nigel S. B. (1978) 'Accidental' Self-Poisoning in Drug-Dependent Individuals. In D. J. West (ed.) *Problems of Drug Abuse in Britain*. Cambridge: Institute of Criminology.

Glanz, Alan, Jamieson, Anne, and MacGregor, Susanne (1980) 'City Roads: Interim Evaluation Report'. London: DHSS. Unpublished.

Gouldner, Alvin W. (1958) Cosmopolitans and Locals: Toward an Analysis of Latent Social Roles. *Administrative Science Quarterly* **II** December – March.

Griffiths, R. (1983) *NHS Management Inquiry*. (Available from DHSS.)

Hartnoll, R. L., Mitcheson, M. C., Battersby, B., Brown, G., Ellis, M., Fleming, P., and Hedley, N. (1980) Evaluation of Heroin Maintenance in a Controlled Trial. *Archives of General Psychiatry* **37**: 877–84.

Helping Hand Organization (1978) *Drugs, Suburbia and Subway: The Pattern of Addiction in the 'Seventies'*. London: Helping Hand Organization.

Homans, George C. (1961) *Social Behaviour*. New York: Harcourt Brace.

Home Office (1980) *Statistics of the Misuse of Drugs 1979*. London: Home Office.

Huntington, June (1981) *Social Work and General Medical Practice*. London: Allen & Unwin.

Interdepartmental Committee on Drug Addiction (The Brain Report) (1965) The Second Report of the Interdepartmental Committee: *Drug Addiction*. London: HMSO.

ISDD (1980) Controlling Addiction: The Role of the Clinics. *Druglink* **13**, Spring.

ISDD Library and Information Service (1982) *Surveys and Statistics on Drug-Taking in Britain*. London: ISDD, August.

ISDD (1983) *Druglink*, No. 18. London: ISDD.

Jamieson, Anne, Glanz, Alan, and MacGregor, Susanne (1981) *Vol. 1. City Roads: Evidence and Analysis; Vol. 2. City Roads: An Assessment*. DHSS. (Available from ISDD and from the British Library Lending Section.)

Johnson, Terence (1972) *Professions and Power*. London: Macmillan.

Kitchener, Paul, MacGregor, Susanne, and Croft-White, Clare (1980) 'Great Chapel Street Medical Centre: Interim Research Report'. London: DHSS. Unpublished.

Kitchener, Paul, MacGregor, Susanne and Croft-White, Clare (1982) 'Health Care of the Young Homeless in Central London: An Assessment of the Great Chapel Street Medical Centre 1978–1981' DHSS. Unpublished. (Available from the British Library Lending Section.)

Leach, John and Wing, John (1980) *Helping Destitute Men*. London: Tavistock.

Lees, Stan (1980) Developing Effective Institutional Managers in the 1980s – Part I: A Current Analysis. *Journal of Advanced Nursing* **5**.

Lemert, E. (1951) *Social Pathology*. New York: McGraw-Hill.

Lemert, E. (1967) *Human Deviance, Social Problems and Social Control*. Englewood Cliffs, NJ: Prentice-Hall.

Lewis, Roger (1982) The Eye of the Needle. *New Society* **62** 9 December.

Marshall, T. F., Fairhead, S. M., Murphy, D. J. I., and Iles, S. C. (1978) Evaluation for Democracy. In *Social Research in the Public Sector: Seminar on Tasks, Possibilities, Limitations, Responsibilities and Vital Issues*. Heidelberg, 6–8 December.

Mechanic, David (1978) *Medical Sociology*. New York: The Free Press.

Menzies, Isabel (1960) A Case Study in the Functioning of Social Systems as a Defense against Anxiety. *Human Relations* **13:** 95–121.

Mitchell, B. and Rose, B. (1975) Barbiturate Abuse – a Growing Problem. *Nursing Times* September 18: 1488–490.

Mitcheson, M., Davidson, J., Hawks, D., Hitchens, L., and Malone, S. (1970) Sedative Abuse by Heroin Addicts. *Lancet* **i:** 606–07.

National Institute for Social Work (1983) *Social Workers, Their Role and Tasks* (Barclay Report). London: Bedford Square Press.

Ogborne, A. C. and Stimson, G. V. (1975) Follow-up of a Representative Sample of Heroin Addicts. *International Journal of the Addictions* **10**(6): 1061–071.

Pahl, R. E. (1982) The Welfare State Intelligentsia. *London Review of Books*, 17–30 June: 15–16.

Plant, Martin (1981) What Aetiologies? In Griffith Edwards and Carol Busch (eds) *Drug Problems in Britain: A Review of Ten Years*. London: Academic Press.

Rees, S. (1979) *Social Work Face to Face*. New York: Columbia University Press.

Rees, Stuart and Wallace, Alison (1982) *Verdicts on Social Work*. London: Edward Arnold.

Smith, Larry L. (1978) A Review of Crisis Intervention Theory. *Social Casework* July: 396–405.

Social Services Committee (1982) *Public Expenditure on the Social Services*. Session 1981–82. Second Report. H.C. 306. London: HMSO.

Spear, H. B. (1969) The Growth of Heroin Addiction in the United Kingdom. *British Journal of Addiction* **64**: 245–55.

Stevens, Barbara (1978) Deaths of Drug Addicts in London during 1970–74: Toxicological, Legal and Demographic Findings. *Medicine, Science and the Law* **18** (2) April.

Stimson, Gerry V. (1973) *Heroin and Behaviour*. Shannon: Irish University Press.

Stimson, Gerry V., Oppenheimer, Edna, and Thorley, Anthony (1978) Seven-year Follow-up of Heroin Addicts: Drug Use and Outcome. *British Medical Journal* **1:** 1190–192.

Stimson, Gerry V. and Oppenheimer, Edna (1982) *Heroin Addiction: Treatment and Control in Britain*. London: Tavistock.

Teggin, A. F. and Bewley, Thomas H. (1979) Withdrawal Treatment for Barbiturate Dependence. *The Practitioner* **223:** 106–07.

Thorley, A., Oppenheimer, E., and Stimson, G. V. (1977) Clinic Attendance and Opiate Prescription Status of Heroin Addicts Over a Six-year Period. *British Journal of Psychiatry* **130:** 565–69.

Thorley, Anthony (1979) Drug Dependence. In Peter Hill, Robin Murray, and Anthony Thorley (eds) *Essentials of Post-Graduate Psychiatry*. London: Academic Press.

Thorley, Anthony (1980) The Nature and Outcome of Treatment. *DHSS Conference on Research into the Careers, Treatment and Rehabilitation of Drug Misusers*.

Trebach, Arnold S. (1982) *The Heroin Solution*. London: Yale University Press.

Waller, Tom and Banks, Arthur (1983) Drug Abuse. Supplement in *General Practitioner*, 25 March.

Webb, Adrian and Wistow, Gerald (1982) *Whither State Welfare? Policy and Implementation in the Personal Social Services 1979–80*. London: RIPA.

Wiepert, G. D., Bewley, T. H., and d'Orban, P. T. (1978) Outcomes for 575 British Opiate Addicts entering Treatment between 1968 and 1975. *Bulletin on Narcotics* **XXX**(1) 21–32.

Wiepert, G. D., d'Orban, P. T., and Bewley, Thomas H. (1979) Delinquency by Opiate Addicts Treated at Two London Clinics. *British Journal of Psychiatry* **134:** 14–23.

Wille, R. (1981) Ten-year Follow-up of a Representative Sample of London Heroin Addicts: Clinic Attendance, Abstinence and Mortality. *British Journal of Addiction* **76:** 259.

Williams, David (1981) The Problem in a Central London Hospital. In R. Murray, A. H. Ghodse, C. Harris, and D. Williams (eds) *The Misuse of Psychotropic Drugs*. London: Gaskell.

World Health Organisation (1964) Expert committee on drug dependence. *Technical Report*, Series no. 116. Geneva: WHO.
Yelloly, Margaret A. (1980) *Social Work Theory and Psychoanalysis*. Wokingham: Van Nostrand Reinhold.

Name Index

Archard, P. 93, 210
Ashton, M. x, 210

Banks, A. 97, 215
Barnes, J. 210
Berger, P. L. 210
Berridge, V. 3, 5, 210
Bewley, T. H. 7–9, 16–17, 157, 195, 210, 215
Blakebrough, E. 210
Blumberg, H. H. 76–7, 82, 210
Brewer, C. 130, 211
Bulmer, M. 211
Busch, C. 3–4, 212
Butrym, Z. 113, 130, 211

Caplan, G. 80–1, 113, 211
Carr-Saunders, A. M. 179, 211
Chapple, P. A. L. 161, 211
Chein, I. 76, 211
'Chris' (case study) 57–60, 66, 201
Clark, D. xiii, 211
'Colin' (case study) 90–1
Connelly, N. 210
Coombs, R. H. 81, 211
Corrigan, P. 129, 211
Croft-White, C. 70, 213

Dorn, N. 211

Edwards, G. 3–5, 210–12
Essen, J. 84, 212
Etzioni, A. xv, 179, 212

Finigarette, H. 10–11, 212
Finsberg, G. 186
Fogelman, K. 84, 212
Fowler, N. 198
Freed, A. O. 130–31, 212

Ghodse, A. H. 15, 18–20, 34–5, 69, 151–52, 168, 192, 194–95, 212
Glanz, A. xvi, 54, 57, 142, 212–13
Gouldner, A. W. 99, 110, 213
Griffiths, R. 213

Hartnoll, R. L. 9, 213
Hasse, A. 10–11, 212
Homans, G. C. xv, 213
Huntington, J. ix, 109, 213

Jamieson, A. xvi, 54, 57, 142, 212–13
'Joe' (case study) 64–6
'John' (case study) 63–4, 66
Johnson, T. 179, 213

Kitchener, P. 70, 213

Lait, J. 130, 211
Leach, J. 93, 169, 213
Lees, S. 109, 214
Lemert, E. 169, 214
Leonard, P. 129, 211
Lewis, R. 197, 214

MacGregor, S. xvi, 54, 57, 70, 142, 212–13
Marshall, T. F. 214
'Mary' (case study) 88–90
Mechanic, D. 81, 214
Menzies, I. 109, 214
Mitchell, B. 17–18, 214
Mitcheson, M. x, 9, 17, 213–14

Ogborne, A. C. 159, 214
Oppenheimer, E. 3, 8, 23, 161, 194, 215
d'Orban, P. T. 7–9, 16–17, 215

Pahl, R. E. 214
Parsloe, P. 131
'Penny' (case study) 60–2, 66, 145
Pinker, R. 129–30
Plant, M. 82, 214

Rees, S. 130, 166, 214
'Robert' (case study) 85–6
Rose, B. 17–18, 214
Ross, N. 21

Smith, L. L. 113–14, 214
Somekh, D. E. 161, 211
Spear, H. B. 214
Stevens, B. 215
Stevenson, O. 131
Stimson, G. V, 3, 8, 23, 70, 78, 92,
    159,161, 214–15
'Stuart' (case study) 87–8

Taylor, W. E. 161, 211
Teggin, A. F. 17, 215
Thorley, A. 8, 12, 93, 155, 161, 215
Trebach, A. S. 195, 215

'Val' (case study) 120
'Vince' (case study) 120

Wallace, A. 166, 214
Waller, T. 97, 215
Webb, A. 154, 215,
Wedge, P. 84, 212
Wiepert, G. D. 7–9, 16–17, 215
Wille, R. 161, 215
Williams, D. 81–2, 215
Wing, J. 93, 169, 213
Wistow, G. 154, 215

Yelloly, M. A. 130–31, 216
Young, Sir G. 186

Subject Index

A and E dept *see* Accident and Emergency Department
ACMD *see* Advisory Council on the Misuse of Drugs
AHA *see* Camden and Islington Area Health Authority
Accident and Emergency (A and E) Department 17–18, 21, 51; Addiction Research Unit study 18–20, 34–5; effects of City Roads on 139–40; referrals to City Roads 29–30, 34, 135–38; views on City Roads 147–51
accommodation for drug users 16, 69–70, 77–8, 159; *see also* case studies; homelessness
Acheson Report 97, 210
activities for City Roads residents 48–9, 115–16, 164
addiction: definition of 4, 10–11; heroin, studies of 8–9; models of 3–6, 11–12, 153–54; notification of xii; theories and treatment of 3–13
Addiction Research Unit study 18–20, 34–5
administration of City Roads 101–02; *see also* operation; staffing
admission to City Roads: barriers to 141–46, 157; policy 29–30; procedure 51–3, 119
Advisory Committee on Drug Dependence 6–7, 15
Advisory Council on the Misuse of Drugs (ACMD) xii, 15, 20–1, 24, 189, 195–98, 210
agencies, voluntary 11–19, 35, 42, 74, 147–51, 198; *see also* Blenheim; Community Drug Project; Hungerford; Lifeline; rehabilitation
ages of City Roads residents 34, 54, 69–70, 143

aims of City Roads xiv–xv, 33–42
alcohol 82–5, 89–91, 93, 207
amphetamines 205
assessment: of City Roads clients 119, 139–41, 145; of City Roads unit 153–71
'atmosphere' at City Roads 40, 48, 146, 170

background of drug users 12, 82–91, 93–5, 116–17, 169, 200–01; *see also* case studies
barbiturates xiii, 14–20, 34, 70–2, 97–8, 143, 206–07
Barclay Report 128, 130, 214
barriers to admission to City Roads 141–46, 157
benefits of City Roads 147–51, 170–71
Birkbeck College ix, 26
Blenheim 14, 198
Brain Committee 4–5, 10, 213
British Medical Journal 6
buildings for City Roads *see* premises

CDP *see* Community Drug Project
CURB *see* Campaign on the Use and Restriction of Barbiturates
Camden and Islington Area Health Authority 25, 28, 39, 100, 180
Campaign on the Use and Restriction of Barbiturates (CURB) 15
cannabis 85, 208
case notes at City Roads 50, 106, 117
case studies of City Roads residents: 57–66, 82–91; Chris 57–60, 66, 201; Colin 90–1; Joe 64–6; John 63–4, 66; Mary 88–90; Penny 60–2, 66, 145; Robert 85–6; Stuart 87–8; Val 120; Vince 120; follow-up 158–61; and social work 118–27
casework 130–32

casualty department *see* Accident and Emergency Department
causes of addiction *see* background of drug users; models of addiction
'chaotic' drug misuse xiv, 13–22
Christian communities 55, 66, 117, 125
City Roads: aims of 33–42; assessment of 153–71; clients of 33–8, 68–95; and links with the environment 134–52; making of 24–43; management of 51–7, 175–91; social work at 113–33; teamwork at 98–111; use of 47–67
clients of City Roads: and aims 33–8; case studies 57–66, 82–91; difficult 68–95; help-seeking of 78–82; motivation of 115–18, 124, 132, 142–44; profile of 69–78; views on City Roads 163–67; *see also* residents
clinics *see* Drug Treatment Centres
cocaine 6, 206
Coke Hole 124
committees for City Roads *see* Management Committee; Steering Committee
Committee on Local Authority and Allied Personal Social Services (Seebohm Report) (1968) 128–29, 211
Community Drug Project (CDP) 14
community services and drug users 12, 128–30, 194, 198, 200
'concept' type of rehabilitation 11–12, 55, 117, 125; *see also* Phoenix House
'confrontational' approach to addiction 10–12
'Cosmopolitans' 99
costs of running City Roads 161–63; *see also* funding
counselling at City Roads 48–50, 101–03, 115–17, 121–22, 130–33, 157, 164–67, 170–71
courts 135–37; *see also* case studies; crime; prison; Probation Service
crime: and activities of drug users 9–10, 74–7, 90–1, 159, 193; and drug supplies xii–xiii, 73, 195
crisis intervention xiv–xv, 13–22, 36, 113–15, 168, 192–93
criticism of City Roads 147–51, 157, 171; *see also* assessment of City Roads

Customs and Excise xii, 200
DDU *see* Drug Dependency Unit
DHSS *see* Department of Health and Social Security
DTC *see* Drug Treatment Centre
Dangerous Drugs Act (1920) 3, 10, 77
deaths of drug users 17, 58, 62, 145, 159
Department of Health and Social Security 25–7, 29–31, 100, 181, 184–91
Departmental Committee Report on Drug Dependence (Rolleston Committee) (1926) 3–4, 211
departure from City Roads 41, 54–5, 144
depressants, central nervous system ('downers') 206–08; *see also* barbiturates; opiates
deprivation *see* background of drug users
detoxification 6–8, 13, 21, 97–8, 143; *see also* Drug Treatment Centres
Diconal xiii, 71, 208
difficult clients at City Roads: 68–95; case studies 85–91; help-seeking of 78–82; problems of 82–95; profile of 69–78
Directors of City Roads 37–41, 47–50, 99–112, 175–84
'dismissal' from City Roads 41, 58, 144
'downers' 206–08; *see also* barbiturates; opiates
Drug Dependency Unit 31; *see also* Drug Treatment Centre
drug misuse: xi–xiv; 'chaotic' 13–22; multiple 14–15, 17, 21; by residents of City Roads 70–2
Drug Treatment Centres (DTCs) 6–12, 42, 74–5, 110, 147–51, 194–95, 198–99
drugs of abuse 204–09
Drugs Acts 3, 10, 20, 77, 168
drugs problem: xi–xiv; as 'social disorder' 5–6; and society 192–201; *see also* addiction
drugs 'scene' 73–8, 114, 130, 142
duration of stay at City Roads 37, 52–4, 118–19, 126

Elizabeth House 55
employment of drug users 17, 76, 92, 95, 200 *see also* case studies

environment, links with City Roads xv, 41–2, 134–52; Accident and Emergency Departments 139–41; barriers to admission 141–46; views of other agencies 147–51; *see also* referrals; rehabilitation
ephedrine 206

families of drug users *see* background
finances for City Roads *see* funding
'fixing rooms' 14–15, 23
follow-up studies of City Roads residents 158–61
funding: of City Roads 25–9, 184–91; of clinics 194; of future services 194, 196–97

GLC *see* Greater London Council
General Practitioners xiii, 6–7, 73, 97, 194–98; *see also* Medical Officer
glue-sniffing 207–08
government response to drug problem xiii, 4–5, 198–200
Greater London Council 186–90
Guardian, The xiii

Health Authorities: Camden and Islington Area 25, 28, 39, 100, 180; Thames Region 186–90
health of drug users 16–18, 73, 79, 86, 96; *see also* case studies
help-seeking of City Roads clients 78–82
Helping Hand Organization 19, 213
heroin xii, 6–9, 208
history of City Roads: 24–32; funding 27–9; Operational Document 29–31; premises 26–7; Steering Committee 31–2
Home Office: addiction records xii, 18–20, 69, 195, 213; Drugs Branch 15; Drugs Inspectorate 27, 136; and funding for City Roads 27–8, 186–90; licensing of doctors 6
homelessness 16, 77–9, 92, 147, 152, 155, 159; *see also* case studies
homes of drug users *see* accommodation; background
hospitals: psychiatric 64, 85, 161; *see also* Accident and Emergency Departments; Drug Treatment Centres; Middlesex; statutory sector; Tooting Bec; University College

hostels 16, 78, 147, 150, 159, 199; *see also* case studies
Hungerford Drug Project 14, 59, 65–6, 74, 198

ISDD *see* Institute for the Study of Drug Dependence
inhalants 207–08
Institute of Psychiatry 18
Institute for the Study of Drug Dependence (ISDD) xiii, 6–7, 213
Interdepartmental Committee on Drug Addiction (Brain Committee) (1965) 4–5, 10, 213

'junkies' 9, 70–6, 78, 81–2, 92

LBA *see* London Boroughs Association
Lancet 7
Leeds Alcohol Detoxification Unit 29
legislation: Dangerous Drugs Act (1920) 3, 10, 77; Medicines Act (1968) 3; Misuse of Drugs Act (1971) 3, 20, 77, 168
Life for the World 55, 66, 125
Lifeline Project 11, 198
lifestyle of drug users 73–8, 114, 127, 130, 142
Link Project 64
links between City Roads and the environment: xv, 41–2, 134–52; Accident and Emergency Departments 139–41; barriers to admission 141–46, 157; views of other agencies 147–51; *see also* referrals; rehabilitation
'Locals' 99, 110
London Boroughs Association (LBA) 25–7, 184–91; Working Party on Addictions 184–86
London: migration to 69–70; *see also* case studies; Greater London Council; Piccadilly

making of City Roads: 24–32; funding 27–9; Operational Document 29–31; premises 26–7; Steering Committee 31–2
management of City Roads 51–7, 175–84; *see also* Management Committee
Management Committee of City Roads 32, 100, 179–84; *see also* Steering Committee

medical: 'model' of addiction 3–4,
    153–54; profession and addiction
    3–6; staff at City Roads see nurses;
    see also General Practitioners;
    hospitals
Medical Officer at City Roads 38, 96,
    100, 103, 105, 110
Medicines Act (1968) 3
meetings at City Roads 104–06, 127
methadone 7–10, 195, 208
Middlesex Hospital 17–18, 21, 61–2,
    81, 139–40
misuse of drugs: xi–xiv; 'chaotic'
    13–22; by City Roads residents 70–2
Misuse of Drugs Act (1971) 3, 20, 77,
    168
models of addiction: medical 3–4,
    153–54; social disorder 5–6, 11–12
motivation of City Roads clients
    115–18, 124, 132, 142–44
multi-disciplinary teamwork see
    teamwork
multiple drug misuse: 14–15, 17, 21;
    by City Roads residents 70–2

NHS see National Health Service
National Child Development Study
    84
National Health Service:
    organization 109; performance
    indicators 202–03; see also statutory
    sector
National Institute for Social Work
    128–29, 214
Nembutal see barbiturates
New Horizon 14
'New Initiatives' 198–200
North East London Drugs Indicators
    Project (NELDIP) xiii
North East Thames Regional Health
    Authority 189–90
North West Thames Regional Health
    Authority 188, 190
notification of addicts to the Home
    Office xii, 18–20, 69, 195, 213
numbers: of City Roads residents 69;
    of drug users xii–xiv
nurses at City Roads 38–41, 47–50,
    100–12

objectives of City Roads xiv–xv,
    33–42; see also assessment of City
    Roads
occupation of City Roads 145–46, 157

one-to-one sessions see counselling
operation of City Roads: 51–7; aims
    38–41; management 175–84
Operational Document for City
    Roads: agreement of 29–31; and
    City Roads' aims xiv–xv, 32–3,
    35–6, 129
opiates and opioids xii–xiii, 6–9,
    70–2, 208
outcome of stay at City Roads 55–7,
    153–54; see also assessment of City
    Roads
overdosing 14, 16, 21, 34, 72, 147,
    151–52, 158–59

performance indicators in the
    National Health Service 202–03
phenobarbitone see detoxification
philosophy of City Roads 107–11,
    128–33, 170, 175; see also
    Operational Document
Phoenix House: 12, 55, 117; and City
    Roads 59–60, 63–5, 86, 124, 132, 165,
    169–70
Piccadilly: 14, 19, 47, 73–6, 89; Advice
    Centre 74
planning for City Roads residents
    123–26; see also rehabilitation
police see crime
policy toward drug misuse: of City
    Roads see Operational Document;
    of government xiii, 4–5, 198–200
Practice Sub-Committee at City
    Roads 182–83
premises for City Roads 25–7, 47–8
prescribing of drugs to addicts: by
    General Practitioners xiii, 73,
    197–98; restriction of 6–7, 195;
    theory of 3–4, 9–10
prison and drug users 58, 91–2; see
    also case studies; crime; Probation
    Service
Prisons Board 15
Probation Service: and addicts 74;
    and links with City Roads 103,
    135–36; and referrals to City Roads
    35, 63–4, 79, 90, 135–38; and
    Steering Committee of City Roads
    32, 180; views on City Roads 147–51
problems of City Roads residents
    115–22
professionalism at City Roads 107–11,
    179
psychedelics 208–09

Psychiatrist, Consultant at City
  Roads 38, 100, 103, 105, 110
Psychiatry, Institute of 18
psychotherapeutic approach to
  rehabilitation 117; *see also* 'concept'

qualifications of City Roads staff 108;
  see also staffing

RHAs *see* Thames Regional Health
  Authorities
readmission to City Roads 126–27,
  144–45
referrals: from City Roads 37, 55–7,
  117–18, 123–26, 160–65; to City
  Roads 34–5, 49–51; 'success rate' of
  136–39
Regional Medical Officers 189
rehabilitation: 'concept' type 11–12;
  referral from City Roads 37, 55–7,
  117–18, 123–26, 160–65; *see also*
  Christian communities; Phoenix
  House
Release 198
research: Addiction Research Unit
  18–20, 34–5; City Roads xiv–xvi,
  182–83; heroin addiction 8–9;
  'junkies' 70–82
residents of City Roads: activities of
  48–9, 115–16, 164; ages of 34, 54,
  69–70, 143; drug use by 70–2;
  duration of stay 37, 52–4, 118–19,
  126; planning for 123–26; problems
  of 115–23; sex of 54, 69–70, 159;
  views on City Roads 163–67; *see also*
  case studies; clients
reviews of City Roads cases 105–06,
  125
Rolleston Committee 3–4, 211
Roma 86
rules at City Roads 41, 144–45

SCODA *see* Standing Conference on
  Drug Abuse
SOS Society 27
St Martin-in-the-Fields Social Service
  Unit 74
Seebohm Report 128–29, 211
sex of City Roads residents 54, 69–70,
  159
smuggling of drugs xii–xiii
Social Services: Committee (1982)
  200, 214; Secretary of State for
  198–99

social work at City Roads: assessment
  of clients 115–18; case studies
  118–27; concept of 128–33; crisis
  intervention 113–15; *see also*
  counselling
social workers at City Roads 38–41,
  47–50, 100–12
society: model of addiction 5–6,
  11–12; response to the drugs
  problem 192–201
sources of drugs: illegal xii–xiii, 73,
  195; legal *see* Drug Treatment
  Centres; General Practitioners;
  prescribing
South East Thames Regional Health
  Authority 187–88, 202
South West Thames Regional Health
  Authority 189–90
staff at City Roads: daily work 47–50;
  meetings 105–06; qualifications of
  108; and residents' problems
  118–21; teamwork 96–112; and
  trades unions 177–78; turnover
  176–79
staffing at City Roads xiv, 30, 38–41,
  99–104, 109–10
Standing Conference on Drug Abuse
  (SCODA): Co-ordinator and City
  Roads 31–2, 185, 188; and funding
  for City Roads 189–91; pressure for
  City Roads 23–5, 179; and referrals
  to City Roads 35, 135; Steering
  Committee on multiple drug abuse
  15–16
statistics of use of City Roads *see* use
statutory sector 176, 194; *see also*
  Accident and Emergency
  Departments; Drug Treatment
  Centres; General Practitioners
Steering Committee for City Roads
  25–32; *see also* Management
  Committee
stimulants, central nervous system
  ('uppers') 72, 205–06
street agencies *see* agencies,
  voluntary
Suffolk House 65, 125

teamwork at City Roads: 36, 38–40,
  47–50, 96–112; care 96–8;
  co-ordination 104–07; philosophy
  107–11; staffing 99–104
telephone use at City Roads 49, 101,
  107, 134–35, 145

Thames Regional Health Authorities 186–90
theories of drug dependence 3–13
Times, The 194
Tooting Bec Hospital 17, 84, 98, 188
trade unions at City Roads 177–78
treatment of drug dependence: 3–13; City Roads' philosophy 107–11, 128–33, 170, 175; justification of a new treatment 155–56
Tuinal *see* barbiturates
turnover of City Roads staff 176–79

UCH *see* University College Hospital
unions, trade, at City Roads 177–78
United States of America 3, 10–11, 13, 80–1, 195

University College Hospital 34, 64, 110, 180
'uppers' 72, 205–06
use of City Roads: 51–67; admissions 51–3; case studies 57–67; departure of clients 54–5; duration of stay of clients 53–4; and other agencies 134–37; outcome of stay 55–7; referrals 51

voluntary sector 11–12, 14, 193–94, 198–99; *see also* agencies; rehabilitation; Standing Conference on Drug Abuse

World Health Organisation, Report (1964) 10, 216